PROPERTY OF
GLENBROOK SOUTH SPEECH TEAM
4000 WEST LAKE AVE.
GLENVIEW, ILL. 60025
(312) 729-2000

Three Screen Comedies
by Samson Raphaelson

PROPERTY OF
GLENBROOK SOUTH SPEECH TEAM
4000 WEST LAKE AVE.
GLENVIEW, ILL. 60025
(312) 729-2000

Other Writings
by Samson Raphaelson include

Plays
Produced and published

1925 The Jazz Singer
1928 Young Love
1930 Boolie
1933 The Wooden Slipper
1935 Accent on Youth*
1936 White Man
1939 Skylark*
1942 Jason*
1944 The Perfect Marriage
1950 Hilda Crane

Screenplays
(from a total list of about 25)

1931 The Smiling Lieutenant†
1932 The Man I Killed†
1932 One Hour with You
1932 Trouble In Paradise
1934 Caravan
1934 The Merry Widow†
1934 Servants' Entrance
1935 Dressed to Thrill
1937 Angel
1937 The Last of Mrs. Cheney†
1940 The Shop around the Corner
1941 Suspicion†
1943 Heaven Can Wait
1946 The Harvey Girls†
1947 Green Dolphin Street
1948 That Lady in Ermine

*Included in Burns Mantle's Ten Best of their respective years.

†Co-screenplay.

Book (Non-fiction)
1949 The Human Nature of Playwriting

Short Stories
In Martha Foley's 1947 Best American Stories *and several other collections*

Three Screen Comedies by Samson Raphaelson

Trouble in Paradise
The Shop around the Corner
Heaven Can Wait

Introduction by
Pauline Kael

Published for the Wisconsin Center for Film and Theater Research by
The University of Wisconsin Press

Published 1983

The University of Wisconsin Press
114 North Murray Street
Madison, Wisconsin 53715

The University of Wisconsin Press, Ltd.
1 Gower Street
London WC1E 6HA, England

Copyright © 1983
The Board of Regents of the University of Wisconsin System
All rights reserved

"Freundschaft" copyright © 1981 Samson Raphaelson; originally published in
The New Yorker, May 11, 1981

Preface, Author's Notes, and emendations to screenplays © 1983 Samson
Raphaelson

Trouble in Paradise © 1932 Paramount Publix Corp. Copyright renewed 1960 by
Emka, Ltd.

The Shop around the Corner © 1940 Loews Incorporated. Copyright renewed
1967 by Metro-Goldwyn-Mayer Inc.

Heaven Can Wait © 1943 Twentieth Century-Fox Film Corp. Copyright renewed
1970 by Twentieth Century-Fox Film Corp.

First printing

Printed in the United States of America

For LC CIP information see the colophon

ISBN 0–299–08780–8

To my wife, Dorshka

Contents

Foreword

Tino Balio

General Editor
Wisconsin/Warner Brothers Screenplay Series

This collection of screenplays by Samson Raphaelson is published under the auspices of the Wisconsin/Warner Brothers Screenplay Series. These pictures were not produced by Warner, yet Raphaelson is linked to our project through his play, *The Jazz Singer*, which was adapted and made into a movie by Warner Brothers.

When I conferred with Raphaelson about the preparation of *The Jazz Singer* volume (which was among the first group of screenplays to launch the series), the discussion inevitably turned to his career as a screenwriter and his famous collaboration with Ernst Lubitsch. This book, bringing together three of Raphaelson's best-known screen comedies, is the result.

Raphaelson provided texts of all three screenplays from his files, and performed the massive job of editing them for publication. In addition, he wrote the "Author's Notes" and the "Freundschaft" memoir which, before its appearance here, was published in the *New Yorker* in 1981.

Thanks are due to Metro-Goldwyn-Mayer and Twentieth Century-Fox, respectively, for permission to publish the screenplays of *The Shop around the Corner* and *Heaven Can Wait*; and to Mrs. Florence Laszlo, widow of Miklos Laszlo, the author of the play *Illatszertar*, we are grateful for the clearance on the underlying rights to *Shop around the Corner*.

Acknowledgments

First, I thank Tino Balio and Herman Weinberg, who came into my life almost fifty years after my time in Hollywood—Tino as General Editor of the Wisconsin/Warner Brothers Screenplay Series, and Herman as a lifetime film savant preparing his book, now well known as *The Lubitsch Touch*. They each "told" me—I was then nearing the age of eighty—that my work as a screenwriter was being remembered. Herman was going to say it in his book, and Tino proposed to say it with a book. I thank also Professor Stefan Sharff of Columbia University, chairman of the Film Division eight years ago, who invited me to be a teacher, which I have been since then.

For the making of this book, I thank Elizabeth Steinberg, Chief Editor of the University of Wisconsin Press, who has been consistently perceptive and watchful, and Diana Cook, who gave generously of her expertise during months of toil over my fifty-year-old studio manuscripts as we struggled to produce readable screenplays. (For details, see p. 49.) Also I thank Florence Laszlo, widow of Miklos Laszlo, the Hungarian dramatist; she has been most gracious about making data of the past available.

I thank Pauline Kael; and here I ask the reader's indulgence. Her introduction in this volume is a distinct honor, of course. However, all my life I have considered it dubious manners to thank a critic for doing a critic's job, and I see no reason to change now. But I have a separate and long-standing gratitude to Pauline Kael, the person, which is inexpressible here and perhaps anywhere else, but I feel that its existence should be on record.

Introduction

Pauline Kael

Early in 1982, when Samson Raphaelson was interviewed on public television by Bill Moyers, he said that he was a better craftsman than O'Neill or Tennessee Williams but that they were better playwrights. It was a clean stab, self-administered. Raphaelson, who was born on March 30, 1896, is wiry and tough-minded; he doesn't sentimentalize himself. When Moyers asked him why he thought that he wasn't as good a playwright, he said that he had never written about the things that mattered most to him, that he hadn't taken the final step—hadn't gone through the agony. Maybe, he said, he lacked the instincts or the emotional richness. However it was, "I never found a way of talking—profoundly and with authority—about what I know." And he explained that if he had died at seventy-five he wouldn't ever have understood this; it was only in the last decade that he had come to have a few little insights into his life. You could hear from his strong, harsh voice that he didn't want comforting assurances; he wanted what used to be called a fair field and no favor.

He was right in his evaluation of his work. But he was also wrong. He didn't give himself his due. He considered what our greatest playwrights have done that he hasn't—how they wrestled with their torments and shocked and disturbed us. But he didn't consider what he has done that they haven't.

Raphaelson's achievement in the theater is the creation of a chimerical world of streamlined elegance. It's a dream of high life, in which lovers are articulate, slim-hipped, and witty. As an adolescent in the thirties I saw his plays performed and, like

13

the plays of S. N. Behrman, they were comedies-of-manners floating in an urban cloudland. I listened to the rhythms of the burnished dialogue and knew that only people on the stage talked like that. The bright talk and the structured quality of Raphaelson's plays, such as *Accent on Youth* and *Jason*, or of Behrman's *Biography* belong to the theatrical past. Actors now don't really know how to move and speak and wear their affectations in the way that the performers of forty or fifty years ago did; they're not trained to be radiant. What then seemed almost-natural-but-better may come dangerously close to being arch, and the actors' consciousness that they're in a period piece can weigh them down. The plays are entertaining in revivals because there's real command of the stage in the way they're put together, but they don't have the glitter and dash they once had, when, just at the right, carefully prepared moment, capricious actresses such as Ina Claire and Gertrude Lawrence made their entrances and stood stock still, with a faint, amused air of surprise, as the audience burst into applause. (That's one of the differences between O'Neill or Williams and Raphaelson: O'Neill's and Williams's plays don't require a "civilized" theatrical style or soigné charmers. They don't make you feel nostalgic, either.) But some of the movies that Samson Raphaelson wrote for Ernst Lubitsch are almost perfectly preserved iridescent, make-believe worlds. They're different from the movies that Lubitsch made with other writers; they're more puckish, and have more texture and fullness and surprise.

It's true that Raphaelson isn't great in the sense that O'Neill is, but surely the poetry of sophistication that he and Lubitsch created in *Trouble in Paradise* (1932) had deep roots in their psyches. They were grown men playing at naughtiness. They were willing—exuberantly eager—to be silly. They prized wit, and the suavity and shimmer of their jokes mattered to them, all right; those are the qualities they wanted life to have (even if they weren't conscious of it).

In the discussion that took place after the showing of *Heaven Can Wait* (1943) at the Museum of Modern Art in 1977, Raphaelson said that he would never have used any of the material that he wrote for Lubitsch in a play of his own but that "looking at that marvellous face I would suddenly think of something that would delight him." Together, they made silliness enchanting. Raphaelson's writing is different in his plays; his comedies don't have a comic vision—they're not really light-headed in the way that his best work for Lubitsch is. They aspired to be more than comedies; there was always a serious kernel—a moral nugget, wisdom. Lubitsch freed him from the literate playwright's obligation to have "something to say." (Generally it was about learning to be "human.") Wanting to see laughter on "that marvellous face," Raphaelson wasn't afraid of frivolousness and nonsense. Since screenwriting wasn't his real work, he didn't have to worry about it; writing for the movies was just coming up with what he has called "wild doodles," and so he could try out the irresponsible thoughts that came to mind. He could trust his impulses, his instinct. But the freedom didn't carry over when he went back to working in the theater. In the plays he held down his own affections, warmth, passion. After the success of his first play, the 1925 *The Jazz Singer*, which in "Freundschaft," his memoir of Lubitsch, he refers to as "heartfelt, corny, and dramatic . . . shamelessly effective," he sought to discipline his emotionalism in the cause of art, and his playwriting lost its rootedness, its tang. From the vantage point of the eighties, it's apparent that he gave up too much. He didn't need to exercise all that rigorous, restrictive control—his sense of structure had become so much a part of him that he could count on it. In the *Citizen Kane* script, Herman J. Mankiewicz brought considerable narrative equipment into operation in order to have shifting perspectives on characters and events; in Raphaelson's scripts he accomplishes this again and again within single scenes.

Writing for Lubitsch, Raphaelson took the giddiest inspirations and then polished his dialogue until it had the gleam of appliquéd butterfly wings on a Ziegfeld girl's toque, but the skeletal strength of his screenplays was what made it possible for the ideas and the words to take flight. At the start of *Trouble in Paradise*, a garbage man in Venice piles refuse into his gondola and paddles off, singing a shade too passionately in a large, rich tenor voice. A few scenes later, the camera moves up, straight above the canal, to show what is going on in the rooms of a busy, expensive hotel: Herbert Marshall, in a tuxedo, stands leaning against a French door and looking into the night as a waiter sets a table for two; down below, Miriam Hopkins, in a slinky evening gown, arrives in a gondola and waves up at Marshall, who bows in acknowledgment and then waves back to her. And we think, "Ah, yes, the low life and the high life." But when we discover that these two are raffish thieves who have improvised romantic titles and backgrounds for themselves, we realize that this Baron and this Countess are lowlifers like the hammy, full-voiced garbage man.

The sequences of *Trouble in Paradise* are so fully shaped that the movie is like an interlocking series of complex vaudeville acts, each with its own specialty. Scene by scene (almost line by line) new light is cast on material that at first seems to be presented at face value, and Raphaelson has the knack of bringing the dialogue around to the opposite point from which a scene started. He uses types, such as Edward Everett Horton, but even his types can have true moments of feeling. When the action moves to Paris, Horton has a scene in which he keeps entering Kay Francis's box at the opera, saying "Goodbye!" and then returning. He doesn't want to go, but he hasn't been made welcome enough to stay, and we know exactly how he feels—we've all played the fool in these situations. Far below Kay Francis's box, Herbert Marshall sits in an orchestra seat, looking up through his opera glasses, and we see only what he sees: her jeweled evening bag. All through the opera sequence, our vision is so limited that we think the moviemakers' game is to present complicated night-at-the-opera maneuvers using just a handful of people; then, suddenly, there's a magical switcheroo—the doors open and crowds pour out. It's much more disorienting than seeing dozens of clowns tumbling from a tiny car, because we've been inside this car and there was practically no one there. (Can a gag be a precursor? A breeze flutters the pages of the opera conductor's score, taking us from the beginning to the end of the first act. It's a spoof of Slavko Vorkapich's montages before he became famous for doing them straight.)

The jokes never seem self-satisfied; the audience isn't left out of the finesse (as we may sometimes feel we are with Noël Coward). Herbert Marshall is so adept at the silky tricks written into his lines that he creates a hushed ambiance, and Miriam Hopkins, quick and darting, always has her feelers out, along with her kittenish claws. The two professional crooks are accomplished seducers, and Raphaelson knows that seduction is a form of flimflam—dust tossed in dazzled eyes. From the moment that the wealthy widow Kay Francis sees Marshall, her face takes on a yearning expression and she can't keep her calf-eyes off him; desire makes her warm and languid. Raphaelson also knows that witty seduction is indistinguishable from love itself. That's what makes him the ideal Lubitsch collaborator. The cynicism about love isn't disillusioning—the cynicism intensifies the lovers' feelings of helplessness. We're all in the same gondola.

The Shop around the Corner (1940) is, I think, as close to perfection as a movie made by mortals is ever likely to be; it couldn't be the airy wonder it is without the structure Raphaelson built into it. His strength is kept in reserve, but you know it's there—it supplies the tension and the elegance of feeling. The delicate, bickering dialogue scenes between Margaret Sullavan and James Stewart have steel underpinnings. (Raphaelson may have been right when he told Moyers that in a couple of hours he could show O'Neill and Tennessee Williams how to be better craftsmen.) The sophisticates of *Trouble in Paradise* were the dupes of one another; in *The Shop around the Corner* the characters are waifs and naïfs—the dupes of circumstance and of love itself. In both films the lines keep the characters twirling, but the sophisticates are the victims of artifice; these naïfs are the victims of sincerity. I doubt that there is any other movie heroine, with the exception of Katharine Hepburn in *Alice Adams*, who makes us feel the almost quivering empathy that Margaret Sullavan's dreamy, pretentious salesgirl does. Her slightly shrill self-consciousness and the scornful tone she uses on Stewart make us laugh, yet take our breath away.

When Sullavan spots a plump woman and improvises a sales pitch for a musical cigarette box by suggesting that it can also be used as a candy box ("This little tinkling song is a message to you: 'Too much candy' "), she is part of an already charged situation that revolves around these idiotic, overpriced music boxes that play "Otchi Tchornya." Raphaelson is so nimble that the sequence might be a demonstration of how many wheels and pranks he can set spinning: the jokes about the music boxes reveal the characters of most of the people in the movie. It's a feat of comic precision, and even when it seems complete, "Otchi Tchornya" returns to haunt those people.

The scripts read spectacularly well, and the attitudes at work in their design are recognizable in the scrupulous gallantry of Raphaelson's remarks about what he thinks are the flaws in *Heaven Can Wait*. He doesn't suggest that the picture wasn't well cast (though it wasn't: Don Ameche rings hollow, and he doesn't have the variety or the shadings to play a Lubitsch rake). And Raphaelson doesn't suggest that in some scenes the director pours on the whimsey and lets it congeal. Raphaelson looks at the movie, registers what embarrasses him in it, and takes the responsibility; he doesn't let himself off the hook. Though we viewers may agree with him about the flaws once he points them out and may even have been dimly aware of them while seeing the picture, it's so ingratiating that we're not likely to have been much bothered by them. They're not as damaging to *Heaven Can Wait* as he thinks, because all along we have a good time. It isn't the ethereal, feathery triumph that *Trouble in Paradise* is—it's a bit too explicit, too talky. *The Shop around the Corner* and *Trouble in Paradise*, though different from each other in almost every aim, are supremely romantic comedies. (If you watch either of them with someone you like, that person may seem enhanced by having seen the movie with you.) *Heaven Can Wait* isn't quite on their level, but it has lovely moments and a marvellously freakish musicale sequence that seems to bubble up out of nowhere. Raphaelson is very tough on himself—the fine critical intelligence with which he examines his own handiwork of decades ago is, possibly, more exhilarating than the movie is. (I sat once with a famous director during the showing of a film he had made many years earlier; he kept up an ecstatic running commentary. I saw weaknesses that knotted my stomach for him, but nothing marred his euphoria.) Raphaelson finds his true voice—comic, generous, unself-conscious—in his satirical observations about his own handiwork. A writer must be a wit right through to the core if he can't resist making fun of his own failures. (And he must have deep intellectual pride to point out those failures.)

Artists are better off when they're not worrying about greatness and posterity; when they take off their frock coats they stand a better chance of being themselves. Raphaelson knows that; just about everybody does. Yet this master of equilibrium undervalues the glories of lightness, because it comes so naturally to him; he thinks he should be wrestling with the higher torments. Blessedly, when he actually sits down to write now, or even just talks, he's as spontaneous as the man who doodled with Lubitsch, and he doesn't lack profundity or authority, though they're kept under wraps. "Freundschaft," which he published in *The New Yorker* in 1981, is perhaps the fullest expression of Samson Raphaelson's temperament; his emotions and his control are in complete harmony. It may be the most deeply felt essay ever written about a moviemaker. It must also be one of the most beautifully sustained pieces of writing ever done by an artist past seventy-five.

Like Lubitsch, Samson Raphaelson is a giver of pleasure. What man can ask more of himself?

Freundschaft:

How It Was with Lubitsch and Me

Samson Raphaelson

I worked on nine talking pictures with Ernst Lubitsch from 1930 to 1947, yet I never quite felt that I knew him or that he knew me. We were too much the creatures of our separate careers. I was a playwright. A play was something you worked on for a year or two, during which you managed to feed, clothe, and shelter your family, and then, if the play had the sheer soaring luck to be produced and even to survive on the stage and become a hit and pile money in your bank, something could sneak up from behind—for instance, the 1929 crash. Thus a pure, unadulterated playwright, which I was, could find himself in good company—other pure, unadulterated playwrights—when he accepted occasional employment in Hollywood, where you were paid while you wrote, week after week. Lubitsch, in contrast, was cinema incarnate. Beginning with his early years as a silent-film director—in Berlin, then in Hollywood—he had captured the imagination of Europe and America; the "Lubitsch touch" was born. In Hollywood, with talking pictures, the "Lubitsch touch" gained in dimension, and soon he stood high and alone as the creator of a special kind of sophisticated, disarmingly warm comedy never seen before or since. When he died, in 1947, I mourned his loss. I stayed away from California for the next three decades, wrote on my own, traveled, "lived"—as ever hot on the trail of the future. But recently the future has been getting more and more predictable, and the past—all I have to do is turn around—has been coming alive, full of enigmas, clues, and challenges. Lubitsch comes up from under. He has been due to reënter my life, even without the reminders from today's seething film culture, because I have begun to feel that he meant much more to me, and perhaps I to him, than I've ever taken the time to realize. Looking back, I can now discern a trail, not so shadowy, of signs we gave each other outside the thousands of work hours we shared—signs of giving a damn about each other as human beings.

Lubitsch was not what a writer would call a writer, nor did he waste time trying to be. I doubt if he ever tried to create a story, a film, even a scene entirely on his own. He had no vanity or illusions about himself. He was shrewd enough to cherish writers, and he welcomed the best available, roused them to outdo themselves, and at the same time contributed on every level and in ways that I cannot measure or define. This much I know: his feel for how good a scene or a picture or a perform-ance could be was that of a genius. Such a gift is rarer by far than mere talent, which is epidemic among the mediocre.

I try to remember what those thousands of hours we spent together were like. I was a film novice; he was the greatest film craftsman of his day. We always worked together in the same room. It might be his or my office in a studio building, a room in his home or mine, or in a New York or Palm Springs hotel. We worked six hours a day, five days a week. There was no clash of egos, no rancor when we disagreed, sometimes vio-lently, about a scene or a line. No matter how loudly we hol-lered, it was always in terms of the given task. We talked our writing. I always wrote by talking, anyway; I was no good alone with a typewriter. Fortunately, Lubitsch was a talker, too, and of course we always had a secretary with us. He wrote some of my best lines, and I supplied some typical Lubitsch touches. I did not keep score, and I never came home from work with details lingering in my mind. I had done the daily stint, earned the precious pay. The screen credit was incidental. The moment I left Lubitsch and movies, I rushed back to my "real" life—the next play, mine and mine alone. I did have a mild curiosity about seeing the finished film, but in all those seventeen years I visited a movie set less than half a dozen times, and then usually because Lubitsch wanted to change a line of dialogue. And I never hung around; there was nothing to learn by watching a three-minute scene being shot over and over.

After our first few films together, Lubitsch almost always wanted me, and I gladly came whenever it was feasible. We were an odd pair. He was short, rotund, eyes brilliant and black, hair shiny black. I was tallish, thin, nearsighted, eyes blue and bespectacled, hair brown. He was a Berlin creature—straight out of *Gymnasium* into Max Reinhardt's theater, educated by clowning in Shakespeare and Molière, a comic star in silent pictures at twenty-one, a world-famous director almost ten years before the advent of talking pictures. I was a Chicago product, middle-class, West Side; my goal was literary and lofty, but my youth had been misspent in four years of journalistic antics on the campus of the University of Illinois, saturated in the cultural ambience of *The Saturday Evening Post*. I soon gravitated to New York and Greenwich Village, where my culture ascended to the level of *The Nation*, *The New Republic*, and *The Smart Set* of Mencken and Nathan, and I vacillated between odd jobs reporting news or writing agency ads for money and unsalable short stories full of integrity. I looked down on movies; to me they were all Douglas Fairbanks jumping over parapets or Rudolph Valentino looking silly. I saw two or three Chaplin films, thought they were funny, and that was that. I had seen none of Lubitsch's silent pictures and barely knew his name. I was theater-mad, yet I never dared aspire to playwriting. I had graduated from O. Henry to Maupassant, but Shaw, Molnár, George Kaufman, Eugene O'Neill, and Sidney Howard were beyond emulation. The mere concept of three successive acts—anything longer than fifteen pages—paralyzed me. I didn't know that drama was my métier until 1924, when, out of the blue, at age twenty-eight, I wrote *The Jazz Singer*, a theater piece—heartfelt, corny, and dramatic. It hurtled me into a lifetime dedicated to never again being so shamelessly effective.

Two plays later, my first time in Hollywood, I met Lubitsch, only four years older but in his prime and, in the new talkies, greater than ever. It was late 1930 at the Paramount studios, where, married and the father of two small children, I was recovering from the 1929 crash. I was more than happy to meet him, because earlier that year I had chanced upon *The Love Parade*, which Lubitsch had produced and directed, and it was the first movie that ever caught me completely. In fact, it sent me cheering into the streets. That is what I had for him when we met—what *The Love Parade* had done to me. And it seems he wanted, for the script of *The Man I Killed*, his first attempt at tear-jerking drama, someone who could write a play like *The Jazz Singer* and really mean it. At the time, neither he nor I suspected that I could write his kind of comedy.

Our work was based always on a play, always European, and usually unknown here. Lubitsch would tell me briefly the general line of the plot. I never read the play, because he wanted me not to be hampered by someone else's writing. He chose material for its possibilities, material that left us free for rampages of invention in what was known as his style, a style I loved and never ceased loving—for him, not for myself. From the first, I found that a certain kind of nonsense delighted him. I would toss in preposterous ideas—"Here's a bad example of what I mean"—while we were struggling over a scene. He encouraged such nonsense, even during the first assignment, the melancholy *The Man I Killed*, and when we got into the next, the prankish *Smiling Lieutenant*,[1] he began actually using the stuff, to my surprise. I soon discovered that these conversational doodlings were serious business. For instance, the opening love scene of *Trouble in Paradise*, in a Venice hotel: Herbert Marshall is a master crook posing as a baron, and Miriam Hopkins is a lady thief posing as a countess. During their first rendezvous in Marshall's suite, their romance flowers when each unmasks the other. It turns out that she has pickpocketed his wallet and his watch and he has lifted her jeweled brooch and then somehow conjured the garter from under her evening dress. It was phony, incredible, and inconsistent with the image of Marshall as a supreme crook. But Lubitsch pounced on the idea, and we juggled

---

[1]*The Man I Killed* was written first, but it was not released until after *The Smiling Lieutenant*.

it past all sanity. He loved my wild doodle of Miriam handing Marshall his watch and remarking, "It was five minutes slow, but I regulated it for you."

We were socially congenial, in the Hollywood fashion. My wife and I were often invited to his home, and he and his wife (the second) were invited to ours, but almost never was it merely a foursome. In Hollywood, anything less than a dinner for ten was a faux pas. I am sure we thought of each other as friends, but my private life held no interest for him, and I had little curiosity about his. As for my plays, they were fiercely my own, and he was the last man on earth I would turn to if I needed advice. I think he preferred it that way. During the long stretches when I was in the East, neither of us wrote or phoned the other, except on business. I hardly ever knew what pictures he was making until long after they were made and I managed to see them. My wife says that we exchanged Christmas gifts when we were working together—boxes of candy or beribboned baskets of fruit and nuts.

I am not quite giving a sense of the fullness of this odd and inconsistent relationship. An example, perhaps, would be how I felt about Lubitsch's courtship of Vivian Gaye and how he gave me the news of their marriage. It was in the mid-1930s. I had done five films[2] with him, and I had been calling him "Ernst" since the first weeks of our first movie. (To Walter Reisch, the writer from Vienna, probably his most intimate friend, he was always "Herr Lubitsch.") He called me "Sam" and occasionally "Rafe," which I am more accustomed to. Yet underneath the informality, especially in the earlier years, I must have held him in awesome esteem. It included my concept of his male charisma. I didn't notice, for months, that he was a short man—about five feet five or six. Only when an envious Berliner mockingly compared him to Napoleon did I think of Lubitsch in terms of height. Actually, not only was he short, but his hands and feet were small, and he walked with a faintly bowlegged, lilting

---

[2] *The Smiling Lieutenant*, *The Man I Killed*, *The Merry Widow*, *One Hour with You*, and *Trouble in Paradise*.

step. He also had a bulge at the waistline. But his remarkable face and those brilliant eyes and his true feeling for every art that went into the making of movies gave him towering stature in my eyes, and I took it for granted that he could have any woman who struck his fancy. I could not conceive of a beautiful woman in her right mind hesitating if she had to choose between, for instance, Gable and Lubitsch. Or take a society man—blue-blooded, handsome, a polo player with a yacht. Hell, take Hemingway. I could write the scene. It would be no contest.

Well, I gradually learned that he was far from being a grand vizier of love. I knew almost nothing of his first marriage and divorce; when I met him he was unattached and freewheeling and, although not a chaser, had an appetite for and did very well with the fabulous cuties of Hollywood. But pretty soon it became clear that a wife to him meant a lady, and as much of a lady as the 1930s would tolerate. He was smilingly unimpressed by glamour women (except for an occasional soupçon of awe in the presence of Garbo), and he treated other men's wives, including mine, with fond boredom. But any female with the icy look of ancestry—unmarried, of course, and not too old or too homely—made him stop, look, and listen. He wanted to marry, and I heard that he had proposed, at one time or another, to several qualified ladies, but without success. This humbly born, self-educated specimen from *unter* no Berlin *Linden*, in his art so hilariously superior to kings and dukes and earls, was touchingly modest in the presence of even an ex-lady-in-waiting to some obscure royal dowager of some distant realm—which more or less described Vivian Gaye.

She was a not untypical European emigrée of the early 1930s, highborn and footloose. Her real name was copious and impressive and (I think) Slavic, and she spoke grammatical English with an expensive accent. My wife and I knew her first as one of the presentable, unclassifiable young women who appeared around the swimming pool of one's house on Sunday afternoons. I haven't the slightest idea who brought her to ours. She was handsome; her figure was good but not ravishing or imperious, and, to the best of my knowledge, she bewitched no one before Lubitsch came along. I believed her when she said she had been lady-in-waiting to the Queen of Denmark, but since I did not know the requirements of such a job I was not impressed. Lubitsch dropped in one Sunday—he had met her some time before, got a whiff of pedigree, a dab of encouragement—and they were now in a courting stage where she smiled but held back and he, truly guileless, was on his best behavior. Being a man of many humors, he couldn't avoid subtleties— deadpan ironies and extravagances. Vivian, who I'd have said had a limited sense of the comic, did seem to know when to smile, when to approximate laughter, and when to nod in recognition of a noteworthy remark—at least two out of three times, and I don't think Lubitsch was counting. I report all this from my own grudging viewpoint. The lady may have been the choicest of choice womanhood, but in my eyes she was not good enough for him.

I did not see Lubitsch for months after that, but one day I heard that he and Vivian Gaye were often together, and it made me, in a comfortable-bystander way, unhappy. Then, in October of 1935—I was in Palm Springs working on a play and must have missed the papers that day—someone told me they were married (something about running off to Arizona), and I readjusted my view of life, deciding that anything could happen to anybody. And, after all, the man and I merely worked together once in a while.

One evening a few months later—I was still in Palm Springs, but the play was going badly—Lubitsch called me. He had a story; was I available? The next day, we lunched in great spirits at Paramount.

"What are you doing, Sam?"

"Oh, you know—a play."

"Ah. How's it going?"

"Bad. I threw it away."

"Fine, fine. I think you're going to like this story."

Back in his office, he began telling me the general idea of *Angel*. The telephone interrupted. "Yes?" His face brightened. "Hello, darling!" He spoke affectionately about domestic matters. When he hung up, his eyes became watchful and his lips curled in a naughty little grin. He said, "Maybe you heard that Vivian and I got married?"

I said, "I think I *did* hear somebody say . . . "

Still with that grin, he said, "Well, it's true." Then, after a moment, brisk and on his feet, "Now, where were we?"

I grinned back and told him where we were.

That is as near as I can come to an indication of how life was between him and me apart from our intimate existence in the more tangible world of applied imagination.

Several years later, Lubjtsch had a heart attack, and there were signs of reaching out, at first mainly on my side. I had last been with him a year before, in the spring of 1942, when we finished our eighth picture together, *Heaven Can Wait*—a blithe experience. Blithe because we were at the height of our productive years. (I had written *Accent on Youth*, *Skylark*, and *Jason*—a head start toward immortality, I thought; Lubitsch, driving for the here and now, had been steadily making Lubitsch pictures with and without me.) Blithe because, separated at last from Vivian Gaye after several years of a troubled marriage, and with a four-year-old daughter to adore, he was in fine fettle. Blithe because we did our work on *Heaven Can Wait* in his Bel Air house, luxuriously at ease, me often laying aside my pipe for one of his special Upmann cigars. Blithe because we combined our individual gifts in that script and felt it was flawless. When the job was over and done, however, we parted with the usual brief handshake, knowing little more about each other than we had known before.

Jump a year, during which Lubitsch, at Twentieth Century-Fox, was bringing *Heaven Can Wait* to consummation on the screen and my wife and I, in Pennsylvania, were purchasing a farm. In the summer of 1943, leaving my family to rural bliss, I returned to Hollywood for a stint at M-G-M. I lived at the Chateau Elysée, and it was there, over the radio at breakfast, that I heard the news of Lubitsch's heart attack. He had fallen down unconscious the night before, at a party in a large tent set over a portable dance floor on a large lawn at the estate of Sonja

Henie. He was brought to Cedars of Lebanon Hospital, where desperate measures were being taken to save his life. The news certainly did something to me. That was thirty-eight years ago; I remember the day in patches. My wife told me later that I had called her and sounded badly shaken. I know that I did not call Lubitsch's home or the hospital and that I felt awful about it. But I hadn't seen him for a year and, as always, was not sure where I stood in his life or he in mine.

I remember the day as a long morning in my office at M-G-M. I arrived and got the latest bulletin from Tildy Jones, my secretary: Lubitsch was dying, if not already dead. Tildy had been with us on *Heaven Can Wait* (the working secretary was always mine), and she was continuing at my side through Hollywood thick and thin. Her news was authoritative and nearly first-hand: with nothing like my qualms, she had called the Bel Air house and simply asked for her friend, Lubitsch's private secretary, Steffie Trondle. Steffie, a dear elderly German woman who had been with Lubitsch since long before I knew him, had just returned from the hospital. She was hysterical, but also apparently in charge, talking with mad efficiency of coffins and pallbearers and, according to Tildy, referring to me as "one of the few who never let him down." (I remember those words exactly, because over the years several people have quoted them—the only precise clue to how Lubitsch felt about me. The rest of the dialogue I am improvising—as close as possible to what was said.) Tildy went on, "Steffie says that she realizes what a terrible loss this must be to you, and that you must express your grief while you feel it most, and I agree. You must write something beautiful to be printed so that future generations will know what a wonderful man Mr. Lubitsch was."

I recall no stirrings of grief. My imagination could not, and cannot, play around death; it is all offstage stuff. I certainly was sorry he was dead. Actually, I must have felt more, because, though I had promised some work to Arthur Hornblow, Jr., an M-G-M producer, I could not get at it. I could not write anything, anything at all. I remember making random telephone calls, and that Tildy looked at me impatiently, perhaps reproachfully.

Then Hornblow dropped in—a cultivated and imaginative man, and one of the few producers with a fine feeling for writers—and told me to forget the assignment. He said, "Why don't you write something about Ernst while you're in this state of mind?" He left, and I turned to Tildy and tried to explain that I didn't know what to write, because, incredibly, I didn't know the man well; I didn't even know what I *felt*. The subject obsessed me, however, and I kept on explaining for an hour or so, until suddenly I said some words, then some more, and they sounded right. She got them down. The rest poured out like a scene suddenly ripe and ready. I did know him. I did feel about him. In no time at all, there was a first draft. Here it is:

Lubitsch loved ideas more than anything in the world, except his daughter Nicola. It didn't matter what kind of ideas. He could become equally impassioned over an exit speech for a character in the current script, the relative merits of Horowitz and Heifetz, the aesthetics of modern painting, or whether now is the time to buy real estate. And his passion was usually much stronger than that of anyone else around him, so he was likely to dominate in a group. Yet I never saw, even in this territory of egoists, anyone who didn't light up with pleasure in Lubitsch's company. We got that pleasure, not from his brilliancy or his rightness—he was far from infallible, and his wit, being human, had its lesser moments—but from the purity and childlike delight of his lifelong love affair with ideas.

An idea mattered to him more, for instance, than where his forkful of food happened to be traveling at a given moment. This director, who had an unerring eye for style, from the surface of clothes and manners down to the most subtle intonation of an aristocrat's heart, was, in his personal life, inclined to reach for the handiest pair of trousers and coat whether they clashed or not, to shout like a king or a peasant (but never like a gentleman), and go through life unaware of many refinements and shadings, with that clumsiness which is the passport of an honest man. He had no time for manners, but the grace within him was unmistakable, and everyone kindled to it, errand boy and mogul, mechanic and artist. Garbo smiled, indeed, in his presence, and so did Sinclair Lewis and Thomas Mann. He was born with the happy gift of revealing himself instantly and to all.

As an artist he was sophisticated, as a man almost naive. As an artist shrewd, as a man simple. As an artist economical, precise, exacting; as a man, he was always forgetting his reading glasses, his cigars, manuscripts, and half the time it was an effort for him to remember his own telephone number.

However great the cinema historians will eventually estimate him, he was bigger as a person.

He was genuinely modest. He never sought fame or coveted prizes. He was incapable of employing the art of personal publicity. You could never wound him by speaking critically of his work. And somehow he never wounded his fellow-workers with his innocent forthrightness. If he once accepted you, it was because he believed in you. Thus he could say, "Oh, that's lousy!" and at the same time you felt his rich appreciation of what you hoped were your hidden virtues. A superb actor, he was totally incapable of acting in his human relations. He did not have one manner for the great and another for the lowly, one style for the drawing room and another for the bar. He was as free from guile and pretense as children are supposed to be, and this made him endlessly various and charming.

I am sorry I was never able to say some of this to him while he was alive.

I was pleased—more than pleased. It was better than a first draft. The real test was its effect on Tildy, a Hollywood product of a kind that I don't think exists today: about thirty, studio-bred since her teens in the silent-picture days, a virgin self-programmed to marry no one less than a thousand-dollar-a-week cinema underling, and very, very script-wise. Here my memory is clear: as I was dictating, I saw a tear rolling down her cheek. Then, after Tildy had typed it—long past lunchtime, but neither of us noticed—I read it aloud to make sure it was heartfelt yet not effusive, laudatory but judicious; and her responses were just right. At one point, she remarked that she hadn't realized how strongly I felt about Lubitsch, and of course I hadn't realized it myself. I had never before seen him defined and clear, framed and final, as by death.

A few weeks later, when I was allowed ten minutes with him at the hospital, I was deeply moved. He had to lie very still; even the use of his expressive hands was forbidden. I reassured him, mentioning John Golden, my producer on *Skylark*, a man over seventy, who was in great shape a year or two after a near-fatal stroke. Lubitsch smiled wanly. "I know, I know. But when I die, this is what I'll die of."

He did not die, and as time went on the accent of death faded. The regular life pattern took over. In the next four years, on the farm, my wife and I went through the ordeals of our children's adolescence, and I was busy with plays and stories. Lubitsch, in Hollywood, was doing his usual incomparable stuff. He probably knew I had a play on Broadway, and I must have heard of his next film, *Cluny Brown*. We were both back to normal. As for my funeral tribute, although it was now distinctly out of order, I kept the two-page script—the original and a few carbon copies—where I could always lay hands on it. I reread it, and found labored adulation, inaccuracies, and a glib style. I didn't do anything about it, but I knew that if the time came I would write more truly. After all, in 1943 I was forty-seven. I was maturing. I could not quite forget the pale man on the hospital bed.

My change consisted of past fragments seen anew—evidence of Lubitsch's humanity, and mine. I felt that one of us had failed the other. Maybe the original fault was mine. How did he take my obvious lack of interest in movies? True, I never received a wire from him on my Broadway openings, never felt he owed one to me. But how had he felt about no word from me on the premières of films we had created together? In many instances, I hadn't even known they had been released until weeks later. I didn't see *Angel* until it came to Bethlehem, twenty minutes from our farm. Conceivably, all this might have chilled him. He might have opened up if I had been a total film man, ambitious to be a director myself. I doubt if there would have been envy. He was too secure in his cinema cosmos.

I began reinterpreting, finding clues in things that had passed me by before. Maybe he had tried and I had failed him. One spring afternoon way back in 1932—we were working on *Trouble in Paradise* in his Santa Monica beach house—he asked me to stay and stroll the beach with him. I was sure he had something special to say, but we walked along with small talk, and after a while he began telling me about his father—unusual, but I gave it no great importance at the time. He was very fond of the old man and maintained him comfortably in a Berlin apartment. The apartment required a housekeeper, and Papa was constantly writing for additional money and sending bills—always for repair work on the main door. It was the housekeepers; there was a great turnover in housekeepers. If they didn't yield to the old boy, out they went. If they did yield, he got tired of them after a while, and the great lover had to have a new door lock to keep a rejected sex-mad female away. Lubitsch told this with his usual glee about fun in bed and with obvious filial pride, but, looking back, I recalled a difference—some pauses, as if he were waiting for me to speak, and a watchfulness that I could sense out of the corner of my eye but that disappeared when I glanced directly at him. But I, enjoying the telling, just smiled and laughed. Then, at the end, there was a long silence. It may well have been an invitation. It was the only time he had ever asked me to stay after work. Probably he was trying to create a more intimate atmosphere and, when I failed to respond, impulsively came up with a random intimacy about his father. Why didn't I tell him about my father? Why didn't I ask for more about Ernst? Was his mother alive? How did he feel about her? How was it between mother and father? Did Ernst have brothers, sisters? We were both Jews. That was something to talk about. My family, before two American generations, had owned, or leased, or labored in vineyards or orchards near Jerusalem. How far back was his family German? And before that—Poland? Spain? Palestine? I had heard, from others, that the father had been a tailor. A little tailor in a shop? An elegant tailor, custom-fitting the rich? I resolved that, next assignment, the very first day together, we would have a fine time bandying childhoods.

I began also to reëxamine some of my own behavior. Often, when talking about Lubitsch, I had said, "I love the guy." It came easily in Hollywood—a common phrase. You might say it about someone who agreed with something you said, or someone you didn't even know who did something you liked. But maybe I really cared. I recalled an evening in the second or third year of his marriage to Vivian Gaye—a dinner party. My wife and I were at the same table with Lubitsch and Vivian. I already knew—felt it, found evidence every time I saw them together— that the marriage had gone bleak. Lubitsch was out on the floor dancing, which he loved. My wife was dancing, too, and so were the others. Vivian preferred not to dance, and we were making talk. I said something about their baby girl, Nicola— that the child was beautiful and exceptionally bright, which was true. Vivian smiled and began praising the American melting pot. She believed in that melting pot, she said earnestly. Here it was not like tired old Europe. Then she said, "I'm all in favor of mixing, for instance, the blood of the aristocrat with the blood of the peasant." I lost my customary aplomb. I said, "I know exactly what you mean, Vivian. You are of course referring to Ernst and yourself—he the aristocrat, and you the party of the second part." I remember the remark well, because I was proud of my wit, and because I felt the lady had inspired it and deserved it. I also remember that we both smiled hideously at each other, pretending that nothing homicidal had been said. Then someone must have returned from dancing. I don't remember any more, but Lubitsch and I did not again work in his home until *Heaven Can Wait*, after he and Vivian had parted.

I often thought ruefully of that gauche and ungentlemanly remark, and I always attributed it to my rugged American resentment of the lady's ladyhood. It did not occur to me that it was an explosion of loyalty, to say nothing of love, for my friend, the husband. But in the years after 1943 I saw it in that light: I hoped and prayed that my words had not added to the dolorousness of his marriage. Did that mean that I cared about the man and hadn't realized it? It was possible, yet in those four years I never wrote Lubitsch or called him on the telephone. Maybe the annual Christmas card, but that is all. I was changing only in the sense that in odd moments I reinterpreted events that seemed to have other values when they happened. (I must add still another view of Vivian: All this goes back forty-five years; I was not as mellow and evenhanded as I am today; and if that episode seems in any way a reflection on the actual Vivian's character, I herewith state that I can be as wrong about fellow-humans as any man. It is quite possible that Ernst was no dreamboat in the dark mazes of matrimony, and, for all I know, Vivian may have had a prodigious sense of humor.)

I thought about Lubitsch again in a new way in 1944, after the ordeal of my play *The Perfect Marriage*. Before production, the script had an extraordinary reception. It was praised high, wide, and handsome by every theater magnifico who read it. All my other plays, especially the ones I brag about, had first been rejected, sometimes by more than a few producers. But this time there was not a single dissenting voice, beginning with my producer and friend Cheryl Crawford and fanning out to financial backers, theater owners, and stars yearning for the leading roles. Even a Hollywood studio hailed the script with a lavish pre-production offer, which Cheryl and I, in the belief that we were outsmarting them, sneered at. Should anyone question my veracity, I have ample evidence in my files. I saved every scrap: letters from the wealthy, the wise, and the glamorous, telegrams, cajoling cards attached to boxes of flowers— every scrap except the reviews of the New York critics, which were unanimously unfavorable.

It was not exactly a box-office failure, however, perhaps because Miriam Hopkins starred in it. But she was also one of the mistakes I had made. I chose her against the advice of others, including Cheryl Crawford. Miss Hopkins did not enhance the part. I might have survived the reviews if I could have put the blame only on my not too bright choice of star. But I knew that the play itself had missed. In the past, I had learned from my failures; there always came a day, not long after, when I saw why I had missed, and that was rejuvenating. But here I remained in the dark. I learned nothing from the critics or from soul searching. Could all those distinguished people who had loved the script be wrong? Yes indeed, they could. I longed for a godlike intelligence, and naturally I thought of Lubitsch. He and I, when going good, had the gift of catching the other on a wrong trail, thus saving what easily could be months of getting nowhere, writing one splendid wrong scene after another. I found

myself thinking, Just five minutes with him after I had finished
that script and five minutes on the phone when we were casting—what a difference it could have made!

In 1947, when Lubitsch called me from Hollywood for *That
Lady in Ermine*, I was punch-drunk from a year with a frustrat-
ing comedy about a young couple who survive the destruction
of the world, and so eager for a break that I welcomed the assignment without fussing about the story. Lubitsch said, "You'll
love it," and I took his word for it. I threw away the cluttered
comedy script. It did not occur to me that I might bring it along
and show it to him and—who knows?—get five life-saving minutes. I did, however, take the almost forgotten funeral piece,
with the vague feeling that anything might happen, and that
with some cuts and careful rewriting it could be made sound
and less irritatingly glib. (I abhorred "love affair with ideas.")

My wife and I arrived in Hollywood on a Sunday morning in
February, called Lubitsch from our rented house, and went to
his Bel Air home in the afternoon. He looked lively and fit. We
greeted each other as always—two fellow-workers starting another job. We did not embrace. Unlike many Middle Europeans,
he did not press lips to ladies' hands, nor did he salute males
with a hug and a two-cheek kiss. We did our usual handshake,
not the long granite grip and eye-to-eye contact of the true
American but a sort of flap—something to get out of the way.

He had changed. He had settled into living a single life, but
Nicola (now nine years old) was there, and he adored her slav-
ishly. He had drawn closer to a few European friends, friends
steeped in the film world—German-speaking cronies like Walter
Reisch, Willie Wyler, Billy Wilder, and Henry Blanke. And he
had, probably for the first time in his life, a real camaraderie
with a lovely woman. She was Mary Loos (niece of Anita)—
young, beautiful, splendidly tall, a blueblood of California-
pioneer ancestry—whose platonic devotion Lubitsch received,
to the surprise of everyone, with gratitude and affection. And
he seemed to have an increased awareness of me as a man with
a family. My wife and I felt it that first evening when we dined
with him. He asked about the school life of our teen-age chil-

dren and about life on the farm. After we told him, however, there were no more questions. And somehow we didn't get around to our own childhood days, his and mine, then or ever. There were also changes in his work life, and I soon found myself involved in them. Two more heart attacks in the past year, slight ones, had somehow been kept secret, especially from Darryl Zanuck, who revered him but might well have hesitated about giving him carte blanche on this expensive production. To impress Zanuck, we worked on the lot, in Lubitsch's executive suite, where I was given an adjoining office.

I did not know about any of these developments on the morning we started work. I saw that Lubitsch no longer smoked his Upmanns but chewed on cheaper cigars; otherwise he was in fine form, acting out every part, selling me his approach to the original old German operetta, while the secretary, taking no chances, was making notes like crazy. (She was new; Tildy was living in Seattle, married, I think, to the owner of a movie theater.) I began finding fault the moment I saw what he was up to—just another variation on the old Lubitsch fun-in-a-castle triangle. He thought the stuff was great, and I felt that he was kidding himself. We had a typical knock-down-and-drag-out hollering session.

Came lunchtime, and as we walked across the lot toward the executive dining room—part of his design to be seen every day, as it turned out—he looked around to be sure no one was within earshot, swore me to silence, and told me about the two "very small, believe me" heart attacks. He added, "And you can see, Sam, I'm taking good care of myself. I'm in great shape. I didn't smoke this morning—I chewed on that cigar. Did you notice?" He went on about taking walks, going to bed early, and eating sparingly—"You'll see at lunch."

I did see. And as I watched this former trencherman diddling with a cup of consommé and an insipid slice of boiled chicken, I decided then and there to forgo my customary integrity (in those days "integrity" was in constant use by eastern writers; so was "truth"; we tried to get them into every story, regardless of what that did to the story), and in the afternoon, after a series of properly reluctant retreats from my uncompromising position, pretended to see the light. So let it be warmed-over 1930 Lubitsch, I decided; it's still good. I rolled with it and developed everything his way—which was no cinch, and nothing to be ashamed of. I don't think I fooled him. Looking back, I believe he knew precisely what we were doing, shared my viewpoint, but preferred survival to glory. That vociferous first morning probably had scared the hell out of him.

Nothing else about his behavior—not a look, a word, a gesture—asked for special treatment. There was no off-moment when those brilliant eyes lost their immediacy and betrayed an underlying colloquy with death. Nor did I have, as I recall it, any sequel to the random stirrings toward him I had experienced when I had been three thousand miles away. Here he was; we had a job to do; his days were numbered; and there was no space for friendship fantasies in the limited workaday future.

My feeling for him, especially in the first few weeks, took a modest form. I merely wanted somehow, somewhere, at his table, at our table, or on his terrace on a weekend afternoon—I wanted to lift a glass, make a little speech, a statement. It sounds easy, but whenever an opportunity seemed to arise I realized, each time, that there was no way of doing it which would not be margined in black. Pretty soon, life was about the same as in earlier years. Lubitsch and I took each other for granted; I began secretly circling around a new play idea and, in my spare time, cheating on *That Lady in Ermine* with a lady who eventually became *Hilda Crane*.

Our last day together, as it reached its end, brought a breakthrough, for Lubitsch as well as for me. It was cockeyed, almost demoralizing, and in some ways perhaps dramatic. The initiative, astonishingly, came from him. Fortunately, I can report in considerable detail on what led up to it. I made notes, dictated them late that same day to my wife, before packing. And the next day, on the Super Chief, I added some observations that are relevant here.

My wife's chicken soup, for instance. In the earlier years, Lubitsch had been inclined to use chicken soup, noodles, and dumplings as lumpen metaphors for domestic felicity. But this chicken soup of 1947—very good but nothing sensational, my wife said, and I agreed—captivated him. He lauded it to one and all, using gourmet terms—on the level, with no mockery.

And his photograph. I had never been a collector of photographs, had never thought of asking or giving. But I saw this one lying loose on his office desk—it was during the first week of work—and I admired it. He said, "Would you like it?" I said, "I certainly would." He picked up the picture as if to hand it to me and, I thought, hesitated slightly—which is why the moment stayed with me. I recall thinking, Isn't he going to inscribe it? Does he expect me to ask? Then he said, after what I may have wrongly seen as hesitation, "Do you want me to sign it?" "Hell, yes," I said. I thanked him warmly for the inscription: "To Raph, with friendship, Ernst." I was not overwhelmed; it seemed a routine, cautious, adequate inscription. But I did know that, in German, "friendship"—*Freundschaft*—is a loaded word, carrying the privilege of using the intimate "*du*" instead of the formal "*Sie*" when saying "you." And he had written "Raph" (his spelling of "Rafe"), which my wife and American friends call me. Conceivably, the inscription was a signal, a message of feeling.

And then there was Steffie Trondle. Steffie is one of the many dear human beings that I failed to appreciate in the graceless interludes of my life. Over the years, I had known her only as a figure behind a desk in Lubitsch's outer office. On my way in, we would exchange descriptions of the weather and assurances of each other's health. On my way out, she would entrust to me, itemized, a series of good wishes for my wife and children, which I would earnestly promise to deliver. Now, daily at the studio, these amenities had expanded, taken on substance. Still unobtrusive, she seemed almost motherly, and I saw her as a person, but I felt no special significance in any of it. I had not seen her at all during the time of Lubitsch's 1943 heart attack. Our only contact had been Tildy's account of her hysterical telephone equivalent of a death announcement, but I doubted if she remembered much of that. Certainly she would have been astonished if I told her I had actually written a funeral piece. Her new family tone merely had meant to me: She's getting older and more chummy, and so am I.

But it turned out that she did know about the funeral piece, had known for a long time. Both she and Lubitsch! Throughout these Hollywood months in early 1947, and long before, they had known, *had read every word of the piece*, with never a hint to me—understandably, for they had got it from Tildy, from whom I had exacted a vow of silence the afternoon of that day back in 1943. I did it the instant I heard that Lubitsch was recovering. You don't want a living man to think you were in such a hurry to eulogize over his coffin that you didn't even bother to inquire if he had stopped breathing. It was more than that. I just could not bear for Lubitsch to know about it, let alone read it. Well, it seems that Tildy had broken her vow. (Tildy Jones is not her real name, by the way.) She kept her shorthand notes, which she had pledged to destroy and, purely as a lover of belles-lettres, had typed a few secret copies. But she had not told anyone, not even inadvertently at lunch that first day; there was a secretarial code, a taboo protecting the inspirations of one's writer. (They might be stolen by another one's writer.) But one fine day, after I had left Hollywood, still in 1943, she ran into her friend Steffie—Steffie, who lived and breathed only for Lubitsch. After all, who had a better right to see his eulogy? Pausing only to extract a hasty duplicate of her vow to me, Tildy delivered a copy to Steffie. Whereupon Steffie, overwhelmed by my prose, and an undiscriminating worshipper of Lubitsch, went straight to her deity and broke *her* vow.

Now comes that last day, a Friday. I stopped at the studio, gathered my things, and said a fond farewell to Steffie. (I never saw her again; she died a few years later.) I drove to the Bel Air home, where Lubitsch and I had a typical windup of a typical job, leisurely checking the mimeographed script. I had long since left behind the sense of imminent death, and I had long relinquished the notion of a love statement. Only the coming evening of packing and last-minute chores was on my mind. Lubitsch, too, seemed to be taking everything in stride. No nostalgia. No "Well, Sam, this is our ninth picture together." We lunched; I don't recall whether Nicola was there. We returned to the study and, as usual, dozed for a half hour in our easy chairs. Then, I smoking a guest Upmann and he chewing his lesser cigar, we cleaned up the last sequence.

About three, we were finished, and we both got up. He seemed to be in great shape—tan, lively, on the beam. He tilted his head a little and took a measuring look at me. Then he said, "By the way, Sam, I heard that you wrote something a few years ago when I was sick—you wrote something very nice about me, and I appreciate it."

It came casually, part of the goodbye—a bit more than a trifle, something even to give pause, calling perhaps for a mutter of surprise and pleasure, and then out with you, I've paid my friendship dues, goodbye and good luck. But I stood there, upset. He said, "What's the matter, Sam? You worried how I heard about it? Come on, you should know how things leak in this town. So what? I'm telling you, I appreciate it."

There was something missing, and—we were still standing in the study, where we had written *Heaven Can Wait*—automatically I turned away from him, a writer with a problem, and began pacing the room. It was easy to guess that the leak had come from Tildy. He, wasting no time in petty deception, admitted it—Tildy to Steffie to himself. And then—of course. Now it came out from under, my awful suspicion: "You read it!" His guilty grin gave him away, and he told me the little story—made a humorous anecdote out of it—dwelling with wry indulgence on the broken vows of Tildy and Steffie, and on his own. "Please, Sam, don't ever tell Steffie I said a word!"

As he went on, I found myself visualizing that piece of writing through his eyes, and its defects became scarifying. My God, it was all about him; he was the subject matter—his *life*, total and complete. Was that the best I could or would do, once he wasn't there to pass judgment?

All he seemed to care about, however, was getting the whole thing over with, and he became serious and brisk. "What's the difference?" he said. "I *liked* what you wrote, Sam. I really appreciated it." This from the man who time and again, through the years, when I had drudged over a scene and he had read it, would say, "Sure it's good. But good isn't enough—you know that. For *us*, it has to be *terrific*." And here he "liked," he "appreciated." It was sinister. It was ironical. The man hated me.

I had to have it out. "It's only a first draft!" I cried, and I floundered on in fragments, saying and not saying and almost saying that I positively would have seen the inadequacies of those two pages the very next day if he had been dead according to expectation. "You know damn well the jumps I can make from the first to the second or third version," I said. I threw his words back at him—"You *liked*, you *appreciated*"—accusing him of insulting my intelligence. I practically called him a monster for waiting four years to tell me, if he truly did "appreciate" and "like" what I'd written, and a double monster for speaking now. I dared him to be honest and specify the defects; I challenged him, betting I saw more than he did; and somewhere along the line he laughed at me, and I laughed, too. Of course it was funny, but part of the laughter came from my relief at discovering that he was not in the least squeamish about his own death or any of the chapel-and-cemetery high jinks it would beget— that to him the whole subject was comic. I laughed, but I returned to what I was really trying, in my writer's pride, to say: that when and if he did die, that piece would be corrected, perfected, illustrious, accurate—a true monument.

It got to the point where, according to my notes, he said earnestly, "I believe you, Sam. I am satisfied absolutely that if I drop dead tomorrow you'll do a polishing job that I would rave about if I read it in advance."

He was not smiling, nor was I, and suddenly we were looking at each other in a very familiar way. I was thinking, "My God— he and I together—right now—it would take just an hour, that's all!" And I saw in his eyes exactly the same thought.

Inevitably, that is what happened. We started working on the piece as if it were a speech in a film. No, it was not like that. I'll come to it. I pause only to caution against false expectations. Let it be clear that this is not heading into a big scene, climactic, revelatory, or dazzling. A scene, to be sure, and worth telling, because, in its awkward way, it was the nearest Lubitsch and I

came to a friendship that now, at eighty-five, I think was there
and waiting to be found.

In that eye-meeting moment, I must have felt that we had
been switched, transposed, as it were, to our private working
domain—two veterans, tried and true, royally at ease, who together could lick anything in the realm of words on paper. It
seemed simple and natural when I leaped up and said, "I have
the script at home—I'll be back in ten minutes." And it seemed
natural—at the time, I'm sure it didn't strike either of us as
funny—when Lubitsch said, "Wait—I think I have a copy here."
He went to his desk, opened a drawer, and the next thing I
remember is the old familiar scene—Lubitsch at the desk,
glasses on, pencil in hand, chewing a cigar, going over a piece
of work line by line, and me, sitting opposite, watching the face
I could read so well.

Halfway down the first page, he marked something with the
pencil, then quoted it: "'An idea mattered to him more, for instance, than where his forkful of food happened to be traveling
at a given moment.'" His tone was impersonal, editorial, as he
looked up over his glasses. He said, "I like the way you describe
my bad table manners, Sam."

The man was obviously not praising my style but rankling at
that single fine careless forkful. I must have made a lightning
readjustment. It was easy, for I was also telling the truth. I said,
"Well, I *don't* like it. I was exaggerating for effect. Your table
manners are damn good ninety-nine percent of the time."

Lubitsch said, "Now, be exact, Sam. Because I don't go around
watching myself—and now that we are on the subject . . . "

I said, "Make it ninety-eight."

He returned to the script. I pulled my chair over beside his
and followed him through that dangerous paragraph. Mumbling, he lingered over phrases like "aristocrat's heart," "handiest pair of trousers and coat whether they clashed or not,"
"shout like a king or a peasant." I trembled at "aristocrat" and
"peasant," praying that Vivian had never, in some twisted,

aberrant moment, added my unfortunate remark to the un-happy vocabulary of their marriage.

Apparently, she had not, for he mumbled on to the end of the paragraph. Then he paused and, in that same phony, workman-like tone, inquired, of all things, about the clashing pants and coats, and, he added, what about shirts and ties? For a moment there, I think he was actually alarmed at the image of himself trotting down the corridors of Time in a series of outlandish ensembles. I said, "Nonsense!" I made the point that his shirts and ties were all too quiet for any glaring contrast, and I gave my word that only once in a while his coat and pants didn't exactly match. He pinned me down: How often? I said, "Twice, maybe, since 1930." I swore that all this was calculated to give an endearing image, to "humanize" him, as he should be the first to understand. He came to his senses and grinned at me. Let me emphasize here that Lubitsch was a modest and unpre-tentious man, and if any of this sounds out of character, so be it.

Then he got to "However great the cinema historians will eventually estimate him," and his tone changed. He said, with a touch of bitterness, "What historians? They'll laugh at you. A movie—any movie, good or bad—ends up in a tin can in a warehouse; in ten years it's dust." He really believed that; I had heard him say it before. He also said, to my surprise, "You're smart that you stick with the theater, Sam. What college teaches movies? But drama is literature. Your plays are published. Someday a student gets around to you—you have a fighting chance." I secretly agreed with him on both counts and made a note to rephrase his greatness.

Toward the end, he got uneasy when he reached the part about lack of guile. He was always leery of people whose word was as good as their bond. He said, "You know better than to call me honest, Sam," and, indeed, in the ambience of Hollywood I did know better. We agreed that he and I—I reasonably in-cluded myself here—were *comparatively* honest. More honest, probably, than Josef von Sternberg and less honest than Abra-ham Lincoln—or even than Samuel Hoffenstein, a lovely man we both admired. Then, completely steeped in his viewpoint, I took over. I went back to the opening paragraph and denounced it as misleading. In truth, as we both knew, he was hardly ever the dominant figure in a group and never wanted to be. He always felt that social life was for the flow of easy talk, and he was against, for instance, Chaplin taking over a party with his pantomimes—"Let him save it for the screen!" I reminded him of all that and promised to cast a benign light on his social unobtrusiveness. He nodded, but said nothing.

I think there was a pause here. Then he looked at me over his glasses, reached for a fresh cigar to chew, and said something like Tildy's remark four years earlier: "I didn't know you had such feelings about me, Sam." And I said something like "Well, I didn't know it, either, but when I thought of you as dead, it gave me . . . " I remember hesitating and his supplying the writer's word: "A springboard?" I said, "Exactly!"—and we both smiled. He questioned whether such feelings would happen to—and he dryly named one or two writers who had worked with him. I told him he was being childish, of course, that he was enormously liked, and I added quite a few more names. He didn't seem impressed.

That was about all. It petered out. Maybe he hadn't even known that our eyes had met. And, actually, what could I possibly have expected? At best, a few lucky minutes in which one of us, preferably himself, would conveniently scintillate—a touch, a phrase, a word—and the room would brighten and Lubitsch would deliver a ringing "Terrific!" to wipe out that grudging "I appreciate."

According to my notes, I looked at him and he looked at me—uneasily, it seemed; but I didn't kid myself into thinking that I could read his mind. I got up. Still in there pitching, I said something like "Well, I'm glad we had this talk, Ernst. A thing like this, a person loses perspective. But now I really begin to see the possibilities. . . ."

He said, "Don't go yet, Sam." An expression of deep thinking had come over his face. He put on his glasses again and picked up the script. "You want to know something?" he said. "This piece is beginning to grow on me. Just the way it is—every single word, from first to last."

I listened in a slight daze as he went on, arguing reasonably to the effect that here was a first-draft spontaneity that had a truth of its own, transcending the literal truth. (I don't remember whether it occurred to me then, but today I suspect he was suddenly smitten with the fear that—behind his back, as it were—I might do a lousy rewrite job.) Well, I kept standing there, probably looking untrustworthy, and suddenly he was up on his feet and around the desk. "Listen, Sam," he said, "this is different from the way we work on a *scene*," and he vigorously argued that here I would not be condemned for literary lapses, that these very lapses, in a person of my taste, were the stammering, decisive evidence that the heart, not the mind, was speaking. As for the inexactitudes about himself, he said, "Who can object? It's your opinion."

The matter had become undisguisedly personal and important to him—much more so than it could be to me. After all, it was his funeral. I saw the point and had no trouble agreeing with him. He was making sense. However, for the record, I carefully reminded him of his own ample critical observations. He dismissed them, reminding me in turn of my ironclad belief that in creative work if you go for the whole truth, honoring every crumb, you're a clerk, not an artist. I accepted that, too, even if it did not exactly apply. But still he wasn't sure of me. "Promise me, Sam," he said, "that you won't change a *single word*." I promised at once, of course. I was on the verge of volunteering a vow, but I refrained; vows were a dime a dozen that day. Anyway, he believed me at last, and all was well.

It was nearly five o'clock when we said a brief final goodbye, both having been thrown off schedule and fretting to get things done. However, as I drove in my rented car to our rented house, I was aware that I most likely would never see him again, and that this last hour had been truly cockeyed, running aslant in all directions, full of implications that might take on meaning in time. I tried to memorize highlights—phrases, expressions on his face, my own thoughts at a given moment. At home, my wife agreed that our packing—everything—could wait, and I dictated to her all I could remember. (I couldn't figure out, and I still can't, whether somewhere toward the end his "I appreciate" had been transmuted into "It's terrific!")

I heard the news of Lubitsch's death over the radio on the farm in Pennsylvania. That was in late November of the same year, 1947. I am sure I sent flowers, telegrams, and letters. I was immersed in a series of short stories, and there was little else I could do until sometime in December, when a letter came from Richard English, editor of *The Screen Writer*. He was publishing a symposium of tributes to the Master, and would I write one. English gave a brief report on the funeral. It was impressive and without pomp. Lubitsch rested not in a formidable crypt but out in the open—a simple tombstone, uncrowded, accessible, and pleasing. English admired the eulogy by Charles Brackett, and he enclosed the text. He also dwelt glowingly on Jeanette MacDonald's rendition of "Beyond the Blue Horizon," adding that it was too bad she hadn't sung it that well originally for Lubitsch in *Monte Carlo*.

I kept my promise to Lubitsch and sent the untouched first draft—untouched except for a brief obeisance to Brackett's graceful and scrupulous eulogy. Otherwise not a comma or a period was altered. I did hesitate about the little postscript in which I regretted not having made my sentiments known to the deceased while he was alive. Lubitsch and I had overlooked that item. I decided to take my promise literally, and launched the dissembling postscript intact, not even revising its sloppy wording. I knew then and there, of course, that I was thus proclaiming myself a liar if ever, in the future, I should find occasion to write what I am writing now, in 1981, when, had he lived, Lubitsch would have been almost ninety and, in my opinion, most amenable.

Author's Notes

Each of these three screenplays is a new creation—totally original in style, in the shape of scenes, and in the dialogue; yet each is based on a stage play and could never have been written if that play had not existed.

These texts have been set in type from the mimeographed studio scripts as they went into production fifty to forty years ago. I have revised for the general reader the detail and phrasing of the continuity, which at the time was intended only for studio personnel—photographers, casting department, costume and setting designers, and so on.

I have retained material that was eventually cut from the finished film. It is set in smaller type. I have added the new material—dialogue, shots, or action—that was inserted during production. ‡It is set between "daggers," like this sentence.‡ There are not many such additions. Lubitsch believed in a script that carried every possible detail. We both distrusted inspired after-moments—our own or from actors. We courted spontaneity and were ready at the drop of a hat to improvise, but only during writing time, when we always made creative elbowroom. That is not inconsistent with cuts and other changes later on; it is simply our way of working.

These texts have not been altered to resemble the final breakdown of a shooting script, which would make them virtually unreadable.

Trouble in Paradise

Trouble in Paradise

SEQUENCE A

FADE IN   NIGHT
MED. SHOT   DOOR OF A HOUSE
A cheap residential district. The house has no architectural character; it is not certain where we are. Near the entrance door is a garbage can, full.

A dog is nibbling at some of the garbage. We hear whistling, footsteps. A garbage man comes into the picture. He shoos the dog away. Without pause in whistling, he lifts the garbage can and, followed by camera, goes to the end of the block, which is only a few steps. Now we discover we are in Venice. In the background is a major canal and a typical bridge—romantic background. Gondolas are passing. In the foreground at the sidewalk is the garbage gondola, piled high with garbage. The man dumps his load, leaves the empty can on the sidewalk, gets in the gondola, and paddles away with the grace of a gondolier. Now, in a beautiful tenor voice which is quite a contrast to the garbage, he starts singing a passionate Italian love song.

LONG SHOT   A GONDOLA
Two tourists. Husband and wife. They are in a sentimental embrace. In back is the gondolier. Camera follows gondola a few seconds, coming closer.

ANOTHER GONDOLA
Camera shoots down. Gondola is covered by a typical little canopy, so that gondolier cannot see the passengers. Camera cuts canopy on one side so that we don't see, at first, who is paddling. In the gondola seat is a woman in evening gown, lots of jewels. She lies in the arms of the gondolier. They kiss. Camera moves up and discovers who is paddling the boat. It is the husband of the lady who is having such a good time with the gondolier. Husband is in tuxedo and straw hat, smoking a long cigar. He is enjoying it like a child with a new toy.

HUSBAND:
    Darling!

WIFE'S VOICE:
    Yes, sweetheart.

HUSBAND:
    What a canal!

SIDEWALK
in front of the hotel. Camera shoots down from the hotel on the sidewalk, including part of sidewalk and canal. The water reflects the electric-lighted name of the hotel. At sidewalk is moored a gondola in which are four people. A man climbs out, starts to sing, the others in the gondola playing accompaniment. We hear a romantic Italian song, irresistible. The four look up to the hotel windows, expecting coins.

HOTEL ROOM INT.
photographed against the open window. In the background is the canal. Through the window we hear the street singers. Near the window is a table where five men are in a poker game, not listening to the music. We hear, over the music, the rattling of the chips. After a few moments the noise of the chips stops and the singing comes through more clearly. Casually one of the men, cards in hand, walks to the window, closes it, and returns to game.

ANOTHER HOTEL ROOM   CLOSE SHOT
at open window. A woman is on a chair by a small table, telephoning.

WOMAN:
    Uh-huh . . . Uh-huh . . .

During the scene we hear the same street singers. The woman, annoyed by the singing, closes the window.

ANOTHER HOTEL ROOM
shooting over the bed toward an open window. Same singers are heard. On the bed, in the foreground, is a woman lying in her chemise and crying. In the background, sitting on the arm of a chair which is by the open window, is an elegantly dressed man. Evening clothes, overcoat, hat, walking stick. Annoyed by the crying and by the outside music, he gets up and slams the window shut with a bang.

FRANÇOIS'S HOTEL ROOM   MED. SHOT
In the background is an open window with French doors leading to a little balcony. This room is on the other side of the hotel, looking out on a side canal. Close outside the window we see trees. The same music is still audible, but much fainter. Near the window is a desk. The drawer is open and all the papers are scattered on the floor. At the

other side of the window is a trunk, open, all the drawers out and the contents thrown around. Room looks as if it has been rifled. For a little while we hear nothing but the faint music. Then we hear the door buzzer. There is no reaction. The buzzer rings again. Suddenly from behind the camera, a man comes into the picture. He is in a tuxedo. His back is to the camera, so we cannot identify him. He goes quickly to the window, jumps from balcony to a tree, and, climbing down, disappears. Buzzer rings again.

Camera goes toward the tree to a very big close-up of a little branch. We see, on this little branch, a false moustache. We hear the man reach ground and receding footsteps as he hurries away. Again we hear, a little fainter, the buzzer.

‡EXT. HOTEL   MED. SHOT
on wall in moonlight. We see shadow of tree and of man as he reaches the ground. In silhouetted shadow, we see him take off moustache and sideburns and toss them out of the picture.

FRANÇOIS'S HOTEL ROOM   MED. SHOT
toward window, low. Camera draws back and comes to a close shot on the feet of a man outstretched on the floor behind the camera. Buzzer is heard again, loud.‡

HOTEL CORRIDOR   CLOSE SHOT
at room door. We see the numbers 253, 5, 7, 9. At the door are two Italian dames, obviously disreputable. One is pushing the buzzer. They speak in Italian, but their emphasis and pantomime make the following clear to English-speaking audiences: Girl No. 1 brought Girl No. 2 to see the gentleman of room 253. Girl No. 1 rings again. Girl No. 2 complains to Girl No. 1 that she should have known better than to have brought her here and wasted her time. Girl No. 1 apologizes and indicates her watch as if to say, "The appointment was definite. I can't understand it." She rings again—viciously this time.

LONG SHOT   FRANÇOIS'S HOTEL ROOM
Sprawled on the floor, his head resting on a chair, François is motionless. We see that a crime has been committed. François is an elegant man, about thirty-five, a conceited bon vivant. He is in a tuxedo. We hear the buzzer, insistent.

CORRIDOR   CLOSE SHOT
at door. Girl No. 1 presses buzzer angrily. Girl No. 2 accuses her loudly. Girl No. 1 answers just as loud. Girl No. 1 now bangs on the door, shouting insults to the occupant of the room. Girl No. 2 joins her.

HOTEL CORRIDOR   CLOSE SHOT
at door across the hall from room 253. It is numbered 254. We hear the voices of the angry Italian girls. The door opens, and an old gentleman, white beard, dressing gown over evening clothes, steps out. He politely but firmly asks, in Italian, for silence.

CLOSE SHOT   DOOR   ROOM 253
The girls turn quickly toward the man. No. 2 says she can talk as much as she wants to.

CLOSE-UP   OLD GENTLEMAN
He states emphatically that he won't stand for this.

CLOSE-UP   GIRL NO. 1
She looks over the old gentleman and makes a nasty personal remark.

CLOSE-UP   OLD GENTLEMAN
He loses his temper and insults the girls venomously.

CLOSE SHOT   TWO GIRLS
They are at the height of their fury. No. 2 walks out quickly toward the old gentleman.

CLOSE SHOT   DOOR   ROOM 254
Old gentleman is in the open doorway. Girl approaches. The two stand toe-to-toe trading verbal punches. The old man, disgusted, retreats. He is about to close door, but girl, still vociferous, follows him into his room and closes door behind her.

CLOSE SHOT   GIRL NO. 1
Still in front of 253. In the sudden silence, she looks amazed toward 254. No. 2 has disappeared!

CLOSE SHOT   DOOR   ROOM 254
Door opens quickly. No. 2 sticks her head out and, with a characteristic jerk, says in Italian, "Come in." She disappears, door slightly ajar.

CLOSE SHOT   GIRL NO. 1
at 253. She goes to 254, enters, closes the door. The camera swings fast to opposite side of corridor and stops at 253. We hear telephone ringing inside.

FRANÇOIS'S HOTEL ROOM
shooting from outside of the window into the room. In the foreground is the window frame. We see François on the floor. Phone is ringing.

François awakes, tries to struggle to his feet. But, still under the influence of dope, he falls. As he falls he drags with him, from nearby little table, a tray with glasses, making a loud noise.

(The window frame in the following moving shot across windows outside will be done with a miniature hotel building.)

Camera swings swiftly along the hotel front, around the corner of the hotel, and up to the third floor. It stops at a little balcony. Behind the balcony, leaning against one of two open French doors, stands Gaston, in a tuxedo, smoking a cigarette, looking romantically into the night. We see, in the room, a waiter setting a dinner table for two. The waiter arranges some flowers; then he comes forward, offering Gaston the menu. Gaston does not respond.

WAITER (breaking into Gaston's reverie):
Yes, sir? (Gaston still looks into the night.) What shall we start with, Baron?

GASTON (coming to):
Oh, yes . . . Well, that's not so easy. (Half to himself.) Beginnings are always difficult.

WAITER:
Yes, Baron.

GASTON (directly to the waiter, presenting a problem):
If Casanova suddenly . . . turned out to be Romeo . . . having supper with Juliet—who might become Cleopatra . . . How would you start?

WAITER (in a professional and prosaic tone):
I would start with cocktails.

GASTON:
Um-hum. Very good. Excellent!

Suddenly Gaston sees something on the canal.

MED. SHOT   GONDOLA
In gondola, Lily, in evening dress, looks up at Gaston and waves graciously.

BALCONY   CLOSE SHOT
Gaston and waiter. Gaston bows—the bow of a gentleman to a lady of high degree—and waves back. This is the woman he is waiting for.

GASTON (still looking at Lily):
> It must be the most marvelous supper. We may not eat it, but it must be marvelous.

WAITER:
> Yes, Baron.

GASTON (turning):
> And, waiter—you see that moon?

WAITER:
> Yes, Baron.

GASTON:
> I want to see that moon in the champagne.

WAITER:
> Yes, Baron. (Writing; very businesslike.) Moon in champagne.

GASTON (groping for words):
> I want to see— (An ecstatic sigh escapes him.)

WAITER (continuing to write):
> Yes, Baron.

GASTON:
> And as for you, waiter—

WAITER (eagerly; expecting a tip):
> Yes, Baron?

GASTON:
> I don't want to see you at all!

WAITER:
> No, Baron! (With a little bow, waiter starts to leave. Suddenly he sees something on the back of Gaston's jacket. Gaston looks at him, puzzled. Waiter reaches over, lifts a leaf that is clinging to the coat, and holds it up.) I beg your pardon.

GASTON (takes the leaf calmly):
> Thank you.

Waiter goes. We hear the door shut. Gaston is thoughtful a brief moment. Then idly he tosses the leaf over the balcony rail into the night.

TELEPHONE ROOM OF HOTEL   CLOSE SHOT
of an operator. In the background we see two other operators. We hear
the girls answering in Italian. Our operator is delivering a lengthy message. While she is talking she looks up to the switchboard because she
sees:

CLOSE SHOT   SWITCHBOARD
at No. 253. The light is flashing on and off very quickly. We hear the
operator's voice, still busy with the message she is delivering. Now she
plugs in on 253.

CLOSE-UP   OPERATOR

OPERATOR:
> *Si, signore.* (We see by her expression that the man in room 253 is
> reporting the robbery; excitedly.) Yes, sir! Right away!

She disconnects 253 and plugs in on the manager. She tells the manager, in Italian, what has happened.

CLOSE SHOT   GLASS DOOR
In Italian, English, French, and German: Manager. Door opens and
manager hurries out.

BIG CLOSE-UP   OPERATOR
talking very fast in Italian, reporting the robbery to someone else.

CLOSE SHOT   A DOOR
opens, and another man, apparently a detective, comes out.

STAIRCASE
Another hotel attendant is running up.

BIG CLOSE-UP   TWO MAIDS
talking excitedly in Italian, apparently discussing the robbery.

ANOTHER PART OF CORRIDOR
Camera shoots down over the back of a waiter. He holds high over his
shoulder a tray on which are several empty dishes. A little bellboy is
standing beside the waiter, looking up and explaining in Italian excitedly what has happened.

‡STAIRCASE

Two maids on opposite landings. Steward comes up stairs and tells them of robbery.

TELEPHONE ROOM

Another operator talking excitedly.‡

CORRIDOR

A hotel official dashes along. We hear many voices talking at the same time. Camera pans with him up to room 253 where he stops. Door is open. Half in room, half in corridor, are hotel attendants, detectives, the manager. With excited gestures, they are discussing the situation in Italian. Their voices become increasingly loud.

MED. SHOT   DOOR

to room 254. It opens quickly. Girl No. 2 appears, hair slightly disarranged. She looks annoyed and shouts in Italian for them to keep quiet.

MED. SHOT

of room 253. The men stop talking, look quickly over toward the girl.

CLOSE SHOT   GIRL NO. 2

Indignantly and crudely, she wants the noise to cease. She closes the door.

MED. SHOT   AT ROOM 253

The men, talking quietly, go into the room and close the door.

GASTON'S HOTEL ROOM   MED. SHOT

at door, inside. Gaston opens it, and Lily enters quickly. Gaston closes the door, looks at Lily questioningly. She is excited and out of breath.

LILY:

Oh, my gracious—he almost saw me.

GASTON (the crook in him worried for a second):

Who?

LILY (almost hysterical):

The Marquis de la Tours. He was in the lobby. But I don't think he saw me. I'm positive he didn't. Thank heaven! . . . But when I came up here, right out in the hall there was King Boris of Alconia!

GASTON:

The tennis player?

LILY:

> The tennis player. He saw me. He bowed. What could I do? I nod-
> ded. (Summing up in panic.) Baron, I shouldn't have come!

GASTON (goes to her, takes her hand; with great feeling):

> But you came. And you must forget everything— (Lily looks at
> him, a little afraid) except that you are here, Countess.

Gaston helps her off with her wrap, puts it on a chair. Lily nervously
walks out of the picture.

CLOSE SHOT   AT WINDOW

shooting from inside. Lily comes in, stops at a chair, sits nervously,
stands, moves to window, and looks off from balcony. Gaston comes
in. He touches her hand. She turns to him.

LILY:

> Out there in the moonlight everything seemed so perfect, so
> simple—but now—but now—

Gaston, thinking her mood is changing to a love mood, is about to
embrace her.

LILY (in a frightened tone):

> Do you *know* King Boris?

GASTON:

> No—no.

LILY:

> Do you know the Marquis de la Tours?

GASTON (with a little smile):

> I would like to.

LILY (agitatedly):

> You'd better not. He's really very dull. But anyhow, when the king
> tells the marquis he saw me, the marquis will tell the marchesa.
> And the marchesa is the best friend of the Duchess of Chambro.
> And *she* will phone the Princess de Costa. The princess doesn't like
> me—but I don't care!

GASTON:

> Why should you?

LILY (as if arguing):
> But she talks a lot. And before this night is over, all Venice will know it. And tomorrow it will be Grand Canal gossip! . . . Oh!

Exhausted, she moves away, drops into an armchair. Gaston goes to her, sits on the arm of the chair, leans over.

GASTON (tenderly):
> Don't stop. Keep right on complaining. It's beautiful.

LILY (looks at him for a moment, quietly; then):
> You know, when I first saw you, I thought you were an American.

GASTON (flattered):
> Thank you!

LILY (with great delight):
> Someone from another world—so entirely different. One gets so tired of one's own class—princes and counts and dukes and kings— ah! And everybody talking shop—always trying to sell jewelry . . . And then I heard your name and found you were just one of us.

GASTON:
> Disappointed?

LILY (leaning back with lure):
> No—proud. Very proud!

Gaston takes her in his arms and kisses her. She returns his embrace. We hear the phone ringing. The embrace breaks, and both look startled. Gaston obviously is nervous because he is a crook. We don't know why Lily is nervous. Gaston goes quickly toward the phone.

CLOSE SHOT   LITTLE TELEPHONE TABLE
Gaston enters, picks up the phone.

GASTON:
> Hello . . . The countess?

CLOSE-UP   LILY
She is still in the chair. Frightened, she rises quickly.

CLOSE SHOT   GASTON

GASTON:
> Just a moment. (Hands over the receiver.) The Duchess of Chambro.

CLOSE SHOT   LILY

at the window. She is perplexed for a moment. Then she hurries out toward the phone.

CLOSE SHOT

at the phone. Lily enters. She makes a gesture as if to say, "You see? They know already!"

LILY:

Hello, Your Grace. Yes, Your Grace. How did you know I was here? Oh, the marquis— (She gestures to Gaston as if to say, "Didn't I tell you?") Yes, Your Grace. I see. (Gaston walks out of the picture.) Dinner tomorrow—at your palace. Oh, I'd be delighted. King Boris will call for me . . . (She makes a gesture of annoyance to Gaston.)

SECOND-CLASS HOTEL ROOM

It is very much in disorder. On the night table is a phone. The woman who speaks is frowsy, fat, common. She is apparently Lily's companion, maid, and intimate friend.

WOMAN (voice guarded and low):

Listen, Lily. When you come home, slip up the back way. I can't talk now, but do what I tell you. (In a loud voice.) And listen, Lily. You know what that darn dog of yours did—?

CLOSE SHOT   LILY

at the phone.

LILY:

So, he really did! How charming! Well, my compliments to the duke. Goodbye. (She hangs up, faces Gaston, makes a desperate gesture.) There you are. The scandal is on!

MED. SHOT   GASTON

standing by the dinner table, thoughtful. He looks over to Lily.

CLOSE SHOT   LILY

She has sunk into a sofa.

LILY (half-despairingly):

Oh! (She puts her head in her hands.)

MED. SHOT   GASTON

He looks sadly at the table, realizing that the dinner he had pictured so charmingly may be spoiled. He goes to Lily.

MED. SHOT LILY

in the chair, still holding head in hands. Gaston enters, touches her hair lightly, controls himself.

GASTON:

Countess, I'm sorry. (With great feeling.) If you think it's best for you to go—well—

CLOSE-UP LILY

She looks up at Gaston, amazed.

CLOSE-UP GASTON

He looks at Lily with great tenderness.

CLOSE SHOT LILY

She looks tenderly at Gaston. She rises, camera rising with her to include both Gaston and herself. She touches his arm. She is moved and confused. Her real feeling starts to break through at this manifestation of chivalry.

LILY (in a tremulous voice):

I think that's very nice—yes, very nice. (They look at each other a few seconds.) I think—I think we should have a cocktail.

Gaston is delighted. He kisses her hand, goes quickly to the dinner table.

CLOSE SHOT

at the dinner table. Gaston walks in, picks up the cocktail shaker. He shakes it, smiles happily at Lily.

MED. SHOT FRANÇOIS'S HOTEL ROOM

François has recovered his memory. His hair is still disarranged, eyes still glazed. For a few moments, he is incoherent, then he gradually becomes almost normal. Grouped near him are five Italian hotel officials, a detective, and the manager. They are gesturing excitedly, all talking at the same time. The dialogue is fragmentary, ad lib, Italian. The manager, who speaks English, turns to François.

MANAGER (indicating the detective):

The representative of the police wants to know how much money you had, M'sieu Filiba.

FRANÇOIS:
I had exactly twenty thousand lire. I had just cashed a traveler's check and put it in my wallet.

Manager turns to the others and translates. They go into a huddle and talk excited Italian.

MANAGER (to François):
Why did you let this man in, M'sieu Filiba?

FRANÇOIS:
Well, he knocked at the door. You see, I was expecting two—uh—two business associates.

Manager turns again to our Italian friends and again we see the same excitement.

MANAGER (again to François):
And then what happened, M'sieu Filiba?

FRANÇOIS:
I said, "Come in." And there he was. A fine-looking man with a moustache and long sideburns. He said, "Good evening. I'm the doctor." I said, "Doctor?" He said, "Yes, the doctor. I came to see about your tonsils."

Manager turns back, translating. It creates a sensation.

MANAGER (to François):
The representative of the police wants to know if there is anything wrong with your tonsils.

FRANÇOIS:
No!

MANAGER (to group):
Niente!

FRANÇOIS:
That's just what I tried to tell him. Well, one word led to another. He really was a very charming fellow. So we talked for about ten minutes.

Manager translates. Again excitement.

MANAGER (to François):
What did you talk about?

FRANÇOIS:
 About tonsils.

MANAGER (to the group):
 Tonsili!

FRANÇOIS:
 So I said to myself, "All right, if he wants to look at them, let him look at them. No harm in that." And then he said, "Say ah." And then I said, "Ah." And that's all I remember . . . And when I woke up, I still had my tonsils, but my pocketbook was gone.

Manager translates. Again excitement.

GASTON'S HOTEL ROOM   MED. SHOT
at dinner table. Gaston and Lily are seated, eating. Waiter is pouring champagne.

GASTON (with casual interest):
 Was it lots of money?

WAITER:
 Oh, it must have been, Baron. The gentleman occupies the Royal Suite—two fifty-three, five, seven, and nine. I think his name is M'sieu Filiba.

Lily apparently is even less interested.

GASTON:
 You're not safe anywhere nowadays.

WAITER:
 But please, Baron. We're not supposed to breathe a word of it. You won't tell anybody I told you?

GASTON:
 You can trust me.

WAITER:
 Yes, Baron. Thank you. (Waiter goes.)

HOTEL CORRIDOR   MED. SHOT
at door of Gaston's room. The number is 300–302. Waiter comes out, closes door.

GASTON'S ROOM   CLOSE SHOT
at dinner table. Lily serenely continues to eat.

GASTON:
That's hotel life. In one room a man loses his wallet (very tenderly) and in another room a man loses—his head. (He tries to kiss Lily.)

LILY (holding him off gently):
Please. (Very sincerely.) When I came here it was for a little adventure—a little game which you play tonight and forget tomorrow. But something has changed me—and it isn't the champagne. (Gaston, also with sincerity, takes her hand.) The whole thing is new to me. Very new. I've got a confession to make to you. (After a slight pause.) Baron, you are a crook. (Gaston's expression doesn't change.) You robbed the gentleman in two fifty-three, five, seven, and nine. (Still Gaston's expression doesn't change. After a slight pause, Lily turns back to the table.) May I have the salt?

GASTON (passes the salt with an elegant gesture):
Please.

LILY:
Thank you.

GASTON:
The pepper, too?

LILY:
No, thank you.

GASTON:
You're very welcome. (There is a short silence as both continue with the meal. Then, with great candor.) Countess, believe me, before you left this room I would have told you everything . . . And let me say this with love in my heart— Countess, you are a thief. (Lily drops her knife and fork.) The wallet of the gentleman in two fifty-three, five, seven, and nine is in your possession. I knew it very well when you took it out of my pocket. (With great charm.) In fact, you tickled me. (Moving closer to her.) But your embrace was so sweet . . . (He caresses her hand lingeringly. Then he gets up, walks out toward the open window.)

CLOSE SHOT
at the window. Gaston enters, closes the window, and pulls the curtains. Looking back at Lily with smiling promise, he returns to the table.

CLOSE SHOT   TABLE
Gaston goes to her, takes her hand, and draws her to her feet. She
looks at him expectantly. Gaston takes her in his arms. It looks like the
start of a passionate love scene. Suddenly, unexpectedly, he grabs her
by the shoulders, shakes her violently.

INSERT
of their feet. Wallet falls from Lily's dress.

CLOSE SHOT   GASTON AND LILY
Gaston reaches down, picks up wallet, puts it casually in his pocket,
then gracefully holds chair, inviting her to sit.

GASTON:
    Countess.

Lily sits with all the poise of a lady. Gaston sits. They continue the meal
as if nothing has happened.

LILY:
    I like you, Baron.

GASTON (fervently):
    I'm crazy about you. (He reaches in his side pocket, takes out a
    diamond brooch which Lily wore when she came in.) By the way,
    your pin.

Lily is flabbergasted. She looks down to her bosom. Indeed, the pin is
missing. She accepts the pin.

LILY (with a little smile of shame):
    Thank you, Baron.

GASTON:
    Not at all, Countess . . . There's one very good stone in it.

LILY (as she fastens the pin):
    What time is it?

Gaston reaches for his watch, discovers it is missing. He gives Lily a
look of admiration and astonishment. Lily smiles triumphantly, opens
her purse, lifts out the watch, hands it to him. He takes it with a bow.

LILY:
    It was five minutes slow, but I regulated it for you.

They bow to each other like two Chinese mandarins.

GASTON (tenderly):
    I hope you don't mind if I keep your garter.

Lily almost leaps out of her chair. She raises her skirt; her hand searches for the garter. It is missing. Gaston takes the garter out of his breast pocket, shows it to her, kisses it, puts it back, and buttons his coat. Lily is delighted. This is the highest compliment ever paid to her. She slides into his lap, embraces him.

LILY:
    Darling! (They kiss; very excitedly.) Now tell me—tell me all about yourself. Who are you?

GASTON:
    You remember the man who walked into the Bank of Constantinople and walked out *with* the Bank of Constantinople?

LILY (thrilled):
    Monescu!

GASTON:
    Gaston Monescu.

LILY (melting away):
    Gaston!

They embrace and kiss again.

COUCH
Lily is lying on the couch, Gaston at her side, leaning over adoringly.

GASTON:
    I love you. I loved you the moment I saw you. I'm mad about you. My little shoplifter! My sweet little pickpocket! My darling!

He takes her in his arms. They embrace and kiss.

                                                              DISSOLVE TO:

COUCH
Camera hasn't moved but has dissolved the two lovers out of the picture. From outside the picture we hear the switch turned, and the light that fell on the couch goes out.

                                                              DISSOLVE TO:

WINDOW
A hand comes in and opens the curtains. The moonlight streams in.

                                                              DISSOLVE TO:

CORRIDOR   CLOSE SHOT

at the door of 300–302. Gaston's arm, in the sleeve of a dressing gown, comes out and fastens on the hook below the number a Don't Disturb sign, clearly printed in several languages. He closes the door.

CORRIDOR   CLOSE SHOT

at the end of the corridor. Around the corner comes our Italian group. Loudly, in Italian, they are still discussing the robbery. Camera goes with them. In front walks the manager, who talks back and forth. The noise increases. Suddenly the manager looks in direction of rooms 300–302.

CLOSE SHOT   DOOR

We see Don't Disturb sign.

CLOSE SHOT   ANOTHER PART OF THE CORRIDOR

Manager, having seen the sign, turns to the others with a loud "Shh!" They quiet down.

CORRIDOR   LONG SHOT

of door to 300–302. The Italians are passing door very quietly. Suddenly the detective wants to say something. We tremble for Gaston and Lily.

Manager again with "Shh!" Detective is silenced. Entire group goes quietly out of picture. We stay a few moments on the empty scene. Camera moves up to Don't Disturb sign.

DISSOLVE TO:

CLOSE SHOT   GRAND CANAL

Camera moves with the garbage gondola. It is filled to overflowing. The garbage gondolier has done a good evening's work. He is paddling with a flourish and singing an operatic aria.

FADE OUT

SEQUENCE B

FADE IN

MINIATURE OF PARIS

Shooting over the roofs and presenting a beautiful view. The camera pans back away from Paris and in the foreground we see factory chimneys, so that we get the impression we are moving into the factory district of Paris.

DISSOLVE TO:

BIG FACTORY WHISTLE

It is blowing loudly.

DISSOLVE TO:

BIG GATE

of the factory. Above gate, in large letters: Colet et Compagnie, Paris. Gate opens. Hundreds of workers, men and women, come out. They are hatless; it is lunch hour.

DISSOLVE TO:

‡FADE IN

PARIS

Shot of Eiffel Tower at night, emitting radio waves. Sound of Morse code signals.

DISSOLVE TO:

RADIO STUDIO

ANNOUNCER AT MIKE   CLOSE-UP

ANNOUNCER (reading copy):
> Geneva . . . From Geneva comes the news that the world-famous international crook, Gaston Monescu, robbed the peace conference yesterday. He took practically everything, except the peace. The police arrested him and confiscated all the stolen goods, but he managed to escape in an unexplainable manner. This is the Paris police reporter speaking.

Announcer exits. A second announcer enters.

SECOND ANNOUNCER:
> Ladies and gentlemen, this program comes to you through the courtesy of Colet and Company, manufacturers of the most famous perfumes in the world. Remember—it doesn't matter what you say; it doesn't matter how you look; it's how you smell. Thank you. (Starts to sing.) "Colet, Colet, Colet and Compa-*ny*"

CLOSE SHOT

Colet et Compagnie sign in front of retail establishment. Song continues.

SECOND ANNOUNCER VOICE:
> "are makers"

Shot of kiosk sign for Colet et Cie.

VOICE CONTINUES:
> "of the"

Shot of flashing neon sign for Colet et Cie.

SONG CONTINUES:
"*best* perfume."

SECOND ANNOUNCER (still singing):
"If you and your beloved can't *agree*,"

NEON SIGN
showing man spraying sleeping woman with perfume atomizer. Woman wakes up and stretches.

SONG CONTINUES:
"permit us to sug-*gest* perfume."

SECOND ANNOUNCER (singing):
"Cleopatra was a lovely tantalizer. But she did it with her little atomizer."

CLOSE SHOT
Girl spraying herself with atomizer bottle.

SONG CONTINUES:
"We'll make you smell like"

ANOTHER GIRL
applying perfume with glass applicator.

SONG CONTINUES:
"a rose; every"

OVERHEAD SHOT
Large factory complex, camera advancing.

SONG CONTINUES:
"nose in Paris knows"

LONG SHOT
Factory gates with sign, Colet et Cie. Hordes of workers pouring out.

SONG CONTINUES:
"Colet and Compagnie."

DISSOLVE TO:‡

DIRECTORS' ROOM
of Colet et Cie. Camera is moving over a long table. We see only the forward half of the table—serious-looking businessmen. Camera stops

at the head in front of M. Giron, chairman of the board, a distinguished elderly man. He is addressing someone at the unseen other end.

GIRON:
> I'm sure, Madame Colet, if your husband were alive, the first thing he would do in times like these—cut salaries.

There is an approving ripple of voices from the other directors.

CLOSE-UP   MARIETTE COLET
in a beautiful light morning dress at the other end of the table.

MARIETTE:
> Unfortunately, M'sieu Giron, business bores me to distraction—and besides I have a luncheon engagement. So I think we'd better leave the salaries just where they are. (Rising.) Goodbye!

CLOSE-UP   GIRON

GIRON (rising):
> Goodbye, Madame Colet.

DIRECTORS' VOICES:
> Goodbye, Madame Colet.

DISSOLVE TO:

JEWELRY STORE, VERY ULTRA   CLOSE-UP
at counter. We see some expensive-looking small purses, compacts, laid out on velvet. Behind counter, an elegant clerk is talking to Mme. Colet, who is out of the picture.

JEWELER:
> This one, Madame Colet, is only three thousand francs.

CLOSE-UP   MARIETTE
at other side of counter, now in a beautiful afternoon gown.

MARIETTE:
> Oh, no. That's entirely too much . . . How about that one?

CLOSE-UP   JEWELER

JEWELER (picks up a handbag, reads the price):
> That's sixteen hundred and fifty.

CLOSE-UP   MARIETTE

MARIETTE:
   Sixteen hundred and fifty! That's outrageous!

CLOSE-UP   JEWELER

JEWELER (pointing to another):
   Here's one for nine hundred.

CLOSE-UP   MARIETTE

MARIETTE:
   Hmm . . . not bad . . . How about *that* one?

CLOSE-UP   JEWELER
He looks down inside the showcase, reaches in, takes out a beautiful handbag, much larger. It is studded with diamonds.

JEWELER (with a smile):
   Oh, this one . . . Madame—well, that's a hundred and twenty-five thousand francs.

CLOSE-UP   MARIETTE

MARIETTE:
   But it's beautiful. I'll take it!

CLOSE-UP   JEWELER

JEWELER:
   Thank you, Madame Colet.

Picks up an elaborate box. As he puts handbag in box we
                                                        DISSOLVE TO:

STREET IN PARIS   CLOSE SHOT
at door to shop of a fashionable furrier. We hear, from outside the picture, the purr of a motor and the sound of brakes as a car comes to a stop. Proprietor opens door from inside, comes toward camera, beaming, bows in the direction of the unseen car.

PROPRIETOR:
   How do you do, Madame Colet?
                                                        DISSOLVE TO:

74

‡SAME SHOT

But now the proprietor has seen her out. Sound of car starting and going.

PROPRIETOR (obsequiously):
Goodbye, Madame Colet.

DISSOLVE TO:‡

CLOSE SHOT

at door in office building, shooting from corridor into a nondescript little waiting room. Door is open so that we can't see sign on it. In doorway stands a fat little Turk with a pointed black beard. He bows repeatedly to someone behind camera.

MAN:
Goodbye, Madame Colet.

He goes back into office, closes door. Now we read the sign: Dr. Isar Ben Marguli, Astrologer.

DISSOLVE TO:

FINE RESIDENCE STREET   MED. SHOT

in front of Mariette's house. Mariette's very expensive car, shooting from house to car. At open car door stands footman, looks toward entrance of the house, bows.

FOOTMAN:
Yes, madame.

DISSOLVE TO:

STAIRCASE   MARIETTE'S HOUSE INT.

shooting from stairs down to hall against entrance door. In foreground, the lower part of staircase. In background, the elaborately furnished hall. Butler stands at foot of staircase, looking up.

BUTLER:
No, madame.

DISSOLVE TO:

UPPER PART OF STAIRCASE

Camera shoots up. On landing at head of stairs, the maid. Background, expensive upper hall. Maid looks at Mariette, who is apparently halfway down staircase.

MAID:
Yes, madame.

DISSOLVE TO:

BEAUTIFUL GARDEN
Background, glimpse of hothouse. Foreground, near flower bed, the gardener.

GARDENER:
　Yes, madame.

DISSOLVE TO:

DRAWING ROOM　CLOSE SHOT
At fireplace stands François Filiba, back to camera; we don't recognize him.

MARIETTE'S VOICE:
　No, no, no, no, François! I tell you no!

ARMCHAIR
Mariette, in a precious armchair by fireplace. We see reflection of the fire. She is in beautiful evening gown. At her side, on a little table, a glass of champagne.

MARIETTE (almost dreamily):
　You see, François, marriage is a beautiful mistake which two people make together. (Sitting up; in a down-to-earth tone.) But with you, François— (Friendly; shaking her head.) I really think it *would* be a mistake.

FIREPLACE
François, still with back to camera. He stiffens at this rejection. He turns, affronted, faces Mariette. Now we discover he is François, the man who had trouble with his tonsils in Venice.

DISSOLVE TO:

GOLF COURSE　CLOSE-UP
of the major, a man about forty-five, in smart golf togs. He looks dejected.

MARIETTE'S VOICE:
　Don't be so downhearted, Major. You're not the only one I don't love.

CLOSE-UP　MARIETTE
on golf course, also in smart sport clothes. She is getting set to swing at the ball and is more concerned with her golf form than with what she is saying.

MARIETTE:
    I don't love François, either.

She swings, hits the ball, turns, watching it, smiles. It was a good shot.
DISSOLVE TO:

STAIRCASE IN MARIETTE'S HOME
Maid comes down, leans over railing, addresses someone behind camera.

MAID:
    Madame will be ready in two minutes.

SOFA IN FRONT HALL
François and Major, seated. Both in full evening dress—overcoats on, top hats on knees, opera sticks in hands. Expressions serious as they nod to maid, then lean back without looking at each other.

FRANÇOIS (after a moment of frigid silence):
    I know you don't like me, Major. And to be perfectly frank, I dislike you intensely. But since we have to be in each other's company this evening, we might as well make conversation. (He expects a reply but gets none.) Well, Major, what's your answer? (Major still doesn't answer. Furiously.) For heaven's sake, man, say something!

MAJOR (turns, looks him up and down; distinctly and slowly):
    Tonsils.

François leaps to his feet, outraged at being reminded of the humiliating episode.
DISSOLVE TO:

OPERA HOUSE   CLOSE SHOT
Part of the orchestra; shooting on an angle down, so that we photograph a part of the orchestra and a portion of the footlights without seeing the singers. We hear the orchestral music and the singers' voices.

OPERA BOX
Door opens. Mariette and Major come in. Mariette looks annoyed. She sits. Major sits.

CLOSE SHOT
Door to box, from interior. Door opens. François appears. He is very angry. The argument with the major apparently reached its peak before

77

they came into the opera house and at the last moment he refused to accompany them.

FRANÇOIS (whispering but final):
> Goodbye! (He closes door, disappears.)

CLOSE SHOT
Mariette and Major. Major paid no attention to François. But Mariette, more annoyed than before, looks toward door, then back to Major.

MARIETTE:
> You should be ashamed of yourselves. Two men of your standing, always quarreling.

MAJOR:
> He started it.

MARIETTE:
> But you're the more intelligent one.

MAJOR:
> That's true.

MARIETTE:
> Then why did you do it?

MAJOR:
> Because I hate him—because I love you!

MARIETTE:
> You should have more self-control. You were in the army.

MAJOR:
> Well, he was in the navy.

CLOSE SHOT   DOOR
It opens again. François appears again.

FRANÇOIS (with increased finality):
> Goodbye! (He closes door again.)

CLOSE-UP   MARIETTE AND MAJOR

MARIETTE:
> I want you to go out and apologize—right away!

Major leaves against his will.

OPERA CORRIDOR   CLOSE SHOT

at door to box. François is in a chair by the door, opera hat and overcoat still on. Door opens and Major comes out. François gets up. They glare at each other.

MAJOR:

> See here, my good man. You've been saying goodbye for the last half hour, and staying on. I wish you would say how do you do, and go!

MED. SHOT   BOX

Mariette, listening to the music. Suddenly door opens. She turns as Major comes in and sits beside her. She looks at him questioningly.

MAJOR (proudly):

> Well, he left. (Mariette is surprised.) I tell you, apologizing is a gift! (He nods pompously as if to say, "I have this gift.")

ORCHESTRA SEATS   CLOSE-UP

of Gaston. He is looking through opera glasses up at Mariette's box. Camera is so close to the opera glasses that we can't see Gaston's face. We see his hand adjusting the opera glasses.

MARIETTE'S BOX

from Gaston's viewpoint, photographed through an opera-glass vignette. We see Major and Mariette. Camera stops in front of the railing. We see Mariette's hand holding the handbag. Camera centers the handbag. We hold this, then camera pans up to Mariette's face. She is looking at the stage. Camera pans quickly down again to handbag. We stay on the handbag. Major's hand comes in and touches Mariette's hand caressingly. She brushes his hand aside. Camera moves quickly up to Major. He is looking ardently at Mariette. He leans over to her. Camera moves with him. Both in the picture. A dialogue scene now follows, but even though it is a close-up, we can't hear them because they are seen through binoculars from a distance. In this inaudible but visually expressive scene, Major tells her he can't understand her attitude toward him. She impatiently asks him to leave her alone to enjoy the opera. Major persistently says he loves her. Mariette insists that he stop it. She takes out of her lap (which is not in the picture) opera glasses and holds them to her eyes. Major gives up, leans back in chair. Camera centers Mariette, alone. Then camera, still framed in opera-glass vignette, pans down and comes to rest on handbag, now lying on the railing unprotected.

CLOSE-UP   CONDUCTOR

from viewpoint of the stage. He is looking up at the singers. Then he looks down to his score.

CLOSE-UP   SCORE

from viewpoint of the conductor. It is the first act, at about page twenty. We hear the soprano singing.

SOPRANO'S VOICE:
    I love you, I love you, I love you!

CHORUS'S VOICES:
    She loves him, she loves him, she loves him!

Without changing camera angle, we see the pages being turned as if by a breeze, and

                                                        DISSOLVE TO:

CLOSE-UP   SCORE

at about page ninety; at least one act has been played. We hear same soprano singing—but a different tune in a different key.

SOPRANO'S VOICE:
    I hate you, I hate you, I hate you!

CHORUS'S VOICES:
    She hates him, she hates him, she hates him!

CORRIDOR   OPERA HOUSE   MED. SHOT

toward the sumptuous down-staircase. We see, in corridor, at opposite sides of staircase, doors to ladies' and men's restrooms. Door to the ladies' restroom is in foreground. A gentleman is pacing up and down. Door opens; a lady comes quickly to the gentleman. They exchange a few words, which we don't hear. (Music of opera comes in dimly.) Gentleman reaches in pocket, gives her a coin. Lady goes back quickly. As she is about to enter restroom Mariette comes out, excited, rushes past gentleman down corridor and out of picture.

MARIETTE'S BOX

Major sits alone. The music comes in full volume. Mariette enters, looks at her chair, at railing, at Major. During the following, both search around in the box.

MARIETTE:
    My bag!

MAJOR:
   Your bag?

MARIETTE (impatiently):
   Yes, my bag!

MAJOR:
   Didn't you take it with you?

MARIETTE:
   Apparently not. Don't you know where it is?

MAJOR:
   No—I'm sorry.

MARIETTE:
   But you saw it here.

MAJOR:
   Yes, I saw it—but—

MARIETTE:
   Well, where is it?

CLOSE-UP   CONDUCTOR
Conductor, disturbed by the agitated sounds, looks up at Mariette's
box, sternly reproving.

BOX
Mariette and Major are standing, searching.

MARIETTE:
   It couldn't have walked out by itself!

Major inadvertently tips over a chair.

GALLERY
Two typical music lovers. One is bent forward, eyes fixed on the stage.
The other leans back, eyes closed in ecstasy. First man, suddenly annoyed by sounds from the box, says, "Psst!" Second man suddenly wakes
up, looks angrily at first man, says, "Shh!" The two glare at each other.

CORRIDOR
outside Mariette's box. (Music continues, slightly muffled.) Door
opens. Mariette and Major come out, shut door. Major is carrying hat

and coat. They are still searching, looking everywhere. Camera moves with them as they go down the corridor. Mariette goes into ladies' room. Major automatically follows her; door closes behind them. An instant later, Major scurries out. Followed by camera, he hurries away, embarrassed, stops, turns.

CLOSE SHOT

at door to ladies' restroom. The maid, a middle-aged woman, looks grimly at Major.

CLOSE-UP   MAJOR

He doesn't know what to say or how to act. At this moment the music stops. We hear the bursting final applause.

CORRIDOR

Doors to first balcony open, and many people hurry out. We still hear applause.

STAIRWAY AND CORRIDOR OUTSIDE BOXES

On either side, a door to a restroom. At top of stairway stands Major. People emerging from boxes. Mariette comes out of ladies' room, goes to Major. We see by her gestures she hasn't found her bag. More people pass from behind camera. Mariette and Major are caught in the crowd and disappear.

DISSOLVE TO:

STAIRWAY   SAME CAMERA ANGLE

Last patrons leaving down the stairs. They disappear; corridor and staircase are empty. Door of men's room opens; out comes a lone figure, Gaston. Immaculate in evening dress, top hat, overcoat, and stick, he strolls toward the stairs and starts down.

FADE OUT

SEQUENCE C

FADE IN

JEWELRY STORE

(Not the one where Mariette bought her bag.) Shooting from inside store through window toward street. In front of window appears Major. He looks, sour and depressed, at the window display. Camera moves with him as he enters shop and goes to counter. Camera pulls back, and now we discover François at the counter. Both look straight ahead; they don't see each other yet. Clerk enters.

CLERK (to Major):
    Yes, m'sieu?

MAJOR:
    I would like to have—

He sees François, and François sees him.

FRANÇOIS (cheerfully):
    Good morning, Major.

MAJOR (embarrassed):
    Good morning. (Stuttering; to clerk.) I'd—I'd—I'd like to look at some cuff links.

CLERK:
    Very well, m'sieu.

Clerk goes. Major ignores François. François smiles, ironical.

FRANÇOIS (with feigned innocence):
    Nice day, Major.

MAJOR (grunts):
    Umm.

FRANÇOIS:
    You're looking fine, Major.

MAJOR (turning):
    Now see here, my good man. I've had just about enough of your insulting remarks!

Another clerk enters. He puts several handbags on counter for François. François regards them smilingly. Major is speechless.

                                                    DISSOLVE TO:

CLOSE SHOT   SIGN
on cheap hotel in suburb of Paris, shooting up from street. Sign reads Paris-Astor Hotel. Camera pans down. In entrance doorway, the bellboy—on his cap: Paris-Astor Hotel—shabbily dressed, leaning lazily against door, bag of cherries in hand. He eats and spits the stones into street with a minimum of energy.

CLOSE SHOT   COUCH IN CHEAP HOTEL ROOM
Lily, in negligee, lying on couch, face covered by newspaper she is reading while she has breakfast, which is on a little table beside her.

The dishes are clean but cheap looking. Lily lowers the paper and looks slyly up. She sees:

OTHER SIDE OF ROOM   CLOSE SHOT
Gaston, in dressing gown, sitting in armchair, reading a newspaper.

CLOSE SHOT   LILY
She watches Gaston, looks down to table, back at Gaston. She wants to put something over without being seen—something important. Now, quick, she decides to do it, come what may. She picks up a French roll—still watching him—dunks it in the coffee, takes a hurried bite, and disappears again behind paper.

CLOSE-UP   GASTON

GASTON (looking up from the paper):
I don't agree with this review at all. I thought Martini's singing was adequate, but to call him a *great* singer—ridiculous!

CLOSE-UP   LILY
still reading her paper.

LILY (without looking up):
I always liked him. Especially last year in Munich . . .

CLOSE-UP   GASTON

GASTON (drops paper):
Last year? It can't be that long.

CLOSE-UP   LILY

LILY (drops paper):
Yes! Don't you remember the day you took that Chinese vase from the Royal Palace (with tenderness) and made it into a lamp for my night table?

CLOSE-UP   GASTON
He looks at her with emotion, gets up, and goes to her.

MED. SHOT   LILY
Gaston sits close to her, caresses her hair.

GASTON:

I remember the lamp, I remember the night table, and I remember the night. (They kiss.) Everything will be all right again. (As he gets up; with a valiant little smile.) Prosperity is just around the corner!

He goes out of the picture. Lily smiles after him with total confidence.

CLOSE-UP   GASTON'S CHAIR
Gaston returns, sits, picks up paper, resumes reading.

CLOSE-UP   LILY
at her paper. Suddenly she stares at something on the page. She leaps to her feet.

LILY:

Gaston!

CLOSE-UP   GASTON
He looks up.

CLOSE-UP   LILY
Paper in hand, followed by camera, she goes to the bureau, opens a drawer, and takes out Mariette's handbag. She looks at the bag, rereads the item in the paper, looks back again.

CLOSE SHOT   GASTON
Puzzled, he gets up.

CLOSE SHOT   LILY
Followed by camera, she hastens to Gaston, hands him the paper, points to the item.

LILY:

Read this.

INSERT
A large classified ad with headline: Handbag Lost—Twenty Thousand Francs Reward. Before we can read the rest, camera moves close to the headline. Under the insert, we hear:

LILY'S VOICE:
The description fits. That's our bag!

CLOSE SHOT   LILY AND GASTON
Gaston has finished reading.

GASTON:
Twenty thousand francs . . . If we sold it we'd get— (He takes the bag from Lily, examines it like an expert.) Well, it's worth forty thousand at the most. She paid probably sixty thousand. When we sell it . . . I'd say five thousand.

LILY:
Darling, then let's be honest and return it to the lady.

GASTON:
And take the twenty thousand francs . . .

LILY:
Right.

GASTON (with sudden emotion):
Sweetheart, what day is today?

LILY:
The fourteenth of May.

GASTON:
And tomorrow is the fifteenth. And the day after tomorrow—

LILY (not knowing what he wants):
The six—

She catches Gaston's eye. Her face lights up. Very tenderly she embraces him.

GASTON:
We'll go to Venice, to the same hotel!

LILY (romantically):
We'll take the Royal Suite!

GASTON:
Two fifty-three, five—

LILY:
Seven and nine!

GASTON:
> And we'll celebrate the second anniversary of the day we didn't get married!

LILY:
> Darling!

They kiss. After they have held the embrace a few moments, we hear a knock on the door. They look toward the door, hide the handbag instantly.

GASTON:
> Come in.

CLOSE SHOT   DOOR
Porter comes in, carrying a pair of shoes.

PORTER (putting them on the floor):
> Your shoes, Professor Bernard.

As he goes

> FADE OUT

‡Their embrace continues. They look at each other dreamily.
> FADE OUT‡

SEQUENCE D

FADE IN
MARIETTE'S LIVING ROOM   MED. SHOT
Mariette and an elderly woman who has seen better days. Her clothes, once elegant, now are shabby. She is unwrapping a package as camera moves toward both to a close shot. She takes out a handbag which also has seen better days, holds it toward Mariette pathetically. Mariette responds with a kindly look.

MARIETTE:
> No, I'm sorry, but that's not the bag.

WOMAN (restraining a sob):
> I know it isn't. But it's pretty—isn't it?

MARIETTE (sympathetic):
> *Very* pretty.

We hear phone ring. Mariette, annoyed at the interruption, goes out of the picture.

CLOSE SHOT   TELEPHONE TABLE
Mariette enters, picks up phone.

MARIETTE:
Hello . . . Yes . . . Where did you find the bag? (Amused.) Where? (Even more amused.) Where? What? (Smiling broadly.) What was in it? (With a change of expression, outraged.) How dare you! (She slams down receiver.)

CLOSE SHOT   ELDERLY WOMAN
bag in hand, with patient hope.

CLOSE SHOT   MARIETTE
at phone. Her expression softens. Followed by camera, she goes to woman.

WOMAN:
You wouldn't have any use for it? (Mariette hesitates.) You see, I have another bag, and I really don't need this. So, if you'd like to buy it . . .

Mariette sees tears in the woman's eyes.

MARIETTE (reaching into drawer of nearby table):
Would two hundred francs be sufficient?

WOMAN (this is much more than she expected):
Yes, madame.

Mariette hands her the money.

WOMAN (overwhelmed):
Oh, thank you, madame!

She goes out of picture toward door. Mariette looks after her with compassion, which is broken by the ringing phone. Increasingly annoyed, she goes to phone, newly purchased bag in hand.

CLOSE SHOT   TELEPHONE
Mariette enters edgily.

MARIETTE:
Hello . . . Yes . . .

She tosses handbag out of picture.

ARMCHAIR
Bag falls on armchair into an assortment of several other bags. Mariette must have been buying bags for hours.

MARIETTE'S VOICE:
>   What? Yes, this is Madame Colet.

CLOSE-UP   MARIETTE
at the phone.

MARIETTE:
>   What? Yes, I lost my bag. Yes. Last night at the opera . . . No, no, I don't
>   want to buy a piano! (She hangs up angrily.)

LONG SHOT   HALL
Shooting from the direction of the living room toward the house entrance door. Hall is filled with men and women, some well dressed,
some shabby. Some carry packages. Several women hold, each, two
"found" bags. One woman carries a crying baby. Butler's voice comes
from behind the camera.

BUTLER'S VOICE:
>   Next, please.

A young Russian Bolshevik, unshaven, with bushy hair, moves toward
camera.

LIVING ROOM   MED. SHOT
Butler at open door. Bolshevik enters, followed by butler, who shuts
door behind them as Bolshevik goes to Mariette. During all this, we
hear:

MARIETTE'S VOICE:
>   No, no . . . No, it was *not* insured. But right now it's too late.

CLOSE SHOT   TELEPHONE

MARIETTE:
>   What? (Bolshevik enters.) I may lose it again? But I haven't found
>   it yet! I'm sorry. Goodbye! (She turns toward Bolshevik distract-
>   edly.) Yes?

BOLSHEVIK (heavy Russian accent):
>   So you lost a handbag, madame?

MARIETTE (impatiently):
>   Yes.

BOLSHEVIK:
>   And it had diamonds in the back.

89

MARIETTE:
>   Yes.

BOLSHEVIK:
>   And diamonds in the front.

MARIETTE:
>   Yes.

BOLSHEVIK:
>   Diamonds all over.

MARIETTE:
>   Well, have you found it?

BOLSHEVIK (screaming):
>   No! (Raising his arm like a prophet.) But let me tell you—any woman who spends a fortune in times like these for a handbag—phooey, phooey, phooey!

Butler enters officiously.

BUTLER (to Bolshevik):
>   I must ask you—

BOLSHEVIK (brushing butler aside):
>   And as Trotsky said— (in Russian) "Any woman who spends a fortune for a silk purse is a sow's ear." (In English.) And that goes for you, too!

CLOSE SHOT   DOOR
to hall. While Bolshevik is ranting, it opens; Gaston enters briskly with an authoritative air, shuts door behind him.

MARIETTE, BOLSHEVIK, AND BUTLER
Mariette is startled; she doesn't know who or what the gentleman is. Bolshevik is frightened. Butler is momentarily nonplussed.

CLOSE SHOT   GASTON
He steps forward commandingly.

MED. SHOT   MARIETTE AND BOLSHEVIK
Gaston goes to Bolshevik, puts his arm patronizingly on his shoulder, and tells him politely but emphatically, in Russian, to leave. Bolshevik

makes a protesting remark. Gaston tells him vigorously and effectively to scram. Cowed, the Bolshevik goes.

CLOSE SHOT   DOOR
Butler, recuperated and full of dignity, opens door to the hall. Bolshevik appears, turns to Mariette and Gaston.

BOLSHEVIK (in a final outburst):
Phooey! Phooey! And— (Looking for another word but failing to find it; twice as loud.) Phooey!

Butler shoves him out, follows, shuts door.

CLOSE SHOT
Mariette and Gaston. Mariette is more bewildered by Gaston than by the Bolshevik.

GASTON (looking after the departed man):
His phooey is worse than his bite. (Turning to Mariette.) I must apologize for entering unannounced. If I am not mistaken, Madame Colet?

MARIETTE:
Yes . . . ?

GASTON:
Will you be good enough to look at this bag, madame? (He brings the bag forth, hands it to Mariette.)

MARIETTE (with instant and joyful recognition):
That's it! Yes, that's it! . . . Jacques!

CLOSE SHOT   DOOR
It opens and butler enters.

BUTLER:
Yes, madame?

CLOSE SHOT   MARIETTE

MARIETTE:
Dismiss all the people in the hall. The bag has been found.

BUTLER'S VOICE:
Very well, madame.

MARIETTE:
>   And Jacques. Call up the major and tell him— No, don't call him. Let him
>   keep on searching! And Jacques— (Phone rings. Mariette picks up receiver
>   and speaks before the other party can speak.) Sorry—the bag's been found.
>   (She hangs up.) And Jacques—

CLOSE SHOT   BUTLER

BUTLER:
>   Yes, madame?

CLOSE SHOT   MARIETTE

MARIETTE:
>   Call Cohen, Cohen, Ginsburg, and Renault. Give my thanks to M'sieu Re-
>   nault. (In high spirits.) Thank them all!

BUTLER'S VOICE:
>   Very well, madame.

We hear door closing. Mariette looks happily at bag, turns to Gaston.

MARIETTE:
>   Where did you—

She discovers that Gaston is no longer standing beside her. She looks
around.

CLOSE SHOT   ANOTHER PART OF THE ROOM
A beautiful Chinese vase on a table. Gaston, looking at vase with ap-
praising eye, is absorbed, unaware that Mariette has addressed him.

CLOSE SHOT   MARIETTE
She goes toward Gaston.

CLOSE SHOT   GASTON
still studying the vase. Mariette appears. He turns to her.

MARIETTE (happily):
>   Where did you find it?

GASTON:
>   You know the main staircase in the opera?

MARIETTE:
>   Yes.

GASTON:
Then you go to the left. There's a landing.

MARIETTE (eagerly):
Yes.

GASTON:
Then you go into the foyer.

MARIETTE:
Yes.

GASTON:
And as you leave the foyer, there is a little niche.

MARIETTE:
I know that niche.

GASTON:
And in that niche, there is a statue of Venus.

MARIETTE:
I remember.

GASTON (irrelevantly):
You like that statue?

MARIETTE (nonplussed):
Not particularly.

GASTON:
Neither do I. (Without any transition.) That's where I found it.

MARIETTE (naively, not suspicious):
I don't know how I could have lost it there. I was nowhere near that niche.

GASTON:
Oh . . . That's strange. Maybe—are you *sure* this is your bag?

MARIETTE (a little nettled):
Of course it is! Are you doubting me?

GASTON (polite but precise):
Not in the least, madame. But you see, it's a very expensive bag and—and one has to be careful.

93

MARIETTE (half-annoyed, half-laughing, and a little conceited):
  Well—I am Madame Colet.

GASTON (urbanely):
  And I am M'sieu Laval—if you will allow me to introduce myself.

Mariette is perplexed. Their relationship has somehow been transformed. She is uncertain. Then she yields.

MARIETTE (with a little laugh; extending her hand):
  Well—how do you do, M'sieu Laval?

GASTON:
  The pleasure is mine, madame.

He bends over and kisses her hand. Camera goes quickly to a close-up of a beautiful diamond ring. As he kisses the hand Gaston's eye appraises the ring.

STREET IN PARIS
François, package under arm, walking. It is apparent that he has purchased the handbag.

LIVING ROOM   CLOSE SHOT
at table. Gaston has just opened the bag.

GASTON (with the air of an honest man taking inventory):
  One purse— (shaking it) empty. One vanity case— (opening it)

MARIETTE:
  But really, m'sieu, this isn't necessary.

GASTON:
  Please, Madame Colet, I believe in doing things correctly. Shall we continue? (He empties the bag.) Two hairpins, one cigarette lighter, one box of real matches, and— Oh, yes, this letter from Major—

MARIETTE (quickly):
  Oh! You didn't read it!

GASTON:
  Naturally I did.

MARIETTE:
  Oh!

GASTON:
>You needn't be embarrassed, madame. A lady as charming as you would, and *should*, get love letters.

MARIETTE (embarrassed and flattered):
>M'sieu Laval!

GASTON:
>But one suggestion, madame. (Shaking his head.) *Not* the major. (Mariette looks startled, as if to say, "How did you know?") I don't mind his grammatical mistakes. I'll overlook his bad punctuation. But the letter has no mystery—no bouquet—no . . . (Changing the subject, taking a lipstick out of bag.) And one lipstick . . . (Reading markings on bottom; disapproving.) Scarlet number four.

MARIETTE:
>What's wrong now?

GASTON:
>With your skin, I prefer crimson.

MARIETTE (now on a vital theme):
>Too much blue in crimson.

GASTON:
>That's what you need!

MARIETTE:
>No, no, no! (She sits on couch. He sits beside her.) I disagree with you completely! I *tried* it once—

GASTON:
>What shade of powder do you use?

MARIETTE:
>Peaches and cream.

GASTON:
>That's too dark.

MARIETTE (fighting for her life):
>Do you realize I have light eyes?

GASTON:
>But, Madame Colet, that's a matter of eye shadow. I can straighten that out in two seconds.

We hear a knock on the door.

MARIETTE (annoyed at interruption):
    Come in!

CLOSE-UP   DOOR
Butler comes in, shuts door quickly behind him.

BUTLER (with a sour expression):
    The major.

CLOSE SHOT   GASTON AND MARIETTE
on couch. She makes a gesture of exasperation. So does Gaston. They
look at each other helplessly. Then Gaston takes charge. He rises and
goes toward butler.

HALL   MED. SHOT
at living room door. Major stands waiting. Door opens; butler comes
out, followed briskly by Gaston.

GASTON (before Major can speak):
    I'm sorry, m'sieu, but Madame had better not see anyone.

Major stares blankly. He never saw Gaston before.

GASTON:
    You see, the bag has just been found, and the reaction of relief
    from her former excitement and strain is just a little too much for
    her. It's not very serious, but just the same we'd better not take
    any chances.

MAJOR (assuming Gaston is a physician):
    Just as you say, Doctor.

GASTON:
    Thank you, Major. (Goes back toward living room.)

MAJOR:
    Good day, Doctor.

GASTON:
    Good day, Major.

The camera goes with Major toward entrance door. Major looks crest-
fallen.

STREET

in front of Mariette's house. François, followed by camera, goes to the door, rings bell. Door is opened by butler, and Major comes out, butler remaining in doorway. Major and François stare at each other. Major looks pointedly at François's package. Then Major turns to butler.

MAJOR:
    Jacques, has the bag been found?

BUTLER:
    Yes, Major.

Major turns with bright smile to François, who looks glum and glances instinctively at his package.

MAJOR:
    Is Madame feeling well?

BUTLER:
    No, Major.

Major is still looking at the unhappy François and having the time of his life.

MAJOR:
    Is Madame seeing anybody this afternoon, this evening, or even tomorrow?

BUTLER:
    No, Major.

MAJOR:
    You may shut the door, Jacques.

Butler closes door. François, miserable, turns away from Major.

MAJOR:
    Well, that leaves you holding the bag. Goodbye!

He lifts his hat, goes out of picture to right. François looks after him angrily, then goes out of picture to left.

LIVING ROOM   COUCH   CLOSE SHOT
Gaston and Mariette. There is a moment of silence.

GASTON (rising):
    Well, I think I'd better be going. Goodbye, Madame Colet.

MARIETTE (rising):
> Goodbye, M'sieu La— Oh, yes . . . This is a rather delicate matter and I don't want to . . . You see, if you read my advertisement carefully, you must have noticed that there was . . .

GASTON:
> In other words, madame, it embarrasses you to offer me the twenty thousand francs reward.

MARIETTE:
> Yes.

GASTON:
> Don't be embarrassed, madame. I'll take it. I need the money. I wish I were in a position to ignore the whole matter. But you know, madame, the stock market, bank crash . . . To make a long story short—a member of the *nouveaux* poor.

MARIETTE (looks at him sympathetically):
> Then I'm glad I lost the bag! I'll write you the check immediately. (Followed by camera, she goes.)

HALL   MED. SHOT
at staircase. Coming from living room, Mariette goes up the stairs, followed by camera. At first landing, as Mariette reaches door—

GASTON'S VOICE:
> Madame Colet!

MARIETTE (turning):
> Yes, M'sieu Laval?

GASTON   BELOW
shooting down from her angle.

GASTON:
> Do you know my first name?

CLOSE SHOT   MARIETTE

MARIETTE:
> No. What is it? Tell me.

CLOSE SHOT   GASTON
Followed by camera, he runs up stairs. At the landing, he goes close to her.

GASTON (whispering ardently):
> Gaston!

She looks at him with a confused smile.

GASTON (still ardently):
> And do you know what I'd like to have you do with that check?

MARIETTE (softly, curious):
> What?

GASTON (passionate):
> Make it out to cash!

MARIETTE:
> As you like. (She opens door and he follows her.)

LONG SHOT   PRIVATE OFFICE OF FORMER SECRETARY, WITH GLIMPSE INTO
ADJOINING ELEGANT BEDROOM
In foreground, at desk, is Mariette. In bedroom background, Gaston is
seen examining a painting on the wall with the air of a connoisseur.
Camera moves to close-up of Mariette. She is opening and shutting
drawers.

MARIETTE:
> Now, where can that checkbook be? Oh, dear me, dear me! She
> must have left it *some*where. It's always the same—when you're
> looking for something, you can't find it. (She continues mumbling
> and slamming drawers.)

CLOSE SHOT   GASTON
at the wall, still admiring the painting. Now he draws painting slightly
away from wall and glances behind as if looking for a safe. He allows
painting to drop back into place. Followed by camera, he goes on looking around. He stops before window, looks out, studying possible entrances and exits.

CLOSE SHOT   MARIETTE
at desk, still searching.

MARIETTE:
> I can't find that checkbook. I should have discharged her six
> months ago! I really don't know what to do. Where can I look
> now? (Turning to Gaston.) M'sieu Laval, I'm very sorry, but—

She stops short. Gaston is not there. She sees:

99

DOOR TO FORMER SECRETARY'S BEDROOM
It is open.

CLOSE SHOT MARIETTE
Followed by camera, she goes to bedroom.

BEDROOM MED. SHOT
at open door. Mariette enters, stops.

CLOSE SHOT BED
Gaston is studying bed with the eye of a connoisseur.

CLOSE SHOT MARIETTE
in doorway. She looks mystified. She moves toward him lightly because:

CLOSE SHOT BED
Gaston apparently doesn't know she is in the room. He is still studying
bed with scholarly concentration. Mariette enters, stops beside him.

GASTON (with respect for the bed):
    Eighteenth century.

MARIETTE (getting it; impressed):
    Yes!

GASTON:
    Early eighteenth century. I should say around—seventeen thirty.

MARIETTE:
    Right!

GASTON (examining headboard):
    Beautiful specimen.

MARIETTE:
    It *is* beautiful. But I got a little tired of sleeping in antiques, so I
    gave it to my secretary.

GASTON (specially interested as he learns this is not Mariette's room):
    Oh? (He wants to hear more.)

MARIETTE:
    This used to be my secretary's room.

GASTON (with affected nonchalance):
> I see. (Going very close to headboard, touching woodwork with expert hand.) She must have been very happy here.

MARIETTE (with a smile):
> Too happy. That's why I discharged her.

GASTON (his eye caught by carving on one of the posts):
> Isn't that wonderful! (He turns to Mariette.) You see, madame— (He stops, noticing something on the wall.)

MED. SHOT
In the wall is a safe. Camera moves to close-up of safe.

CLOSE SHOT   MARIETTE AND GASTON

GASTON (inspired):
> Let me tell you something, madame, as a man who has had all kinds of secretaries . . . I wonder if she put that checkbook in the safe!

MARIETTE:
> I hardly think so. But let's look. (She goes toward safe.)

CLOSE SHOT   SAFE
Mariette enters, starts turning knob, lips moving silently as she articulates numbers to herself. The camera pans her out and stops before Gaston, who is now close behind her, concentrating on the combination.

CLOSE SHOT   MARIETTE'S HAND
turning knob back and forth.

CLOSE SHOT   GASTON'S HAND
It is instinctively turning an imaginary knob, following Mariette's pattern.

CLOSE SHOT   MARIETTE AND GASTON
Mariette opens safe. Gaston takes a swift good look into safe, but acts casual, in case Mariette turns around.

MARIETTE (rummaging with her hand):
> No, no. No, it's not here. (Suddenly.) Oh! What do you think of

that? (She brings out two crisp packages of bank notes.) A hundred thousand francs! (With a half-smile.) You know, I didn't have the slightest idea—

GASTON (severely):
But, madame, you keep a hundred thousand francs—in your safe—at *home?*

MARIETTE (worried):
You think that's too much?

GASTON (emphatically):
No! Not enough! (With the air of a banker.) In times like these, when everything is uncertain, every conservative person should have a substantial part of his fortune within arm's reach.

MARIETTE (nodding with the gravity of a woman accepting her banker's advice):
That sounds sensible. (She goes out of the picture, thinking it over.)

CLOSE SHOT   LITTLE SETTEE
Mariette enters, sits.

MARIETTE:
Very sensible!

Gaston enters, sits beside her.

GASTON (sternly; an uncle):
Madame Colet, I think you deserve a scolding. First, you lose your bag—

MARIETTE (gaily):
Then I mislay my checkbook—

GASTON:
Then you use the wrong lipstick—

MARIETTE (almost laughing):
And how I handle my *money!*

GASTON:
It's disgraceful!

MARIETTE (with a flirtatious look):
>   Tell me, M'sieu Laval, what else is wrong?

GASTON:
>   Everything! . . . Madame Colet, if I were your father— (with a smile) which, fortunately, I am not—

MARIETTE (coquettish):
>   Ye-es?

GASTON:
>   And you made any attempt to handle your own business affairs, I would give you a good spanking—in a business way, of course.

MARIETTE (complete change of expression; businesslike):
>   What would you do if you were my *secretary?*

GASTON:
>   The same thing.

MARIETTE:
>   You're hired!

>   FADE OUT

SEQUENCE E

FADE IN

BOARD OF DIRECTORS ROOM
Camera moves along the table in close shots of members of the board. An excited murmur runs along the table. Camera stops in front of M. Giron, the chairman, who is talking to the man beside him. Now he turns to opposite end of table, rises.

GIRON:
>   Speaking for the board of directors, as well as myself, if you insist, in times like these, on cutting the fees of the board of directors, then we resign.

CLOSE SHOT   GASTON
at opposite end. He gets up with an air of authority.

GASTON:
>   Speaking for Madame Colet as well as myself—resign!

CLOSE-UP   GIRON

GIRON (haughtily):
   Very well! (He hesitates.) We'll think it over, M'sieu Laval!

DISSOLVE TO:

INSURANCE OFFICE   CLOSE SHOT
of insurance agent at his desk. He is looking over Mme. Colet's policies.

AGENT:
   Now, M'sieu Laval, as for Madame Colet's life insurance, it totals one million francs. There is five hundred thousand fire insurance and four hundred thousand against burglary.

CLOSE-UP   GASTON
in a different suit. He begins to calculate with his fingers and murmurs figures.

GASTON (after a moment):
   Then we'd better increase the burglary insurance to eight hundred and fifty thousand francs.

CLOSE-UP   AGENT

AGENT (happily; with a little bow):
   Thank you, M'sieu Laval!

CLOSE-UP   COOK
in the kitchen. Big, fat, motherly looking.

COOK:
   No potatoes, M'sieu Laval?

CLOSE-UP   GASTON
In still another suit. He is standing, looking stern.

GASTON:
   No potatoes!

CLOSE-UP   COOK

COOK:
   Yes, M'sieu Laval.

QUICK DISSOLVE TO:

CLOSE-UP   BUTLER
in hall.

BUTLER (answering a question):
> No, M'sieu Laval!

DISSOLVE TO:

CLOSE-UP
A fluffy, pretty little maid in Gaston's bedroom, holding a duster.

MAID (playing naughty):
> *Maybe*, M'sieu Laval!

DISSOLVE TO:

GYMNASIUM   CLOSE SHOT
of Mariette's feet and legs in gymnasium outfit, shooting down on an angle. Feet rise and camera follows movement arc-wise, comes to rest on Mariette's face.

MARIETTE (holding the position):
> Is this what you mean, M'sieu Laval?

CLOSE SHOT   GASTON
erect in sweater, arms folded.

GASTON:
> Absolutely, Madame Colet.

DISSOLVE TO:

CORRIDOR   CLOSE SHOT
Gaston in doorway to his office. Evening; lights are on. He wears a dark business suit.

MARIETTE'S VOICE (coaxingly):
> Now, M'sieu Laval, please!

GASTON:
> Frankly, madame, I'm too tired.

UPPER STAIRCASE
from Gaston's viewpoint. Mariette, in evening dress, is near landing. From downstairs, the music of a tango and laughter of guests.

MARIETTE:
> Don't you want to come down and join the party? Just a little tango—no? Oh, you with your messy old papers and contracts and money-money-money—all those uninteresting things!

CLOSE SHOT GASTON
in doorway.

GASTON:
> They're very interesting to *me*, madame. And *somebody* in this house
> should worry about money. No, madame, really, I have to be up
> early in the morning.

DISSOLVE TO:

OFFICE CLOSE SHOT NEXT MORNING
of Gaston at window, walking up and down dictating, followed by
camera. We hear click of a typewriter.

GASTON:
> New paragraph. Furthermore, it is Madame's wish—

CLOSE SHOT SECRETARY
Typing away at an appropriate desk is none other than our Lily. She is
demure in a little blouse and skirt.

GASTON'S VOICE:
> —that while half of the interest shall be deposited as usual in Ma-
> dame's account—

CLOSE SHOT GASTON

GASTON:
> —the other half, contrary to custom, shall be delivered in cash into
> Madame's personal custody. (Followed by camera, he goes to Lily
> and takes her in his arms.) Darling, that means that on the second
> of June we'll have eight hundred and fifty thousand francs.

LILY (ecstatically):
> And her *jewelry* is worth a fortune!

GASTON:
> No jewelry! Hands off jewelry! If we're broke—all right. I might
> pick up a million-franc necklace. But in times like *these* when we're
> doing a *cash business*—why take a chance on jewelry?

Lily gets up, goes to him.

LILY (the way a wife talks to a husband when she wants something
special):
> I know you're awfully busy, and I don't like to trouble you. But

she has *one little necklace*—you know, that one with the seed pearls? It's so *quiet* and *simple*. It would go just beautifully with my neck.

Gaston takes her in his arms, moved. They kiss. There is a knock at the door. They leap into employer and employee positions.

GASTON:
Come in!

DOOR
Butler enters.

BUTLER:
M'sieu Laval, Madame would like to talk to Mademoiselle Gautier for a moment.

CLOSE SHOT   GASTON AND LILY

GASTON:
Very well, Jacques.

We hear door close as butler goes. Lily turns to Gaston. He looks her over, straightens her hair a little, then pulls the zipper on her blouse high up to the neck.

DISSOLVE TO:

MARIETTE'S BEDROOM   CLOSE SHOT
of Mariette in bed. Breakfast table. She is reading a magazine. Knock on door.

MARIETTE (putting down magazine):
Come in.

DOOR   CLOSE SHOT
Lily enters. She is now wearing glasses. (Under no circumstances shall her appearance be exaggerated. Lily is *playing* the *part* of a modest, polite little secretary.)

LILY:
Good morning, madame.

CLOSE SHOT   MARIETTE

MARIETTE:
Good morning, mademoiselle. (She makes a gesture inviting Lily to come closer.)

CLOSE SHOT   LILY
She approaches Mariette.

CLOSE SHOT   MARIETTE
in bed. Lily enters.

MARIETTE (indicating a chair):
    Please.

LILY:
    Thank you.

Lily sits on a small chair by the bed. Breakfast table is between them.

MARIETTE (busy at the breakfast tray):
    You've had your breakfast—oh, but of course you have.

LILY:
    Yes, madame. You see, I have to get up very early. (Chattering.)
    My little brother goes to school— (With controlled pathos.) You
    see, Mother is dead.

MARIETTE (pouring her own coffee; making conversation):
    Yes, that's the trouble with mothers. First you get to like them and
    then they die.

Lily nods sad agreement. Her glance drops to the floor.

INSERT
of a diamond ring on floor by bed.

CLOSE SHOT   LILY
She looks at ring with undisguised desire for an instant. Then she
reaches for it.

INSERT
Lily's hand lifts ring from floor.

CLOSE SHOT   MARIETTE AND LILY
Seeing that she has been observed, Lily hands ring to Mariette.

MARIETTE:
    Oh, thanks. (With indifference she throws it over toward night
    table on the other side of the bed.)

NIGHT TABLE
A little jewel box, open. The ring falls in.

CLOSE SHOT   LILY
She looks toward the jewel box with regret, fingers itching. She pulls herself together and sits on her hands.

CLOSE SHOT   MARIETTE AND LILY
Mariette is just about to reach for the cream. Lily, quick and polite, takes the cream pitcher and pours for Mariette.

MARIETTE:
   Thank you! . . . Now, mademoiselle, the reason I asked you to come—

LILY:
   Two lumps, madame?

MARIETTE:
   Please! (Lily puts sugar in coffee.) Thank you.

LILY (taking a spoon):
   May I?

Mariette nods graciously. Lily stirs the coffee. Then she sits and resolutely puts her hands under again.

CLOSE SHOT   MARIETTE
She lifts cup, sips coffee. She looks over at Lily.

CLOSE-UP   LILY
Looking downward modestly.

CLOSE-UP   MARIETTE
She watches Lily a moment to make sure she is not looking. Then she quickly dunks a roll in the coffee and takes a quick bite.

CLOSE SHOT   MARIETTE AND LILY

MARIETTE:
   Now, Mademoiselle Gautier—

LILY:
   Yes, madame?

MARIETTE:

You see— (She has just picked up some potato a la Julienne—thinly shredded, noodlelike and crisp—on her fork. Then she speaks furtively as she suddenly remembers.) Oh, not a word to M'sieu Laval!

LILY:

About what?

MARIETTE (almost in a whisper):

Potatoes. He doesn't want me to eat them— (with a little laugh) and naturally I don't want to upset him.

LILY (with a poisonous little giggle):

Naturally not! (Slowly her giggle dies out, and she looks at Mariette with sly contempt.)

MARIETTE:

Now. Uh—mademoiselle—in the short time you have been M'sieu Laval's secretary, have you noticed any change in him?

LILY (on guard):

Well—uh—yes and no.

MARIETTE:

To me he seems rather nervous.

LILY:

Nervous? (She takes a chance.) Um-hum. He smokes too much!

MARIETTE:

No, he *works* too much. (Lily nods with great relief.) He's chained to his desk. Too much detail. Now, if you could take over some of his work—

LILY (with deadly sweetness):

So he wouldn't be confined so much to his office—

MARIETTE (innocently pleased):

Yes! And he would have a little more time for—

LILY:

For all the really important things—

MARIETTE:

Right!

LILY (rising):

I'll do my best, madame, even if I have to work every night.

MARIETTE (frightened):
 Oh, no, no, no, no, my dear child! That's ridiculous. You go home
 as usual—five o'clock every day. Now I'm going to be a little bit of
 a tyrant—I insist. It'll be nice for your little brother, too. *Five
 o'clock*—remember!

LILY:
 Very well, madame. Thank you. (She starts to leave.)

CLOSE SHOT   DOOR
Lily opens door.

MARIETTE'S VOICE:
 And, my dear—

LILY (turns):
 Yes, madame?

CLOSE SHOT   MARIETTE

MARIETTE:
 How much is your salary?

CLOSE SHOT   LILY
in doorway.

LILY:
 Three hundred francs.

CLOSE SHOT   MARIETTE

MARIETTE:
 Well, in times like these most people are cutting salaries, but suppose we say, in your case, three hundred and fifty?

CLOSE SHOT   LILY

LILY:
 Oh, madame, you're just too sweet for words! (She goes, shutting
 door.)

MED. SHOT   OFFICE
close to door. Gaston is pacing up and down. Lily enters, quickly closing door behind her. She takes off her glasses. She is seething.

GASTON:
Well, what does she want?

LILY (bitterly):
You! And she's willing to pay as high as fifty francs!

GASTON:
What?

LILY (violently):
But it's not enough!

MARIETTE'S BEDROOM   CLOSE SHOT
Mariette, still in bed, talking into phone.

MARIETTE:
Now, François, don't be silly. I have nothing against you . . . Oh, no, that's all forgotten . . . What? . . . Not this week, François . . . (Happily.) Business, François, business!

OFFICE   MED. SHOT
which during the scene moves to a closer shot of Gaston and Lily. As we pick them up both are pacing up and down at the height of unpleasantness.

GASTON:
You're talking like a child. You know exactly what we're here for and what it's all about.

LILY (stopping):
This woman has more than jewelry.

GASTON (dismissing it):
Ah!

LILY:
Did you ever take a good look at her—uh—

GASTON:
Certainly!

LILY:
They're all right, aren't they?

GASTON:
Beautiful. And what of it? (Going close to Lily; with conviction.)

Let me tell you something: so far as I'm concerned, her whole sex appeal is in that safe!

LILY (looks at him a moment; suddenly fearful):
Gaston. Let's open it—right now! Let's get away from here! (With great unhappiness; holding back her tears.) I don't like this place!

GASTON (taking her in his arms):
Oh, no, darling. There's *more* sex appeal coming on the first of the month. It's only ten days . . . (Rolling it on his tongue.) Eight hundred and fifty thousand francs.

LILY (clinging to him):
Darling, remember you're Gaston Monescu. You're a crook. I want you as a crook. I love you as a crook. I worship you as a crook. Steal, swindle, rob—but don't become one of those useless, good-for-nothing gigolos!

FADE OUT

SEQUENCE F

FADE IN
OFFICE   CLOSE SHOT
of clock on desk. It is 5 P.M. We hear five chimes. Against this shot of the clock:

LILY'S VOICE:
Good night, Gaston darling.

GASTON'S VOICE:
Good night, sweetheart.

We hear sound of a kiss.

LILY'S VOICE:
Well, I leave you alone with that lady—but if you behave like a gentleman— (Slowly.) I'll break your neck! (With tenderness.) Goodbye, darling!

We hear door open, close, and the sounds of Gaston returning from the door, humming.

DISSOLVE TO:

CLOSE-UP   SAME CLOCK, SAME ANGLE
It reads 5:12. We hear a knock at the door.

GASTON'S VOICE:
Come in.

Sound of the door opening.

MARIETTE'S VOICE (pretending surprise at not seeing Lily):
Oh, M'sieu Laval . . .

GASTON'S VOICE:
Yes, Madame Colet?

MARIETTE'S VOICE:
Has Mademoiselle Gautier gone?

GASTON'S VOICE:
Yes—uh—

MARIETTE'S VOICE (with feigned regret):
Oh, that's too bad. You see, I wanted her to do something . . .
Well, I guess I'll have to do it myself.

GASTON'S VOICE:
What is it, madame?

MARIETTE'S VOICE:
I wanted to ask her to ask you if you'd be good enough to go out
to dinner with me tonight.

We hear her laugh. He joins her. As the laugh gets louder we

DISSOLVE TO:

CLOSE-UP   SAME CLOCK
Five past nine. Light is different, room being almost in darkness. We
hear phone ring several times. Nobody answers.

DISSOLVE TO:

CLOSE-UP   SAME CLOCK
Ten to eleven. So dark that we can barely see the hands. From outside,
faint voices. We hear door open, and a bar of light falls across clock.

GASTON'S VOICE:
Good night, Madame Colet. And let me tell you again—you dance
like a dream.

MARIETTE'S VOICE (coyly):
Oh, no, it's the way you lead.

GASTON'S VOICE:
 No, madame, it's the way you *follow*.

MARIETTE'S VOICE:
 No, m'sieu!

GASTON'S VOICE:
 Yes, madame!

MARIETTE'S VOICE:
 Well, the evening is still young. Let's go down to the living room
 and talk it over. (Cheating by an hour.) It's only ten o'clock.

She laughs. He apparently joins her again.

 DISSOLVE TO:

LIVING ROOM CLOSE-UP
of a different, more decorative clock on mantel. Hands stand at eleven.
As clock strikes eleven, with dainty, rapid chimes, pan along one side,
following mantel, until clock is out of picture, and we see two half-
empty champagne glasses.

 DISSOLVE TO:

CLOSE SHOT WINDOW
Open window frames a view of garden. Foreground is dark. Above
trees, a church steeple with a clock large enough so that we can read
the time. It is twelve. As we hear, in splendid tones and a slower
rhythm, the tolling of midnight, pan over to the side.
 Steeple is out of picture and full moon comes in.

 DISSOLVE TO:

HALL UPPER END OF STAIRS
Close shot of hall clock near Mariette's bedroom door. Hands indicate
the hour of two, and deep tones strike the hour. Apparently there is
only a dim light. Camera pans to door of Mariette's bedroom. In half-
open doorway stands Mariette, evening dress, looking toward office
door, eyes languorous.

MARIETTE (reluctantly):
 Good night, M'sieu Laval.

CLOSE SHOT OFFICE DOOR
In half-open doorway stands Gaston, white tie and tails.

GASTON (low tone):
  Good night, Madame Colet.

MED. SHOT   HALL
At one end, at her open bedroom door, is Mariette. At other end, as
we have seen, is Gaston. They look at each other for a vibrant moment.

MARIETTE (since nothing happens; sadly):
  Good night.

GASTON (also sad):
  Good night.

Mariette goes into her room, closes door. Gaston stands a moment in
his doorway, undecided. Then, with a decisive air, he goes halfway
toward Mariette's door. He stops abruptly at the one light, a lamp on
the wall. He turns it out. Then he goes back to his office-bedroom
slowly. Camera moves closer to him and up to his door. He goes in,
shuts door, and we hear the lock click from inside. Camera pans
quickly to Mariette's door. We hear similar click.

                                                            FADE OUT

SEQUENCE G

FADE IN
LIVING ROOM
A large window, consisting of four or five framed units, fronts on a
terraced garden in which a small informal party is underway.
  Close shot of the first frame, showing part of garden and terrace.
Windows are shut; we cannot hear what is going on. Beyond window,
on terrace: a group of society people, teacups, butler serving cakes
from tray. Mariette comes from garden to join group, a cordial hostess.
As she moves her eye is caught elsewhere.

CAMERA PANS QUICKLY
to the last window frame, following her glance, and stops before Gaston and two very attractive young ladies who seem delighted at what
he is saying. Mariette comes quickly into the picture and, pretending
she wants to introduce him to someone else, takes Gaston from his
dangerous companions.

CAMERA MOVES

back along window with them. As soon as the two young ladies are out of the picture, Mariette brings Gaston intimately close toward window and camera. (Assumption is that living room is empty and no one can see them from behind camera.) Charmingly and with a twinkle in her eye, she reprimands him, in a guarded whisper, about flirting. He answers and apparently says something that makes her laugh, disarming her. With a sudden return to party manner, she moves with him along the framed windows. Camera goes with them as she introduces him to a few little groups. By this time, they are back in the first window frame, and now they move out of picture.

CAMERA CONTINUES

past window and discloses inside corner of living room. In a chair, sitting stiffly as if in a waiting room, is M. Giron, the chairman of the board, briefcase on knees, flower in buttonhole. He seems in a bad mood—apparently the financial cut hasn't agreed with him. We hear a door opening.

BUTLER'S VOICE:
  M'sieu Giron, Madame will be with you presently.

GIRON:
  Very well, Jacques.

We hear door closing. Giron, irritated, gets up and, followed by camera, goes toward the window.

TERRACE   CLOSE SHOT

at window shooting into living room. Giron comes toward window and looks into garden. His face gets stern and angry as he sees:

GARDEN   CLOSE SHOT

Giron's view, of Gaston and the major, animatedly conversing. Camera angle must be so that Gaston is more prominent, thus giving impression that Giron's attention is focused on Gaston.

GASTON:
  No, no, my dear Major. There's a limit to what you can do with infantry. If you have the proper artillery backing, I would say—maybe.

TERRACE   CLOSE SHOT

toward window. Behind window stands Giron, muttering imprecations under his breath.

CLOSE SHOT   MAJOR AND GASTON

MAJOR:

> No, no, no! I disagree with you absolutely. That's the trouble with you artillery men.

GASTON:

> Now just a minute, Major—

MAJOR:

> No, Captain, I tell you—

Mariette comes into the picture.

MARIETTE:

> Now, Major, you mustn't monopolize M'sieu Laval. (To Gaston.) Please! (She leads Gaston away, camera with them. They stop before another group. She introduces Gaston.) May I present M'sieu Laval? Madame Chotard, Madame Leconte, Madame Poncelet. (Camera moves with them to a lady and a gentleman.) Madame Rudaux, M'sieu Legrand—M'sieu Laval. (They move to François and a lady.) M'sieu Laval—Madame Boucher. M'sieu Filiba. (François bows, not recognizing Gaston. Camera moves along with them to others.) M'sieu Laval—Madame Jeantaud, M'sieu Gentil.

Gaston, his back to camera, bows politely; then suddenly—a second "take"—he looks over his shoulder toward François. It is apparent he has recognized François. Mariette moves Gaston along.

CLOSE SHOT   FRANÇOIS AND LADY

LADY:

> That's that M'sieu Laval.

FRANÇOIS:

> Laval? Who is M'sieu Laval?

LADY:

> *I* don't know. *She* says he's her secretary.

François turns and looks searchingly at Gaston, who has paused with Mariette at another group.

FRANÇOIS:
> Oh? . . . So!

LADY:
> And *he* says he is her secretary. Maybe I'm wrong—maybe he *is* her secretary. (She laughs cynically.)

CLOSE SHOT   GASTON
Mariette has apparently left the last group, and he remains. The others, at the moment, are busy with tea and cakes; no one talks. Gaston, standing, back to camera, steals another look over his shoulder at François.

CLOSE SHOT   FRANÇOIS
from Gaston's viewpoint. He is staring at this new and dubious figure in Mariette's life—Gaston.

CLOSE SHOT   GASTON
with the group. He sees that François is staring at him, becomes a little uncomfortable. With sudden decision, he turns to the group.

GASTON:
> Excuse me, please. (Followed by camera, he steps over to François. Camera stops in a close shot on Gaston, François, and lady. Gaston bows to lady, faces François.) Pardon me, m'sieu, but I have the feeling we have met somewhere before.

FRANÇOIS (snobbish, polite):
> I'm sorry, but I don't seem to recall the occasion. No, I'm afraid
> . . .

GASTON (courteously):
> Well—then it must be my mistake. (Bowing.) I beg your pardon.

He smiles, ignoring the snub, as François stands with frozen superiority. Gaston goes. François looks after him.

FRANÇOIS (to the lady):
> That man never met me, and he knows it. Trying to make social connections!

LIVING ROOM   MARIETTE AND GIRON
On a table is a pile of business papers and an empty briefcase. Giron has fountain pen in his hand, ready to turn it over to Mariette for signature.

MARIETTE (with a despairing little laugh):
> But my dear M'sieu Giron, I'm having a tea party. Must I be bothered with all these papers now?

GIRON:
> I'm sorry, madame, but there are still certain matters which I think you should attend to yourself. And I, personally, would not care to refer them to—to— (He hesitates.)

MARIETTE:
> To M'sieu Laval?

Giron doesn't answer. There is a pause.

GIRON (with dignity):
> Madame Colet, I've enjoyed the confidence of your family for more than forty years. (With great feeling.) I was a school friend of your husband's . . .

MARIETTE (looking at his white hair, which tells the whole story of her marriage; grimly):
> I know!

GIRON:
> Madame, let me ask you: *Who is M'sieu Laval, anyhow?* Where does he come from? *What is he?*

MARIETTE (crisply):
> He is my secretary! I hope that answers all your questions, M'sieu Giron.

GIRON (after a pause):
> You know what Paris is saying about the Countess Falconier and her chauffeur?

MARIETTE (outraged—furious, then icy; turning to door):
> Jacques!

CLOSE SHOT   DOOR
It opens; butler enters.

BUTLER:
> Yes, madame?

CLOSE SHOT   MARIETTE AND GIRON

MARIETTE:
>Ask M'sieu Laval if he will be good enough to come in.

BUTLER'S VOICE:
>Very well, madame.

We hear the door closing.

GARDEN   CLOSE SHOT
of lady and François at a table. François is very fidgety.

LADY:
>Now, please. Please calm yourself!

FRANÇOIS:
>I'm like that—I can't help it! I *know* I never met that man, and yet—
>(Looking in Gaston's direction.) Laval, Laval . . . You know, if I
>*like* a man, I remember him. And if I *don't* like a man, I never *forget*
>him. In a nutshell, madame, it's little things like that that drive me
>crazy! Excuse me! (He gets up and walks out of the picture.)

CLOSE SHOT   GASTON
in garden. He is about to join another group when François stops him.

FRANÇOIS:
>M'sieu Laval . . .

GASTON:
>Yes, M'sieu Filiba?

FRANÇOIS:
>You see— (He stops to look Gaston over from all angles, tortured
>with uncertainty. Shaking his head and smiling.) No, no! And
>*yet*— (He looks at Gaston intently again.) *Did* I—did—now *where*
>could we have—

They are interrupted by entrance of butler.

BUTLER (to Gaston):
>Pardon me, m'sieu. Madame Colet would like to see you in the
>living room.

GASTON:
>At once, Jacques. (To François.) We'll continue later.

He goes. François now has jealousy added to his confused suspicion. As he glares after Gaston the major enters.

MAJOR:
> Now see here, my good man, let's face the facts. I'm having a dinner party, and one man turned me down at the last minute. (Very cutting.) Have you a dinner jacket? (François stiffens.)

MED. SHOT   LIVING ROOM
Giron and Mariette. The situation is tense. Gaston enters.

GASTON (with a bow):
> Madame.

MARIETTE:
> Will you be good enough to run through these papers with M'sieu Giron?

GASTON:
> I'll be delighted.

MARIETTE (to Giron, sharply):
> And so will M'sieu Giron.

Giron bows. Mariette turns.

LIVING ROOM   DOOR
Mariette goes out.

CLOSE SHOT   GIRON AND GASTON
For a moment the men eye each other. Gaston smiles, but Giron maintains a frigid face. Gaston calmly takes the papers, sits, and starts to go over the figures.

GIRON:
> M'sieu Laval, there are several things I've wanted to ask you for quite a while. I understand you are from Marseilles.

GASTON (pretending to be absorbed in the figures; absently):
> Um-hum . . .

GIRON (persistently):
> You must be related to the Lavals of Marseilles.

GASTON (with pretense of being mildly distracted):
> Just a second. (He goes over the papers even more thoroughly,

turns several pages, then turns back, apparently comparing items, muttering figures to himself.)

GIRON (sarcastically):
I hope you find the figures correct.

GASTON (pointedly):
I hope so, too.

GIRON (with indignation):
M'sieu Laval, I have enjoyed the confidence of this family—

GASTON (not looking up):
For more than forty years. So Madame told me.

GIRON (change of tone; very deliberately):
And I have known the Lavals of Marseilles for more than thirty years.

CLOSE SHOT   GASTON
Deaf to Giron, concentrating on figures, he turns absently to the window—and suddenly comes awake, for he sees:

CLOSE SHOT   WINDOW
from Gaston's viewpoint. Outside window, on terrace, stands François. He is staring at Gaston as if to say, "*Where* did I see him?"

BIG CLOSE-UP   GASTON
He smiles cordially at François.

CLOSE SHOT   FRANÇOIS
through window. He begins to smile, then shakes head as if saying, "No, that's not the fellow." He goes out of the picture.

CLOSE SHOT   GASTON AND GIRON
Gaston still smiling toward window. Now he turns back to the papers and begins muttering more figures.

GIRON (in a cutting voice):
M'sieu Laval, you seem to be avoiding my questions.

GASTON:
And you, M'sieu Giron, seem to be disturbing my examination of *this report*.

GIRON:
Examination! M'sieu Laval, what are you insinuating? I have enjoyed the confidence of this family for more than forty years. How
long have *you* enjoyed Madame's confidence? Three weeks, I believe.

GASTON (coolly):
Two weeks and three days.

GIRON (nastily):
Um-hum!

GASTON (very softly):
Are *you* insinuating anything, M'sieu Giron?

GIRON (with equal softness and a sudden smile):
No, not at all!

GASTON (beaming):
Well, that's fine. Then you are not insinuating that I am avoiding
questions. And I am not insinuating that you won't let me examine
this report.

GIRON (continuing the friendly note; with an innocent chuckle):
I was only asking if you are related to the Lavals of Marseilles.

GASTON (even more friendly):
And I was only asking you if you would let me examine your report without interruption.

GIRON (like a man about to make a new friend):
I don't see why any man should get excited when he is asked
about his hometown.

GASTON:
And I don't see any reason for any man getting nervous when
somebody checks over the figures of his report.

GIRON (sudden change; enraged):
Are you insinuating that this is not an honest report?

GASTON (with vigor):
I am only insinuating that you are nervous.

GIRON (furious):
Nervous! Why should I be nervous?

GASTON (with deadly sincerity):
I don't *know*, M'sieu Giron!

Outraged, Giron picks up the batch of papers, shakes it in Gaston's face.

GIRON:
>Are you trying to say that there is anything in these figures to make me nervous?

Gaston pauses, and we see his suspicion has become a certainty.

GASTON (with a quiet smile):
>No, not at all.

With quick, casual movement, Gaston takes the report from Giron's hand, drops it in desk, locks desk, and puts key in his pocket. Giron is speechless, frightened to his heels.

GASTON (getting up; amiably):
>We'll keep these papers here. (Taking Giron by the arm, he leads him toward door. Camera follows them from behind.) And tomorrow morning I'll drop in at your office, and I'll tell you all about the Lavals of Marseilles. (Giron looks back over his shoulder toward the desk in a panic.) And there won't be any tea party to interrupt us! (They reach the door. He escorts Giron out, follows, closes the door.)

GARDEN   CLOSE SHOT
at a table. On table is an ashtray. François is sitting by table, an unlighted cigarette in his hand, very thoughtful, still trying to place Gaston. He puts cigarette in his mouth, takes a match from ashtray, which is equipped with matchbox. He lights cigarette and suddenly looks at ashtray.

CLOSE SHOT   ASHTRAY
It is made in the shape of a gondola.

CLOSE-UP   FRANÇOIS
staring at the gondola. We see that his mind is grappling, trying to connect gondola, Venice, and Gaston. He rises, brain working.

MED. SHOT   DOOR IN ENTRANCE HALL
In the half-open doorway stands Gaston.

GASTON (out toward street):
>Goodbye, M'sieu Giron! (He shuts door quickly and goes out of picture toward stairway.)

LONG SHOT STAIRWAY
Gaston runs quickly up.

OFFICE MED. SHOT
at the door. Gaston opens door, enters, closes it quickly with great excitement.

CLOSE SHOT DESK
Lily is typing. She is startled at Gaston's sudden entrance and gets up.

CLOSE SHOT GASTON
at door. Followed by camera, he goes to Lily.

GASTON:
Do you know who is here? (There is a knock on the door. Lily goes quickly back to typewriter.) Come in!

CLOSE SHOT DOOR
Butler opens.

BUTLER:
M'sieu Laval, M'sieu Filiba would like very much to see you.

CLOSE SHOT LILY AND GASTON

GASTON:
In a moment.

We hear door shut. Lily gets up, puzzled. The name sounds slightly familiar to her.

LILY:
Filiba . . .

GASTON:
Yes—Filiba! Venice—Grand Hotel—room two fifty-three—

LILY (it dawns on her):
Five, seven, and nine—

GASTON:
Yes! (With swift reassurance.) Now don't worry! (Followed by camera, he hastens out, closing door behind him.)

LONG SHOT STAIRWAY
Gaston comes quickly down, goes out toward entrance door.

ENTRANCE HALL   CLOSE SHOT

of François, waiting, hat in hand, ready to leave. Gaston enters.

FRANÇOIS:
I wanted to say goodbye to you.

GASTON (quickly):
Goodbye, M'sieu Filiba. (He starts away. François stops him.)

FRANÇOIS:
But before I say goodbye I want to ask you one question: Have you ever been in Venice?

GASTON:
No.

FRANÇOIS:
You've *never* been in Venice?

GASTON:
No . . . (Suddenly.) Have *you* ever been in Vienna?

FRANÇOIS (taken aback):
No.

GASTON:
Amsterdam?

FRANÇOIS:
No.

GASTON:
Constantinople?

FRANÇOIS:
No.

GASTON (with astonishment):
You've never been in Constantinople?

FRANÇOIS:
No!

GASTON:
But you *have* been in Venice?

FRANÇOIS:
Yes!

GASTON:
  Let me tell you, Venice *can't compare* with Constantinople.

FRANÇOIS:
  But—

GASTON:
  I don't care *what* you say! In Constantinople at least you have streets, sultans, pashas—

FRANÇOIS (up a new alley; with a new, naughty interest):
  And harems . . . ?

GASTON:
  All kinds.

François leans over and whispers a question. Gaston nods vigorously, then leans over and whispers in François's ear. François's eyes get bigger and bigger. The two men look at each other with a big smile. François extends his hand.

FRANÇOIS (as they shake; almost singing):
  Well—Con-stan-ti-*nople!*

Followed by camera, François goes toward street door, opens it, then stops and turns around. His face suddenly sobers. He looks at Gaston.

CLOSE SHOT   GASTON
at foot of staircase. He bows smilingly to François.

CLOSE SHOT   DOORWAY
François looks searchingly at Gaston for a long moment, then turns and departs, still puzzled.

MED. SHOT   GASTON
Once door is shut, there is a swift change on his face. He turns and dashes upstairs.

OFFICE   CLOSE SHOT
at door. Gaston enters and, followed by camera, goes swiftly to desk, past Lily, who stands fearful and ready for action, straight to the phone.

GASTON:
  Élysée seven, eight, nine, two. (To Lily.) We have to clear out. (Into phone.) Railroad station? Ticket office, please.

LILY (excitedly):
He recognized you!

GASTON:
No—not yet—but— (Into phone.) Two tickets to Berlin—first class and sleeper—night train . . . Right . . . Right . . . Leave them in the name of—Don Ignacio Fernandez . . . Right . . . Thank you. (Hangs up.)

LILY (who already has got at a telephone directory):
Spanish passports?

GASTON
Correct. Now the train leaves—

LILY:
At twelve twenty. I know. (She grabs phone.) Lyons two, four, seven, one. (Hand over mouthpiece.) Two more days and we'd have seven hundred and fifty thousand francs more!

GASTON:
Well, we'll have to take what's here. A bird in hand is worth two in jail.

LILY (into phone):
Hello . . . Is this the Spanish consulate? This is Doña Ignacio Fernandez. (In Spanish.) My husband and I are leaving tonight for Berlin . . . Is it too late to get a visa this afternoon . . . ? Thank you, thank you. (She hangs up. To Gaston; in English.) How long will it take you?

GASTON:
I don't know. Fortunately, she has a dinner engagement tonight. I'll meet you at the station—midnight. (Lily hastens out. Phone rings. Gaston answers.) Hello . . . Yes? What? . . . You found a handbag? Well, you're three weeks too late! (He hangs up. Lily swiftly returns, wearing hat and jacket.)

LILY:
Well, see you at the Berlin Express.

GASTON:
By the way, how is your German?

LILY:
Grossartig—kolossal!

GASTON:

> *Also, um zwoelf Uhr.*

LILY:

> *Am Berliner Zug.*

GASTON:

> *Auf wiedersehn.*

LILY:

> *Auf wiedersehn.* (A quick kiss. She speeds out.)

GASTON (into phone):

> Marchand two, nine, one, one . . . Hello . . . Is this the Petit Flower Shop? This is Don Ignacio Fernandez. I'd like you to take five dozen roses—deep red roses—and I'd like you to put them in a basket and send the basket tomorrow morning to Madame Mariette Colet. The Madame Colet . . . Yes . . . You have the address? . . . Good! And attach a card: "In memory of the late M'sieu Laval" . . . Tomorrow morning—ten o'clock . . . Yes. ‡What? . . . Charge it to Madame Colet. Yes.‡ Thank you.

FADE OUT

SEQUENCE H

FADE IN

DINING ROOM   MAJOR'S APARTMENT

Table is for twenty-four people. Butler at table. Major enters, half-dressed: tuxedo trousers, stiff shirt without collar, dressing gown. Butler gives him the place cards, already stacked in order. Major puts first card at head of table. As he does:

INSERT   TABLE

Major's hand puts down card reading Major.

CLOSE SHOT   MAJOR

Looks at second place card, smiles, puts it at next place. As he does:

INSERT   TABLE

Major's hand puts down card reading Madame Colet.

CLOSE SHOT   MAJOR

Looks at next card. Smile disappears. He gives butler a reproving look. Followed by camera, he goes with the card to other end of the table.

INSERT   TABLE

Major's hand puts down card reading M. François Filiba.

DISSOLVE TO:

FRANÇOIS'S BATHROOM

François, in underwear, shaving brush in one hand and safety razor in the other, sitting on edge of bathtub, still trying to figure out where he saw Gaston.

DISSOLVE TO:

STAIRCASE   MARIETTE'S HOUSE   MED. SHOT

at door to her bedroom. Mariette, in evening gown and wrap, comes out. About to go downstairs, she stops. Followed by camera, she goes to office door, knocks. Door opens, and Gaston appears.

GASTON:
Yes, madame?

MARIETTE (very charming):
What are you going to do with my day tomorrow, M'sieu Laval?

GASTON (looks at her a moment with real feeling, knowing he is saying goodbye):
Well, we'll have breakfast in the garden.

MARIETTE (nodding):
Um-hum . . .

GASTON:
Then riding together.

MARIETTE (nodding):
Um-hum . . .

GASTON:
Then lunch in the Bois—

MARIETTE:
Together.

GASTON:
Then a little nap—

MARIETTE (restrains an automatic "together" and smiles, a bit embarrassed):
How do you like my dress?

GASTON (meaning it):
Beautiful.

131

MARIETTE (seductively):
    Hair?

GASTON:
    Marvelous.

MARIETTE (closer; softly):
    Lipstick?

Gaston leans to inspect her mouth; any moment they might kiss.

GASTON:
    Crimson!

MARIETTE (still softer):
    Correct! (After a slight pause; extending her hand.) Good night.

GASTON (taking hand; slowly):
    Good night. (He kisses her hand.)

MARIETTE (without withdrawing hand):
    Good night.

GASTON (slowly letting hand drop; in a slightly different voice):
    Goodbye.

He remains in doorway looking after her as, followed by camera, she goes to the staircase. When she is down a few steps:

GASTON'S VOICE:
    Madame. .

MARIETTE (pausing on steps):
    Yes?

CLOSE SHOT   GASTON
in office doorway.

GASTON:
    Are you staying out late?

STAIRCASE
from Gaston's view. Big close-up of Mariette. She looks at him with eagerness, thinking he has amorous designs.

CLOSE-UP   GASTON
He sees she misunderstood, is a little embarrassed.

STAIRCASE
Close-up of Mariette. She misinterprets his embarrassment.

MARIETTE:
    Why do you ask?

CLOSE-UP   GASTON
He cannot tell the truth and is so truly smitten that he hates to lead her
on.

CLOSE-UP   MARIETTE
convinced he is shyly in love with her and needs assistance.

MARIETTE (repeats softly):
    Why do you ask, M'sieu Laval?

CLOSE SHOT   GASTON

GASTON
    (with a helpless smile): Do I have to answer?

CLOSE-UP   MARIETTE
Her lips form the inaudible whispered answer.

MARIETTE (soundlessly):
    No!

CLOSE SHOT   GASTON
in doorway. He bows, returns into office; door shuts.

CLOSE SHOT   MARIETTE
Looks after him an instant, then, followed by camera, goes slowly
downstairs, very happy; her love affair is coming to a head. She stops.
On impulse, she turns and, followed by camera, goes quickly up stairs
to his office and enters, closing door behind her.

                                                    DISSOLVE TO:

LILY'S HOTEL ROOM
Lily is packing—Gaston's clothes and her own. She gaily hums a well-
known Spanish fandango.

LONG SHOT   UPPER STAIRCASE
In Mariette's home, including office door and door to Mariette's bedroom. Butler comes up stairs, goes to Mariette's door, knocks. Door to
office opens and Mariette comes out, now without her wrap.

MARIETTE:
　　Yes, Jacques?

CLOSE SHOT　BUTLER
Turns, puzzled to see Mariette in office doorway.

BUTLER:
　　The car is waiting, madame.

CLOSE SHOT　MARIETTE

MARIETTE:
　　I won't need the car, Jacques. I'm not going. (She turns back, shuts office door.)

CLOSE SHOT　BUTLER
at bedroom door.

BUTLER (dazed):
　　Very well, madame! (Followed by camera, he starts down staircase, muttering to himself.)

CLOSE SHOT　OFFICE DOOR
Door opens; Gaston comes out quickly.

GASTON:
　　Jacques!

BUTLER
on staircase; from Gaston's point of view. He stops.

BUTLER:
　　Yes, M'sieu Laval?

CLOSE SHOT　GASTON

GASTON:
　　Madame has changed her mind. She'll be down in a minute. (He goes into office, shuts door.)

CLOSE SHOT　BUTLER

BUTLER (still one beat behind):
　　Very well, m'sieu! (Followed by camera, he continues down stairs, punch-drunk.)

CLOSE SHOT MARIETTE AND GASTON
in office. Gaston has just closed door.

MARIETTE:
> But I told you I don't want to go.

GASTON:
> But you have an engagement, and I don't want people to talk.

MARIETTE:
> Talk? About me—about us?

GASTON:
> Precisely.

MARIETTE (ironically):
> Afraid I'm ruining your reputation, M'sieu Laval?

GASTON:
> No—yours, madame.

MARIETTE (after a slight pause):
> M'sieu Laval, I've got a confession to make to you . . .

Gaston, remembering that Lily once used the same phrase before she dubbed him a crook, turns with a flash of alarm.

MARIETTE:
> You like me. In fact, you're crazy about me. Otherwise, you wouldn't worry about my reputation. Isn't that so?

Gaston looks at her with relief and delight. She is as charming as if she herself were a crook.

MARIETTE:
> But incidentally, let me tell you, *I* don't like *you*. I don't like you at all! (Going close to him.) I wouldn't hesitate one instant to ruin *your* reputation—like that! (She snaps her fingers.)

GASTON (loving the game; stepping closer):
> You would?

MARIETTE (even closer):
> Yes, I would!

GASTON (snapping his fingers):
> Like that?

MARIETTE (snapping her fingers again):
> Like that!

GASTON (playing tough):
> I know all your tricks.

MARIETTE (also tough):
> And you're going to fall for them.

GASTON:
> So you think you can get me?

MARIETTE:
> Any minute I want!

GASTON:
> You're conceited—

MARIETTE:
> But attractive—

GASTON:
> *Now, let me tell you—*

MARIETTE:
> *Shut up—kiss me!* (Gaston embraces and kisses her. She kisses him ardently, then frees herself for a moment, holds him off.) Wasting all this marvelous time with arguments! (Kisses him again. He takes her in his arms.)

CLOSE SHOT   GASTON'S TELEPHONE
It rings several times. No one answers.

LOWER HALL TELEPHONE   CLOSE SHOT
It is ringing—a different tone from the one we have just heard. Butler enters and answers.

BUTLER:
> Hello . . . Well, I'll try him again. (He pushes a button.) Yes, he's in his office, but he's busy . . . Madame Colet? She's still here—yes . . . But she's busy, too . . . Well, I'll ring again.

LANDING ON UPPER STAIRCASE   MED. SHOT
office door. Telephone still ringing inside. Nobody seems to answer.

LILY'S HOTEL ROOM   CLOSE SHOT
Lily at phone, putting down receiver. She sits, very thoughtful. She tries to hum the fandango she had been humming so gaily before. Now

it comes in fragments as she moves about, sits, gets up. She is worried and suspicious.

DISSOLVE TO:

MED. SHOT   UPPER STAIRCASE
Hall clock is striking eight. Butler comes up stairs, goes to office door, and knocks. To his multiple confusion, behind him *Mariette's* door opens, and *Gaston* appears.

GASTON:
Yes, Jacques?

CLOSE SHOT   BUTLER
He turns to Gaston's new location.

BUTLER:
M'sieu Giron is downstairs.

GASTON (with vast authority):
Tell M'sieu Giron I can't see him now. Impossible! (Butler is about to leave.) And, Jacques. Dismiss the car! Madame is not going. (He turns back into Mariette's room, shuts door.)

BUTLER (by now a confirmed cynic):
Yes, M'sieu Laval! (Followed by camera, shaking his head, he goes down.)

CLOSE SHOT   MARIETTE'S BEDROOM DOOR
It opens. Mariette appears.

MARIETTE:
Jacques!

CLOSE SHOT   BUTLER

BUTLER (looking dizzily in wrong direction):
Yes, madame— (Turning.) *Yes*, madame!

CLOSE SHOT   MARIETTE

MARIETTE:
Don't dismiss the car! I'll be down in a few minutes. (She shuts door.)

CLOSE SHOT   BUTLER
He finds his jittery way down the stairs.

BEDROOM   CLOSE SHOT
Mariette and Gaston at foot of bed. Bed is untouched. On bed is her wrap. Mariette picks up wrap.

GASTON (passionately):
I want you to stay, Mariette. You've *got* to stay. You can't go now!

MARIETTE:
I *must* go.

GASTON:
I'm crazy about you!

MARIETTE (holding him off):
I know it.

GASTON:
I love you.

MARIETTE:
I *believe* you.

GASTON:
Then why do you want to go?

MARIETTE:
Because I want to make it tough for you.

Gaston takes her in his arms, kisses her passionately. She returns kiss with even greater passion.

MARIETTE (still in his arms; genuine feeling in its full wisdom):
We have a long time ahead . . .

CLOSE-UP   A MIRROR IN THE ROOM
The couple are seen at one angle, as dialogue continues.

MARIETTE:
Weeks . . .

CLOSE-UP   ANOTHER MIRROR
Another angle on the couple as she says:

MARIETTE:
months . . .

MED. CLOSE SHOT ON THE EMPTY BED
Their embracing shadows lie the length of the bed, giving the effect of two bodies in a sex embrace on the bed, as she says:

MARIETTE:
years! . . .

CLOSE SHOT   BOTH STILL EMBRACING
She continues:

MARIETTE:
Think of that, Gaston—the future lies bright before us!*

A real struggle goes on in Gaston. She kisses him tenderly, frees herself, and, followed by camera, goes to door, stops, turns.

MARIETTE (breathless; in a very low voice, making the rendezvous for later):
Eleven o'clock! (She is gone; door closes.)

CLOSE SHOT   GASTON
A man in love, completely shaken. He sits on bed, thinks, then takes telephone slowly, decisively.

GASTON:
Élysée seven, eight, seven, nine.

LILY'S HOTEL ROOM
The luggage is packed and in order. Followed by camera, Lily, dressed for travel, paces nervously up and down. Phone rings. She rushes to phone.

LILY:
Hello . . . Darling! Oh, darling, it's good to hear your voice! I thought you'd *never* call! I *tried* to get you . . . What? *What?* (Camera moves to big close-up of her.) *Tomorrow morning? Why?* (Tears come into

---

*NOTE: It is difficult to indicate changes that were made in the scene between Gaston and Mariette in her bedroom. Let me say simply that the scene as originally written had no mirror shots or shadows on a bed. The camera was on Gaston and Mariette, and we saw them both as Mariette said, "We have a long time ahead. Weeks, months, years! Think of that, Gaston—the future lies bright before us!" The evocative mirror shots and the erotic shadow on the bed of the embracing couple were inspirations of Lubitsch while shooting the picture. This is a rare and perhaps isolated instance. As the scripts show, Lubitsch almost always planned the visual wit as part of the working script.—S.R.

her eyes.) Of course . . . Um-hum . . . Um-hum . . . (With a brave, cheerful tone.) That sounds reasonable—very reasonable . . .

FADE OUT

SEQUENCE I

FADE IN

LIVING ROOM   MAJOR'S HOME   CLOSE-UP

of Mariette. It is after dinner. We hear voices and music. Her thoughts are with Gaston. She sips from a champagne glass. Medium close-up to include her chair and a small table. She puts glass on the table and, oblivious to other guests, leans back dreamily, anticipating a night of love, eyes closed.

Camera pans to a couch not too near Mariette. François and the major, smoking cigars. Camera moves to close-up. They are watching Mariette. They exchange a look of understanding. They have become friends, realizing that neither has a chance with Mariette.

MAJOR (intimately):
No doubt about it—it's that secretary.

FRANÇOIS:
Funny, the kind of men women fall for.

MAJOR:
No color, no sparkle—but dependable.

FRANÇOIS:
The type they marry.

MAJOR:
You know, I'm not the marrying type. I like to take my fun and leave it.

FRANÇOIS (inspecting the major; friendly):
Nice suit.

MAJOR:
Like it?

FRANÇOIS:
Smart. London, eh?

MAJOR:
Ogilvie and Oglethorpe.

FRANÇOIS:
I thought so.

Both men lean back. A moment of silence.

FRANÇOIS (patronizingly):
He's really not a bad fellow.

MAJOR:
Just dull.

FRANÇOIS:
Insignificant . . . He's a secretary, always *was* a secretary, always *will* be.

MAJOR (with a smile):
Funny—the first time I saw him I thought he was a doctor!

FRANÇOIS (sitting up suddenly):
Doc—!

He looks stricken. Major, worried, thinks François has a heart attack. François gets up; Major gets up. François stares into space, then unseeingly at Major. Major becomes alarmed. François sits. Major sits with him. With sudden decision, François snaps his fingers, stands up. Major also stands up. François, followed by camera, goes straight to Mariette. Major, in a daze, follows. Mariette is still dreaming. François taps her on the shoulder. She looks up. His expression frightens her. François, waving his hand, tries to talk. The words don't come. Finally one word escapes him.

FRANÇOIS:
Tonsils! (Major and Mariette think the man has gone insane.) *Positively tonsils!*

DISSOLVE TO:

VERY CLOSE SHOT   GASTON'S BEDROOM WINDOW
from outside. Behind the glass, Gaston's hand drumming on the pane nervously. Camera pulls back, and we see Gaston looking into the night, waiting restlessly. Suddenly he turns around sharply toward the door. Apparently someone has knocked at the office door. Camera swings over to the next window, and we recognize the office, which adjoins Gaston's bedroom. Through office window we see butler, who has knocked on bedroom door, waiting. Bedroom door opens, and Gaston emerges. It is apparent that butler delivers a message. Camera moves

down one floor and stops in a close shot of living room window from outside. Behind the glass stands Giron. He also drums nervously on the pane.

LIVING ROOM   CLOSE SHOT
at door to the corridor. Door opens. Gaston enters.

CLOSE SHOT   GIRON
He turns. Gaston comes into picture.

GASTON (impatiently):
I'm very sorry, but this is no time, M'sieu Giron—

GIRON (emphatically):
I've got to see you.

GASTON:
But not now.

GIRON:
Right now! It's very important, M'sieu Laval.

GASTON:
It may be important to you, M'sieu Giron—

GIRON:
No, to you—M'sieu *Monescu*.

Pause, as they face each other.

GASTON (cordially):
Won't you sit down?

EXT. MAJOR'S VILLA
In entrance driveway stands Mariette's car.

CLOSE SHOT
of entrance door. Mariette comes out, followed by Major and François. All are excited.

MAJOR AND FRANÇOIS:
But, Mariette, *please* . . . Now *listen*—it's *true* . . .

Followed by camera, they approach car.

MARIETTE:
It's absolutely ridiculous! I don't believe it!

MAJOR AND FRANÇOIS:
But, Mariette—

MARIETTE:
I'm awfully tired anyhow. So please leave me alone. Good night!
(She steps into car. Chauffeur shuts car door and goes out of picture to driver's seat. François and Major linger awkwardly. Door opens and Mariette leans out.) I had a very lovely time! (Door closes.)

LONG SHOT
Shooting toward the car from opposite side. View of house and Major and François is covered by car. Car pulls away. We see Major and François moving toward house, chummy, animatedly talking.

FRANÇOIS:
So I said to myself, "All right, if he wants to look at them, let him *look* at them. No harm in that." And then *he* said, "Say *ah!*" And that's all I remember . . .

They disappear into house.

MARIETTE'S LIVING ROOM   MED. SHOT
of Gaston and Giron at door to hall.

GIRON (thinking he is the winner):
So . . . You will pack your things at once!

GASTON (with deceptive humility):
Yes, m'sieu.

GIRON:
And you will be out by tomorrow morning.

GASTON:
Very well, m'sieu.

GIRON:
Otherwise I'll call the police.

GASTON:
Yes, m'sieu. (Giron is about to leave.) M'sieu Giron!

GIRON:
What is it?

GASTON (opening a new subject):
You have enjoyed the confidence of this family for more than forty
years. You must be a man of about—about sixty-five. (Giron looks
puzzled and uneasy.) Let's see— (Gaston counts on his fingers.)
You will be exactly eighty-seven when you come out of prison.

GIRON (outraged):
What do you mean?

GASTON:
You say I am a crook.

GIRON:
I know it!

GASTON (amiably curious):
Then why didn't you call the police? Why *don't* you call the police?
(Conversationally.) I'll tell you why—you crook, you.

GIRON (trembling with indignation):
M'sieu . . .

GASTON (helpfully):
Monescu.

GIRON:
M'sieu Monescu!

GASTON (with a smile):
Just call me Gaston.

INT. MARIETTE'S CAR
as it drives along. Close shot of Mariette. She knows that François told
the truth.

MED. SHOT   ENTRANCE DOOR
to Mariette's house. It opens, and Giron emerges, full of dignity and
indignation. Gaston, in the doorway, is a smiling host.

GASTON (calling after him):
Good night, Adolph!

Giron stops in his tracks as Gaston shuts door.

STAIRWAY

Gaston hastens up. He reaches landing and is about to enter his office, when outer doorbell rings. Exasperated, he hastens down.

HALL   CLOSE SHOT

at entrance door. Gaston opens. There stands Giron, furious.

GIRON:

   Don't you dare to call me Adolph!

Gaston slams door in Giron's face and turns back.

STAIRWAY

Gaston starts up.

UPPER LANDING

Gaston is about to enter office, thinks a moment, then goes toward Mariette's bedroom door.

LONG SHOT   HER BEDROOM INT.

It is dark. Door opens. Gaston enters, shuts door, turns on wall switch, flooding room with light. He moves to a night table by the bed, on which is a small lamp, turns on the lamp, then goes back to wall switch and turns off main lights. Room is now in soft shadow, with only the one small light. He turns to window, sees that shade is not down, goes toward the window.

CLOSE SHOT

of same window from outside. Gaston appears, is just about to pull down shade when he glances toward his own bedroom in other wing of house. He sees:

CAMERA PANS QUICKLY

to other wing of house and stops outside Gaston's bedroom window. Behind window stands Lily looking across at him. The situation is clear; she knows the worst. She looks menacingly calm.

MARIETTE'S BEDROOM WINDOW

from outside. Gaston is in trouble and he knows it. He goes quickly toward door.

GASTON'S BEDROOM WINDOW
from outside. Lily, having seen Gaston leave Mariette's room, pauses, makes up her mind, then draws the curtains closed.

GASTON'S BEDROOM   INSIDE   CLOSE SHOT
at door. It opens. Gaston rushes in, looks toward window, doesn't see Lily, turns, and sees:

CLOSE SHOT   LILY
at the wall safe. She has one hand on the dial and is facing Gaston defiantly.

CLOSE SHOT   GASTON
Followed by camera, he goes to Lily.

GASTON:
Are you insane? You've to get out of here at once! She may come back any minute.

LILY (grimly):
What time is your rendezvous?

GASTON (frantic):
Now, Lily—

LILY:
Yes, *M'sieu Colet?*

GASTON (staggered; recovering; desperate):
You *have* to get out of here!

LILY (bitterly):
That's what I'm here for—to get out! I want to get away from here, from you—as fast as I can and as far as a hundred thousand francs will take me. (She returns to the safe, hand on dial.) Sixty-five, ninety-four—

GASTON:
Don't you *realize*—

LILY:
Thirty-five to the left—sixty-three, eight . . . I wouldn't fall for another man if he were the biggest crook on earth . . . Seventy-six, eighty-four, fifty-five— (Suddenly facing him; bitterly.) What has she got that I haven't got?

GASTON:
    Lily, you *must* listen to me.

LILY:
    Shut up! Don't make up any stories!

GASTON:
    But, Lily—

LILY:
    Don't you dare lie to me! (Ironically.) I know you love me. (Pause.
    He is helpless.) Well, why don't you say something? Come on—be
    brilliant. Talk yourself out of it—bluff yourself in! (Gaston makes
    an effort to speak.) Shut up, you liar, you! (She turns back to safe,
    opens it, looks inside.) That's what I want! (Taking out the stacks
    of bank notes.) This is real! Money! Cash!

STREET
in front of Mariette's house. Her car comes, stops.

MED. SHOT   HALL
Gaston's door. Lily comes out, very excited, closing door behind her.
Followed by camera, she runs down steps, across hall, toward entrance
door. Doorbell rings. She stops.

BUTLER'S PANTRY
Butler in a chair, half-asleep. Bell rings again. He gets up and goes out.

HALL   MED. SHOT
at entrance door. Lily has disappeared. Butler comes, opens door. Mariette enters.

BUTLER:
    Good evening, madame.

Sweeping past him, followed by camera, Mariette goes up stairs. She
pauses at her bedroom door. Changing her mind, she goes to Gaston's
door. She knocks.

MED. SHOT   MARIETTE'S BEDROOM DOOR
from hall. Gaston opens the door. He sees Mariette, smiles, and opens
her door very wide, welcoming her to her own room.

CLOSE SHOT   MARIETTE

at Gaston's door to his office-and-bedroom suite. She smiles at him enigmatically. Instead of responding, she opens his door and goes in, leaving door open. As she goes she gives him another smile, as if to say, "This is where it's going to be."

CLOSE SHOT   GASTON

puzzled, but not worried. He closes her door and goes toward his own door.

GASTON'S BEDROOM

Mariette stands in the center of the room. Gaston enters, closes door, goes toward her. Camera moves to close shot of both. She embraces him—they kiss. Then, languorously, she takes off her wrap. He helps her. She drops wrap on bed. Then she reaches for her necklace with the seductive air of a woman about to disrobe. She takes off the necklace, the jeweled pin on her bosom, then her bracelets and rings.

MARIETTE (as he watches her; a lover, but careful):
    When a lady takes her jewels off in a gentleman's room, where does she put them?

GASTON (gallantly):
    On the night table.

MARIETTE (provocatively):
    But I don't want to be a lady. (She kisses him lightly and moves out of the picture, the jewels in her hand.)

CLOSE SHOT   SAFE

Mariette enters with the intention of opening the safe.

CLOSE-UP   GASTON

He is startled. He goes quickly toward her.

CLOSE SHOT   SAFE

Mariette is about to turn the dial. Gaston enters.

GASTON (helpfully):
    May I?

MARIETTE (again with that smile; playful):
    Ah, let me have a little fun.

GASTON (playing the game; graciously):
Please! (He moves away.)

CLOSE SHOT   ARMCHAIR
Gaston enters, sits on the arm of the chair, and leans back, smiling, on guard.

CLOSE-UP   MARIETTE

MARIETTE (beginning to dial):
Now let me see—sixty-five, ninety-four—

CLOSE-UP   GASTON

GASTON:
Thirty-three—

CLOSE-UP   MARIETTE

MARIETTE:
No—thirty-five! (She laughs.)

CLOSE-UP   GASTON
He laughs, too. They are apparently having a jolly time.

CLOSE-UP   MARIETTE
She continues to dial.

MARIETTE:
Thirty-five . . . (Very casually.) You know, François—M'sieu Filiba—thinks you're a very remarkable man.

CLOSE-UP   GASTON
For one swift instant his face tells us that now he knows the worst.

MARIETTE'S VOICE:
He was at the dinner tonight.

CLOSE-UP   MARIETTE:

MARIETTE (continuing to dial):
Sixty-three, eight—

CLOSE-UP   GASTON

GASTON:
Mariette!

CLOSE-UP   MARIETTE
She turns toward him charmingly.

MARIETTE (with pretended innocence):
Yes, Gaston?

CLOSE SHOT   MARIETTE AND GASTON

GASTON:
What would you say if you found your safe had been robbed?

MARIETTE:
I wouldn't say anything—I would act.

GASTON:
Call the police?

MARIETTE:
Instantly.

GASTON (as if to say, "It's a good idea"):
Um-*hum* . . .

MARIETTE (lightly):
But why talk about robbery on a night like this?

She pauses—is it ironically? He is not quite sure. He takes a last chance.

GASTON (ardently):
You look beautiful.

MARIETTE:
Thank you. (Turning back coolly to safe.) Seventy-six, eighty—

GASTON (rising; the game is over):
Mariette!

MARIETTE:
Yes, Gaston?

GASTON:
You have been robbed—for years. And not a hundred thousand francs, but millions. And you know who did it? Adolph.

MARIETTE:
 Adolph?

GASTON:
 Adolph J. Giron.

MARIETTE (laughing at him):
 And you expect me to believe that?

GASTON:
 Naturally not. But I expect the police to believe it. (He goes out to night table.)

CLOSE SHOT   NIGHT TABLE
Gaston enters, picks up telephone.

CLOSE-UP   MARIETTE
at the safe. Frightened, she goes quickly to telephone.

CLOSE SHOT   TELEPHONE
Mariette enters, takes receiver out of Gaston's hand, sets it back.

MARIETTE:
 No!

GASTON:
 Why not? He's a thief—he's a criminal.

MARIETTE:
 I don't believe it!

GASTON:
 Then why are you afraid to let me prove it?

Mariette turns away. She is beginning to suspect there might be truth in what he says.

GASTON (ironically):
 It would be a terrible scandal, wouldn't it?

MARIETTE (to herself):
 Giron . . . !

GASTON:
 Yes, Giron! Chairman of the board of Colet and Company. Honorary president of the Orphans' Asylum. Adolph J. Giron—distin-

guished citizen! . . . Well, shall I call the police? (Mariette's silence eloquently says no.) I see! You have to be in the social register to keep out of jail. But when a man starts at the bottom and works his way up—a self-made crook—then you say, "Call the police! Put him behind bars! Lock him up!" (He glares at her indignantly, then goes to the safe.)

CLOSE SHOT SAFE
Gaston enters, gives the dial one turn, and safe opens. The papers inside are in complete disorder.

CLOSE SHOT MARIETTE
staring at the open safe.

CLOSE SHOT GASTON
He goes toward her.

CLOSE SHOT MARIETTE
Gaston enters, bows formally.

GASTON:
> I don't seem to have my calling cards with me, Madame Colet. So permit me to introduce myself informally—Gaston Monescu. I assure you in my own circles I am very well known.

Mariette looks at him sadly for a moment. She gets up, restraining tears.

MARIETTE:
> You wanted a hundred thousand francs, and I thought you wanted me.

Gaston is deeply moved. Mariette turns, moves sadly toward window.

CLOSE SHOT WINDOW
Curtains are now open. We see the church steeple—the same one we saw romantically before. Mariette enters and leans her head against the window, her back to the camera. The church clock strikes eleven.

CLOSE SHOT GASTON
He is crushed. Followed by camera, he goes to her, stops at her side.

GASTON:
> I came here to rob you—but unfortunately I fell in love with you. (No reaction.) Mariette!

She turns, looks at him.

MARIETTE (bitterly):
> Why did you take the money?

Gaston is speechless; the truth is too complicated. Despairing, she goes. He stands looking after her. We hear her steps as she crosses the room; then we hear the door shut. He turns to the window. Suddenly he stares toward Mariette's bedroom window.

CLOSE SHOT
Mariette's bedroom window from outside. Behind the window is Lily, looking across at him implacably. She has witnessed the scene at the opened safe and has come to her own conclusions.

GASTON'S BEDROOM WINDOW
from outside. Close-up of Gaston. He looks at Lily, dumbfounded.

MARIETTE'S BEDROOM   CLOSE SHOT
at door to corridor, from inside. Mariette enters. Suddenly she turns, and she too is dumbfounded, because she sees:

CLOSE SHOT   WINDOW
from Mariette's viewpoint. Lily is still looking out at Gaston, her back to Mariette. She hears the door close, turns, sees Mariette, takes in the situation at a glance, and goes, proudly direct, toward her.

CLOSE SHOT   MARIETTE
Lily enters. They face each other.

LILY:
> Madame, the only thing that seems to stand between you and romance is a hundred thousand francs. Well, he didn't take it. (She brings the bank notes out of her jacket.) I took it—all by myself. Now you can have your romance!

MARIETTE (scornfully):
> I think you'd better go.

LILY:
> Ever had a romance with a crook?

MARIETTE:
> I beg your pardon!

LILY:
> Let me give you a little advice. When you embrace him, be sure to put on your gloves. It would be too bad if your fingerprints were found . . .

MARIETTE:
> Mademoiselle Gautier—or whatever your name is—I thank you for your advice, but I must ask you to go. You've got your money—

LILY (violently):
> I don't want your money!

MED. SHOT   ALL THREE
as Gaston appears. He stops inside the door. Both women turn.

LILY (looking at Gaston, but talking to Mariette):
> You wanted to buy him for fifty francs. Well, you can have him for nothing! (She tosses the money out of picture.)

CLOSE SHOT   BED
The money falls on bed.

CLOSE SHOT   GROUP
Lily walks toward Gaston.

LILY:
> And you—

GASTON (pleadingly):
> Lily— (He takes her arm.)

LILY (freeing herself):
> Leave me alone! You were willing to sacrifice a hundred thousand francs for her. (She turns to Mariette, sizes her up.) Well— (she has a sudden idea) she's worth it! ‡(To Mariette.) You were willing to pay a hundred and twenty-five thousand for a *handbag*. You can pay a *hundred* thousand for him!‡

CLOSE SHOT   BED
Lily enters, takes the money she had gallantly relinquished.

CLOSE SHOT   MARIETTE AND GASTON
standing like two guilty schoolchildren. Lily comes into picture, walks past them to door, opens door, turns.

LILY:
    Goodbye—Madame Colet and Company! (She leaves, slamming door.)

GASTON (calls):
    Lily!

He dashes to door, goes out, closes door. Behind the door we hear their excited voices. Mariette goes a step closer to the door. She is in a state of confused suspense. Suddenly the voices cease. We hear, muffled, a woman's footsteps running down the stairs. Then, following, a man's footsteps. Then silence. Now, Mariette, followed by camera, goes to the bed and sinks into it heartbroken: she will never see Gaston again.

MED. SHOT   DOOR
Outside we hear the slowly returning footsteps of Gaston.

CLOSE SHOT   MARIETTE
sitting up on bed. She turns toward door with hope.

CLOSE SHOT   DOOR
Gaston enters, closes door, and moves toward Mariette. He looks very grave.

CLOSE SHOT   MARIETTE
still sitting on bed. Gaston goes to her. Pause.

GASTON (with great feeling):
    Goodbye . . .

MARIETTE (getting up; also with feeling):
    Goodbye . . .

GASTON:
    It could have been marvelous . . .

MARIETTE:
> Divine . . .

GASTON:
> Wonderful . . . But tomorrow morning, if you should wake out of your dreams and hear a knock, and the door opens, and there, instead of a maid with a breakfast tray, stands a policeman with a warrant—*then* you'll be glad you're alone.

MARIETTE (sighs):
> But it could have been glorious.

GASTON:
> Lovely.

MARIETTE:
> Divine . . . But that terrible policeman!

GASTON:
> Goodbye . . . (He takes her in his arms. They kiss. He goes to door.)

CLOSE SHOT   DOOR
Gaston opens door, turns to her.

GASTON:
> You know what you're missing?

CLOSE-UP   MARIETTE
She shuts her eyes and dreamily nods.

CLOSE-UP   GASTON
in doorway.

GASTON (shaking his head):
> No . . . (Out of his coat pocket he takes the necklace of seed pearls.) *That's* what you're missing! . . . Your gift to her.

CLOSE-UP   MARIETTE
For an instant she is taken aback; then she smiles.

MARIETTE (graciously):
> With the compliments of Colet and Company!

CLOSE SHOT GASTON
He bows, goes. Door shuts behind him.

CLOSE SHOT MARIETTE
She looks after the departed Gaston a moment. Her mood is broken by ringing of telephone.

MARIETTE (into phone):
> Hello . . . Yes . . . What? . . . Yes . . . No, no. Thank you very much, but the handbag has been found (sadly and with another meaning) exactly two weeks and three days ago. (She hangs up.)

> DISSOLVE TO:

INT. TAXICAB MOVING AT NIGHT ALONG PARIS STREETS
Close shot of Gaston and Lily. There is a strained silence between them. Gaston smiles toward her. He is trying to make up, but she sits frozen. He smiles again, anticipating the surprise he has in store for her. He reaches for the pearls in his pocket. A look of dismay crosses his face—the pearls are not there! He looks in all his pockets, can't find them. Suddenly, with suspicion, he looks sidelong at Lily. She responds to his look with a triumphant smile. From her bosom she brings forth the string of pearls and holds it up. He is amazed, can't figure it out. She reaches behind and brings forth a handbag, which we recognize as the one originally stolen from Mariette, and she drops the pearls into the bag. Gaston is now smiling with admiration, yet he looks sly. As Lily drops in the pearls she glances into the bag. Her expression changes. Something is missing. She looks suspiciously toward Gaston. Nonchalantly, he draws, from his inside breast pocket, the precious bank notes, and slips them too into the bag. They smile at each other. Together forever, they embrace and kiss.

> FADE OUT

THE END

Production Credits

Produced and directed by	Ernst Lubitsch
Screenplay by	Samson Raphaelson
Based on the play	
The Honest Finder, *by*	Aladar Laszlo
Adaptation (from the Hungarian)	
by	Grover Jones*
Photography by	Victor Milner
Art Director	Hans Dreier
Music by	W. Franke Harling
Lyrics by	Leo Robin
Costumes by	Travis Banton

Studio: Paramount
Shooting: July 25 to mid September 1932
   —approximately eight weeks
Running Time: 83 minutes
New York Premiere: November 8, 1932

*This adaptation credit is occasionally misunderstood. Jones had nothing to do with the screenplay. According to the studio, he had helped with the translation of Laszlo's play.—S.R.

Cast

Lily	Miriam Hopkins
Mariette Colet	Kay Francis
Gaston Monescu	Herbert Marshall
The Major	Charles Ruggles
François Filiba	Edward Everett Horton
Adolphe J. Giron	C. Aubrey Smith
Jacques (the butler)	Robert Greig
Russian	Leonid Kinsky
Waiter	George Humbert
Salesman	Rolfe Sedan
Irritated opera fan	Luis Alberni
Insurance agent	Hooper Atchley
Madame Bouchet	Nella Walker
Radio announcer	Perry Ivins
Singer	Tyler Brooke
Guest	Larry Steers

Author's Notes

In the script, and in the prints I have viewed in recent years, I miss a shot which would establish that the secretarial suite mentioned on page 99 opens from its office to the hallway. If that is an oversight, I herewith supply the information.

Also, in the rapid click of shots introducing a tree-climbing thief, a few agitated call girls in the hotel corridor, and the hotel officials in a tizzy about the robbery, some deplorable cuts have been made, perhaps for television, and for a few moments the action may be too fast to follow. Nothing of actual value is lost, but I assure the reader that it was extremely lucid when I first saw it, in pre-television days.

These are small matters, but to any viewers of the film who find one or two fleeting moments unclear, I raise a hand in baffled and regretful agreement.

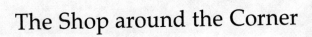

The Shop around the Corner

The Shop around the Corner

‡After credits, the silhouette of the Metro lion fades into a title:

TITLE

    This is the story of Matuschek and Company—of Mr. Matuschek and the people who work for him. It is just around the corner from Andrassy Street—on Balto Street, in Budapest, Hungary.‡

DISSOLVE TO:

SEQUENCE A

STREET IN BUDAPEST   A FEW MINUTES BEFORE 8 A.M. ON AN AUTUMN DAY

MED. CLOSE SHOT   PEPI

the fifteen-year-old errand boy of Matuschek and Company. He is riding a delivery bicycle, on the box of which we read:

MATUSCHEK & COMPANY

NOVELTIES & LEATHER WARE

Camera moves with Pepi along a Budapest street. He whistles cheerfully. In the background we see people going to work and shops being opened. Camera moves with Pepi around the corner, and he stops at Matuschek and Company's shop. The shop is still closed. In front stands Mr. Pirovitch, a middle-aged timid clerk. Absorbed in his newspaper, he ignores Pepi's arrival. He is smoking what is left of a small, cheap cigar. Pepi jumps from the bicycle and goes whistling toward Pirovitch.

CLOSE SHOT   PIROVITCH

Pepi enters.

PEPI:

    Good morning, Mr. Pirovitch.

PIROVITCH (without looking up):

    Good morning.

163

PEPI (typical fresh kid):
Always the first one, huh?

PIROVITCH:
It's none of your business. And let me tell you, it doesn't hurt to be too early.

PEPI:
What for, and why? Who sees you? Me. And who sees me? You. What does it get us? Can we give each other a raise? No.

PIROVITCH (folding paper):
What are you doing with that bicycle? You're not supposed to take it home—better not let Mr. Matuschek see it.

PEPI:
Why don't you tell him? It's all right with me. Do you know where I was last night while you were home soaking your feet in hot water? Running my legs off for *Mrs.* Matuschek. (Imitating Mrs. Matuschek's voice.) "Pepi, go to the dressmaker." And when I come back, "Oh, Pepi, will you please pick up a package at the drug-store?" Then she remembers that she forgot some nail polish, and I have to go again. And then, when I think I'm all through . . . Did you ever take Mrs. Matuschek's poodle for a walk? You wouldn't think a dog as small as this— (indicating with his hands a very small dog) could be so stubborn!

PIROVITCH:
Don't speak disrespectfully of your employer's poodle.

MED. CLOSE SHOT   THE TWO
Flora, the cashier, enters the scene. She is about thirty, modestly dressed.

FLORA:
Good morning.

PIROVITCH:
Good morning, Flora.

PEPI:
Morning, Miss Flora.

Camera moves to a close shot of Flora and Pirovitch.

FLORA:
How's your little boy?

PIROVITCH:
Much better, thanks. We called Dr. Hegedus.

FLORA (impressed):
Oh . . . he's a high-priced doctor!

PIROVITCH:
Well, what can you do? I figured I'd cut down on cigars for a few weeks. Better not take a chance.

Ilona enters. She is the bookkeeper. About twenty-eight, somewhat sexy.

ILONA:
Good morning.

FLORA:
Oh, that's a new jacket! It's stunning!

ILONA (a little self-consciously):
Thank you.

PIROVITCH:
It must have been pretty expensive.

Pepi joins the admiring group.

ILONA:
It is. I hesitated a long time before I bought it. I said, *no, I can't* afford it—and yet, I couldn't take my *eyes* off it. And then I said no, I have *no right*—

PEPI:
And then *he* said, "Aw, go on and take it!"

ILONA (annoyed):
Trying to be clever!

PIROVITCH:
Shut up, will you!

MED. LONG SHOT   THE WHOLE GROUP
Alfred Kralik enters. He is the head clerk, a young man of character.

KRALIK:
Good morning.

THE OTHERS:
Good morning, Mr. Kralik.

KRALIK (to Pepi):
Pepi, run over to the drugstore and get me some bicarbonate of soda.

He gives Pepi money. Pepi goes.

PIROVITCH:
What's the matter—aren't you feeling well?

KRALIK:
It's nothing—I'll be all right.

Vadas enters the scene. He is loudly dressed, cocky, conceited.

VADAS:
Good morning, morning, morning. Want to hear a joke?

EVERYONE:
No.

There is a little pause. Kralik and Pirovitch open up their papers, ignoring him. Vadas looks them over, unsnubbed.

VADAS:
What's the matter, folks? Aren't you awake yet? I bet I haven't slept half as much as you . . . Friends, Romans, countrymen, to tell you the truth, I had quite a time last night.

CLOSE SHOT   ILONA AND VADAS

ILONA:
And we don't want to hear the poor girl's name. We're not curious.

VADAS:
Jealous, huh?

He tries to chuck her under the chin. She slaps his hand down.

MED. CLOSE SHOT   GROUP:

PIROVITCH (to Kralik):
How was the dinner last night?

Vadas leaves Flora, comes closer to Kralik.

VADAS:

Oh, yes! Mr. Kralik had dinner with the boss! How was it? Are you a partner now, Mr. Kralik?

KRALIK:

Don't be funny. (To Pirovitch; earnestly.) It was a very nice evening. I really enjoyed it.

PIROVITCH (with the curiosity of the underdog):

I bet the food was good.

KRALIK (almost smugly):

Well, you can imagine.

By now the whole group has gathered around Kralik.

ILONA:

Tell me—is it true Mrs. Matuschek had her face lifted?

KRALIK:

How could I know?

ILONA (hot on the trail):

How old did she look to you last night?

KRALIK:

Well, I would say—around forty.

ILONA (to Flora; without malice, matter-of-fact):

Then she *had* her face lifted.

This is the moment for Mr. Vadas to start trouble.

VADAS (reproving Ilona):

I think Mrs. Matuschek is a charming woman.

FLORA (wise to Vadas's ways; sharply):

Who said she isn't?

ILONA (angrily):

And don't you try to make something out of nothing. I didn't say Mrs. Matuschek is *not* charming.

VADAS:

And I said she *is* charming—what's wrong with that? (Patronizingly.) Now don't get excited—take it easy! Calm down, folks!

The whole group subsides. There is a moment of uncomfortable silence.

CLOSE SHOT   PIROVITCH AND KRALIK

PIROVITCH (returning to his real interest):
So the food was good!

KRALIK (unable to conceal his pride):
Seven courses—not counting the hors d'oeuvres.

Vadas joins the two, still unsquelched.

VADAS:
I bet you were sitting next to Mrs. Matuschek.

KRALIK (coolly):
I was—what do you think of that?

VADAS:
I bet you were brilliant.

KRALIK:
No—I just kept still and tried to learn something.

MED. CLOSE SHOT   THE GROUP
Pepi enters.

PEPI:
Here's your bicarbonate of soda, Mr. Kralik.

KRALIK (taking it and sticking it into his pocket):
Thank you.

VADAS (smelling a rat):
Bicarbonate . . . ?

KRALIK (innocently):
I guess I had a little too much goose liver last night.

VADAS (moving in):
What's the matter? Wasn't it good?

KRALIK:
Now look here, Vadas—! (To everybody.) Folks, I want you to hear this. Did I make any derogatory remark about the goose liver?

EVERYONE:
No, no, no!

KRALIK (with precision):
I simply said I had too much goose liver.

PIROVITCH:
A *little* too much goose liver.

KRALIK:
Correct. A *little* too much goose liver. Not one word more, not one word less.

EVERYONE (seriously; assuming the roles of witnesses):
That's right, that's right!

VADAS (quickly shifting):
I didn't mean anything wrong. I was simply worried because you didn't feel well. (He puts his hand with affected concern on Kralik's shoulder.) Better take care of yourself, young man!

There is another uncomfortable pause.

PEPI:
In other words, Mrs. Matuschek's goose liver is not so hot!

Everybody turns almost violently on Pepi, but the next moment they stop, for they see:

SHOOTING FROM SHOP TOWARD THE STREET
A taxi has just stopped. Hugo Matuschek, the owner, steps out. He is a dignified businessman, about fifty-five. He is both kindly and stern. This morning he seems to be more on the stern side. He pays the taxi driver and goes toward the shop.

MED. SHOT   IN FRONT OF THE SHOP
The employees are waiting respectfully. Matuschek enters the scene.

MATUSCHEK:
Morning.

EVERYBODY:
Good morning, Mr. Matuschek. Good morning.

Matuschek walks toward the door, takes out his keys.

‡MATUSCHEK (stops; staring at the window display):
Who put this thirty-two fifty suitcase in the window?

PIROVITCH (worried):
I did, Mr. Matuschek.

MATUSCHEK (thinking it over):
I guess it's all right.

PIROVITCH (happy):
Thank you, Mr. Matuschek!‡

MATUSCHEK:
Pepi—run across to the drugstore and get me some bicarbonate of soda.

PEPI (humble and quick):
Yes, Mr. Matuschek!

The employees exchange looks over this bicarbonate of soda coincidence. There can't be any doubt that Pepi was right about the goose liver.

Matuschek opens the door with a big old-fashioned key, and all follow him in.

DISSOLVE TO:

LONG SHOT   INT. SHOP
It is a medium-sized shop, prosperous, middle class, with a pretense of style. Near the door is the cashier's booth, Flora's territory. The rest is typical leather goods and gift shop. Handbags, belts, cigarette cases, compacts, leather and silver photograph frames, wallets, briefcases, suitcases.

In the background are: one door leading to Mr. Matuschek's office, another door to the stock room, and a third leading to the locker room. There is also a spiral staircase leading up to a small, narrow balcony containing shelved merchandise.

The employees are at their morning routine, taking covers off the counters, dusting, rearranging small items.

CLOSE SHOT   AT A COUNTER
Pirovitch picks up several boxes. The camera pans with him as he goes to the stock room door.

INT. STOCK ROOM   MED. SHOT

Leaning against a table stands Kralik, reading a letter. Pirovitch enters, starts to place the boxes on a shelf.

KRALIK:

Pirovitch . . . You want to hear something nice?

PIROVITCH:

Yes. What is it?

KRALIK:

A letter from a girl. (Reading with poetic fondness.) "My heart was trembling as I walked into the post office—and there you were, lying in box two thirty-seven. I took you out of your envelope and read you—read you right there—oh, my dear friend—"

PIROVITCH (puzzled):

What *is* all this?

Kralik puts the letter back in his pocket, begins to help Pirovitch put the boxes on a shelf.

KRALIK:

You see, I wanted to buy an encyclopedia—

PIROVITCH:

Encyclopedia! What are you talking about!

KRALIK:

Well, you come to a time in your life when you get tired of going to a cafe or a dance hall every night, and you want to improve yourself. For instance, you want to know something about art, history, or literature—or how many people live in Brazil—

PIROVITCH:

Tell me, what has all this to do with the letter?

KRALIK:

You *know* I can't afford an encyclopedia. But I was looking through the ads in the Sunday paper—I got on the wrong page—and then I came across an ad— (As he takes out his wallet and extracts a clipping.) Here. Let me show you. (Hands it to Pirovitch.)

PIROVITCH (reads):

"Modern girl wishes to correspond on cultural subjects anonymously with intelligent, sympathetic young man." (Gives Kralik a slightly kidding look. Continues.) "Address Dear Friend, Post Office Fifteen, Box Two Thirty-seven." (He gives the ad back to Kralik.) I know those ads—the papers are full of them. How long has this been going on?

KRALIK:
We've exchanged four letters— (He stops working, goes closer to Pirovitch.) And, Pirovitch, she's no ordinary girl. Listen . . . (Quickly looks through the letter, turning at least five pages.) "Are you tall? Are you short? Are your eyes brown or blue? Don't tell me!" (Poetically.) "What does it matter—so long as our minds meet?"

PIROVITCH (impressed):
You're right—it's beautiful.

KRALIK (continues):
"We have enough troubles in our daily lives. There are so many great and beautiful things to discuss in this world of ours. It would be wasting these precious moments if we told each other the vulgar details of how we earn our daily bread. So don't let's do it! Oh, I do agree with you when you say"—she means me— (with proud emphasis, reading his own line) "'What are men and women for, but to rise above the stupid necessities of the eight-hour day!'"

This beautiful moment is broken by the realistic call of the boss.

MATUSCHEK'S VOICE:
Kralik!

Kralik shoves the letter into his pocket as he goes.

KRALIK:
Yes, Mr. Matuschek! (Camera pans with Kralik as he hastens toward the door.)

SHOP   MED. CLOSE SHOT   DOOR TO THE STOCK ROOM
Kralik enters. Camera pans with him as he hurries to Mr. Matuschek, who is standing by a counter and has a medium-sized cigarette box in his hand.

KRALIK:
Yes, Mr. Matuschek?

MATUSCHEK:

I can get two dozen of these cigarette boxes at Miklos Brothers. What do you think of it? (To make sure that Kralik agrees with him.) I think it's great. (Kralik takes the box.) Open it.

Kralik opens the box, and it plays a song, like a music box. Kralik instantly closes the box.

KRALIK:

No, Mr. Matuschek—that's not for us.

MATUSCHEK (irritated):

You haven't even listened to it—it plays "Otchi Tchornya."

KRALIK (businesslike):

Even if it played Beethoven's Ninth Symphony, I still would say no. I just don't like the *idea*.

MATUSCHEK:

It's wonderful how quickly you can make up your mind! I've been in this business thirty-five years and it took me a whole hour to decide that I like the box. But I guess you're a genius—you know so much more than I . . . (Signaling out into shop.) Mr. Vadas!

MED. CLOSE SHOT   VADAS

He is standing on a ladder, putting goods high on a shelf.

VADAS (responding big):

Coming, Mr. Matuschek! (He flies down.)

CLOSE SHOT   MATUSCHEK AND KRALIK

As Vadas enters, Matuschek calls.

MATUSCHEK:

Miss Novotni!

Ilona, the bookkeeper whom we have seen in the background, comes quickly.

CLOSE SHOT   PIROVITCH

He is standing behind a counter at the far end of the shop. In no mood for a crisis, he slips quickly through the locker room door.

CLOSE SHOT   MATUSCHEK, KRALIK, VADAS, AND ILONA

MATUSCHEK:

Look here—what do you think of this? I want your honest opinion. Don't let me influence you. (He opens the box. It plays "Otchi Tchornya.") It's a very popular classic.

There is a moment of silence. Vadas makes sure that Matuschek sees how delighted he is as he listens to the music.

ILONA (taking no chances):

I think people who smoke cigarettes . . . and who love to hear "Otchi Tchornya" . . . will like it.

VADAS:

I'd even go further. I think it will make music lovers out of cigarette smokers, and cigarette smokers out of music lovers! I think it's sensational!

MATUSCHEK (triumphantly):

Well, Mr. Kralik. Have you thought it over?

KRALIK (quietly, but firmly):

Yes. I still think it's inadvisable.

MATUSCHEK (losing his temper):

But give me *one reason!*

KRALIK (starting calmly, but gradually warming up):

Let's say a man smokes twenty cigarettes a day. That means he opens the box twenty times, and twenty times he has to hear "Otchi Tchornya." It's a horrible idea! And besides, this is imitation leather and cheap glue. In two weeks the whole thing will come apart—and all you have left is "Otchi Tchornya"!

MATUSCHEK:

I know that's imitation leather—you don't have to tell me. You just *sell* things, and let *me* do the buying!

Flora enters the scene.

FLORA:

Excuse me, Mr. Matuschek—Miklos Brothers is on the phone.

Camera moves with Matuschek and Flora as they go to the phone, but at such an angle that Vadas, Kralik, and Ilona are in background.

MATUSCHEK:

Yes, Mr. Miklos . . . (He looks toward group in background a little

174

uncomfortably. They all pretend to be busy with other things. In a lower voice.) Can I call you back? I'd like to have a little more time to think about it. No, it's not the price. I'm not so sure about the whole idea . . . (Forgetting himself; loud.) You can't expect me to make up my mind in five minutes! . . . Well, if that's the case, I have to say no. Sorry. (He puts down the receiver with a bang and goes, passing Kralik with a resentful look.)

CLOSE SHOT   MATUSCHEK'S OFFICE DOOR
Matuschek goes in, slams the door behind him.

CLOSE SHOT   VADAS AND KRALIK
Vadas realizes that despite the boss's anger, Kralik has won. He makes a gesture as though to say, "Life is full of puzzles."

KRALIK:
  If you want the bicarbonate of soda, it's on the second shelf in the locker room.

VADAS (now a serious man):
  Always clowning!

He picks up an armful of boxes. Camera pans with him as he goes indignantly into the stock room.

MED. CLOSE SHOT   ENTRANCE OF STORE
Klara enters. She is a quiet, modestly dressed girl. She stops with shy hesitancy before a display of bags. She looks at one of the bags, but something else seems to be on her mind.
  Kralik enters, goes through his customary act.

KRALIK:
  Good morning, madame.

KLARA:
  Good morning.

KRALIK:
  Lovely bag, don't you think?

KLARA:
  Yes—very.

KRALIK:
  It's an imported model. We have it in pigskin and alligator and in several colors—with or without fitted accessories.

KLARA (uncomfortably):

Well, I didn't really come in to buy a bag.

KRALIK (quickly):

I beg your pardon, madame. What can I show you?

KLARA (hesitating):

To tell you the truth, I really didn't come to buy *anything*.

KRALIK:

That's perfectly all right. If you wish to look around, please make yourself at home.

KLARA:

Thank you . . . (With sudden resolution.) I wonder if I could see Mr. Matuschek?

KRALIK:

Unfortunately, Mr. Matuschek is very busy at the moment. Of course, I'd be glad to call him . . .

KLARA (quickly):

I'd appreciate that very much.

KRALIK:

But if you'll tell me your wishes, it's quite possible I could take care of them to your satisfaction.

KLARA:

Well—I noticed in your shop window that you're having a summer sale.

KRALIK:

Yes, madame. Everything is reduced twenty-five percent—several articles even more. For instance, this compact. Yesterday you couldn't have bought it for one penny less than three ninety—and today you can have it for two twenty-five.

KLARA:

Really? That's a wonderful bargain.

KRALIK:

Everything in the store is a bargain today.

KLARA:

I imagine you'll do a big business.

KRALIK (bragging):

No question about it. You're very lucky to come so early. We'll probably have such a big rush we won't be able to take care of the customers.

KLARA:

Then you should have some extra help.

KRALIK:

We probably will.

KLARA (finally daring):

In that case, maybe you can use me? I'm looking for a job.

KRALIK (injured but not unfriendly; at once changing the status to that of two clerks):

Now listen, that wasn't very nice, letting me go through this whole routine!

KLARA:

I'm terribly sorry—I didn't mean to . . . Do you think you could help me get a job here?

KRALIK:

I'd like to, but I'm afraid there's absolutely no opening.

KLARA:

But you just told me you'd need some extra help because of the rush.

KRALIK:

Look around for yourself. You can see what kind of business we're doing.

CLOSE SHOT   ENTRANCE DOOR

A cranky, middle-aged woman is standing by the door, looking into the show window from inside of the shop. Kralik enters.

WOMAN CUSTOMER:

How much is that belt in the window—the one that says two ninety-five?

KRALIK:

Two ninety-five, madame.

WOMAN:

Oh, *no* . . .

She leaves the store. Camera moves with Kralik as he goes back. For a moment he has forgotten about Klara. He moves around the store, resuming some of his duties, putting things in order, but Klara follows him.

KLARA:

Excuse me, but may I tell you my qualifications?

KRALIK (helplessly):

If I could do anything for you, I'd do it—

KLARA:

You know, I'm not an inexperienced girl—

KRALIK:

But I know the situation here—there isn't a chance—

KLARA:

I worked for two years at Blasek and Company—and I left of my own accord. And before that I was with Latzko Brothers for ten months.

KRALIK:

My dear child, even if you worked at Kramer and Kramer—

KLARA:

I did! I can take care of the finest clientele.

KRALIK:

We don't deal with that type of people. We have middle-class trade.

KLARA:

What kind of trade do you think Blasek and Company have? And they'd be glad to have me back right now.

KRALIK:

Why don't you go back?

KLARA:

Well, that's another story.

KRALIK:

Listen, if it were up to me, I'd put you to work right away—but I'm not the boss.

KLARA:
Then why don't you let me see him?

KRALIK (with great patience):
He's in a very bad mood today.

KLARA (still hanging on):
I'll take a chance. Maybe I can cheer him up!

DOOR TO MATUSCHEK'S OFFICE   MED. CLOSE SHOT
Matuschek comes out of the office. Camera moves with him as he walks along, inspecting things. We gradually pick up Klara and Kralik in the foreground, with Matuschek in the background. Neither Klara nor Kralik is aware of Matuschek several feet away. Matuschek, in turn, pays no attention to them.

KRALIK (as Matuschek passes):
My dear young lady—I've been here nine years. I know Mr. Matuschek inside and out— (Matuschek turns and listens with great interest.) I know exactly what his attitude would be. I can predict his every reaction. I could tell you word for word what he would say—

MATUSCHEK:
Mr. Kralik! (Beckoning, his tone very polite.) Just a moment, please.

Kralik goes to Matuschek.

CLOSE SHOT   KRALIK AND MATUSCHEK

MATUSCHEK (in a low voice, not so nice):
So—you know every reaction of mine, hmmm? You know everything about me. You know exactly what I think—even before I thought of it! You're not only a genius, you're a mind reader!

KRALIK:
But, Mr. Matuschek—

MATUSCHEK (waving him off):
Never mind! (He leaves Kralik behind, goes toward Klara.)

MED. CLOSE SHOT   KLARA AT COUNTER
Matuschek enters, bows.

MATUSCHEK:
Good morning, madame. I am Mr. Matuschek.

KLARA (unprepared; this is too sudden):
Good morning, Mr. Matuschek.

MATUSCHEK:
Please have a seat.

Klara, not knowing what to do, sits.

KLARA:
Thank you.

CLOSE SHOT   KRALIK
who has watched. He grins. Then he turns and goes quickly toward
the background.

CLOSE SHOT   MATUSCHEK AND KLARA

MATUSCHEK:
I don't know what the difficulty is, but I can assure you there is no
such word as impossible in the vocabulary of Matuschek and Company.

KLARA:
I'm so glad to hear you say that!

MATUSCHEK:
And I mean it!

KLARA (realizing that she can't monkey around any longer):
Mr. Matuschek, I was at Blasek and Company—

MATUSCHEK:
I'm sure you'll find much nicer things in my shop.

KLARA (getting up; with dignity):
No, I mean I *worked* there . . . (Matuschek stares at her, suspicious.) I'm looking for a job.

MATUSCHEK (turning in a split second from salesman to boss):
No, no, no! That's impossible. It's out of the question.

KLARA:
But, Mr. Matuschek—

MATUSCHEK (moving away):
>I have no time, no time—I'm very busy!

He goes. Klara stands, awkward and pathetic. Kralik enters.

KRALIK (sympathetic but realistic):
>I told you there's no use . . . You're just wasting your time.

KLARA (hopelessly):
>I've *got* to have a job!

CLOSE SHOT   DOOR OF MATUSCHEK'S OFFICE
Matuschek is already inside, the door open.

MATUSCHEK (calling):
>Kralik!

CLOSE SHOT   KRALIK AND KLARA

KRALIK:
>One moment, Mr. Matuschek.

The tension increases. Kralik does not want to walk out on Klara; on the other hand, he must respond to Mr. Matuschek.

KRALIK (speaks hastily, low tone; question and answer come rapidly):
>Have you tried Baum's department store?

KLARA:
>Every entrance.

KRALIK:
>I don't know what to say—maybe after inventory—

KLARA:
>When will that be?

KRALIK:
>Well—in a week or two.

MATUSCHEK'S VOICE:
>*Kralik!*

KRALIK:
>*Coming*, Mr. Matuschek!

KLARA:
>Please—may I leave you my address?

KRALIK:

All right. (Pulls out pencil and paper.) And if we need anybody, you'll be the first one.

KLARA (with lightning speed while Kralik scribbles it down):

My name is Klara Novak—Albert Street, forty-six. If you need me in a hurry, you can phone six, two, two, four, two—that's the grocery store downstairs. Ask for Johanna; tell her you have a business message for Klara . . .

KRALIK:

All right—I've got it all. (He hurries out of the scene.)

MATUSCHEK'S OFFICE   MED. SHOT

Matuschek is pacing up and down. Kralik appears in the doorway.

KRALIK:

Yes, Mr. Matuschek.

MATUSCHEK:

Close the door.

Kralik does. Camera moves up to a closer shot on the two.

MATUSCHEK (like a hurt parent):

Why do you put me in a situation like that, in front of the whole shop?

KRALIK:

I'm sorry, Mr. Matuschek, but it wasn't my fault.

MATUSCHEK:

Whose fault was it? Mine?

KRALIK:

Well—yes.

MATUSCHEK:

What's the matter with you, Kralik? You're my oldest employee. I try to show my appreciation in every way. I invite you to my house . . .

KRALIK:

And I'm very grateful.

MATUSCHEK:

You have a funny way of showing it! You know how much I value your judgment—and on every occasion you contradict me. Whatever I say, you say no.

KRALIK (angry):
All right, Mr. Matuschek—from now on I'll say yes . . . *Yes*, Mr. Matuschek—*certainly*, Mr. Matuschek—*yes*, Mr. Matuschek—

MATUSCHEK (sees he has been overdoing; changing completely):
It was a nice party last night, wasn't it?

KRALIK (not giving in entirely; a little sulky):
Yes, sir.

MATUSCHEK (trying to make up):
I had lots of fun, didn't you?

KRALIK:
Yes, sir.

MATUSCHEK (insisting on making up):
Well, I'm glad you enjoyed it. By the way, that little poem you wrote in Mrs. Matuschek's guest book—did you make that up yourself?

KRALIK (embarrassed):
Not exactly. It's half and half. Half me, and half Shakespeare . . . I changed it a little to suit the occasion. I had the last line rhyme with Matuschek . . . that's all.

MATUSCHEK:
Well, Mrs. Matuschek liked it. You made a very fine impression on her. Yes, Mrs. Matuschek thinks an awful lot of you— (His face beaming with love for his wife.) And, you know, I think an awful lot of Mrs. Matuschek . . .

Matuschek pats Kralik on the shoulder in a fatherly way. From the shop we hear the sound of the music box playing "Otchi Tchornya." Matuschek and Kralik look at each other in suspense. Next moment the door opens and Vadas comes in triumphantly.

VADAS:
I think I've found a customer for the cigarette box! What price shall I quote, Mr. Matuschek?

Matuschek gives a little patronizing smile to Kralik. Going to the door, followed by Vadas and Kralik, he begins figuring.

MATUSCHEK:
Well, let's see—two eighty-five—and I think we'll get five percent discount. (He opens the door.)

SHOP   CLOSE SHOT   DOOR TO MATUSCHEK'S OFFICE
Matuschek comes out, still figuring, when suddenly he sees:

CLOSE SHOT   AT COUNTER
Klara stands listening to "Otchi Tchornya."

CLOSE SHOT   MATUSCHEK, KRALIK, VADAS
Matuschek is puzzled. Kralik, quickly sizing up the situation, pushes Vadas aside.

KRALIK:
Let me take care of this, Mr. Matuschek. (He goes quickly.)

CLOSE SHOT   AT COUNTER
Kralik and Klara.

KRALIK (very patiently):
Look—there's no use waiting. Please believe me—if there's an opening you'll be the first one—

Before the girl can answer, Matuschek enters. He has an idea.

MATUSCHEK (to Klara):
Would you buy a box like this?

KLARA:
Mr. Matuschek—I couldn't buy *anything* at the moment.

MATUSCHEK:
No, no. I just want your opinion—*your honest opinion.*

‡CLOSE SHOT   PIROVITCH
near the spiral stairway at rear. At the words "your honest opinion" he scuttles up and out of sight.

BACK TO SHOT OF MATUSCHEK, KLARA, AND KRALIK‡

MATUSCHEK (continuing to Klara):
Do you like it?

KLARA (meaning it):
Yes, I do—it's marvelous.

MATUSCHEK:
>   Why?

KLARA (after a moment's thought):
>   I—I think it's romantic.

KRALIK:
>   Romantic? What's romantic about it?

KLARA:
>   Well—cigarettes and music . . . I don't know—it makes me think of—of moonlight—and . . . cigarettes and music!

MATUSCHEK (triumphant):
>   There's the woman's point of view!

This is too much for Kralik. He walks out.

KLARA (making the most of the moment):
>   How much are you selling it for?

MATUSCHEK:
>   Well—I would say—four twenty-five.

KLARA:
>   Oh, that's a bargain! That's a real bargain!

A slightly plump woman customer is passing in the background, and the word "bargain" catches her. She turns, looks at the box. Klara, seeing her great chance, swiftly takes her hat off, tucks it behind the counter, instantly is a salesgirl. The woman is examining the box with great approval.

KLARA:
>   It's lovely, isn't it?

WOMAN:
>   Is it a candy box?

Matuschek, who has joined them, is about to answer, but Klara is ahead of him.

KLARA:
>   Yes, madame—a candy box! And I would say a *very unusual* one.

She opens the box with a look of anticipation. But the box doesn't play. Klara and Matuschek exchange worried looks.

CLOSE SHOT   KRALIK AT ANOTHER COUNTER
watching, smug. His opinion of the bad workmanship is confirmed.

CLOSE SHOT   MATUSCHEK, KLARA, AND WOMAN

WOMAN:
> I like it. How much is it? (Suddenly the music decides to start. The woman's expression changes.) Is *that* coming out of *this box?*

MATUSCHEK:
> Yes, madame. It's "Otchi Tchornya"—a very popular classic.

WOMAN:
> Oh, no—that'll never do! Where do people get such ideas? Can you imagine—every time you take a piece of candy you have to listen to that!

CLOSE-UP   MATUSCHEK
He is upset. Kralik's argument has been confirmed in terms of candy.

CLOSE-UP   KRALIK
He beams.

CLOSE SHOT   MATUSCHEK, KLARA, WOMAN CUSTOMER
The woman shuts the box.

WOMAN:
> Oh, no!

She is about to leave. Now Klara goes to work.

KLARA (with finished salesgirl technique):
> I know *just* what you mean, madame. And *yet*, do you know, some of our customers *like* it for the very thing you *object* to. We've sold quite a few—and especially to ladies. There's no denying we all have a weakness for candy—and when I say weakness, I don't mean to say *anything* against *candy*—I only mean we're inclined to overdo it a little.

WOMAN (indifferently):
> That's true, I suppose.

KLARA:
> Now, for instance, madame—have you any idea how many pieces of candy you eat a day?

WOMAN:
Well, no—I never gave it a thought.

KLARA:
That's just it. We pick up a piece of candy absentmindedly, and then we take another piece—and before we realize it, we've gained a pound or two. That's when our troubles begin. Masseurs, electric cabinets—

WOMAN (with feeling):
Don't I know it!

KLARA:
Now this little box makes you *candy-conscious*. That's what Matuschek and Company *designed* it for. Every time you open it, this little tinkling song is a message to you: (In the rhythm of the song.) "Too much candy—now be careful!"

WOMAN (succumbing):
How much is it?

KLARA (thinking fast, raising the price):
Five fifty— (Matuschek, feeling that she is going too far, wants to correct her. But she shakes her head—she knows what she is doing.) —reduced from six ninety-five. It's a real bargain.

WOMAN:
I'll take it!

CLOSE-UP   MATUSCHEK
He is very happy and turns with a smile toward Kralik, camera including both.

CLOSE SHOT   KRALIK
He is a defeated man.

FADE OUT

‡MATUSCHEK:
Well, what do you think now?

KRALIK
I think people who like to smoke candy and listen to cigarettes will love it.

MATUSCHEK (annoyed, serious):
Don't misunderstand me. All I want is your opinion—your honest opinion . . .

CLOSE SHOT   CIRCULAR STAIRWAY
Pirovitch's legs are coming down, but at "your honest opinion," they instantly reverse and hasten up.

FADE OUT‡

SEQUENCE B

FADE IN
CLOSE SHOT   ONE OF MATUSCHEK'S TWO SHOW WINDOWS EXT.
It is a slushy day, a dark December morning, about ten minutes before eight. A Christmas tree is in the window; around it are displayed a variety of articles. Camera moves back to a medium shot of the window. A policeman in a winter overcoat, back to camera, is looking at the Christmas tree. Camera pans with him as he strolls along. At the next window he passes Pirovitch, also in a heavy overcoat, leaning against the window corner, reading his morning paper—as usual, the first.

POLICEMAN:
   Morning.

PIROVITCH (tipping his hat):
   Good morning, sir.

The policeman, continuing past the second show window, glances idly at the display.

CLOSE SHOT   THROUGH GLASS
on what the policeman sees. It is a montage of about twenty music boxes. They are grouped around a prominently lettered card which reads:

SPECIAL CLEARANCE SALE
OTCHI TCHORNYA CIGARETTE BOXES
REDUCED FROM 4.25 TO 2.29

MED. CLOSE SHOT   PIROVITCH
The policeman is gone. Kralik arrives.

KRALIK:
   Good morning.

PIROVITCH:
   Good morning, Kralik.

KRALIK:
   Well, I have a big dinner date tonight.

PIROVITCH (his face lighting up):
  With the boss?

KRALIK:
  Oh, no, he doesn't invite me anymore . . . How do you figure him out?

PIROVITCH:
  I give up. It's certainly difficult to get along with him these days.

KRALIK:
  He hardly talks to me anymore. Well, I hope he feels more cheerful today. He'd better—because I'm going to ask him for a raise.

PIROVITCH:
  A raise!

KRALIK:
  Pirovitch—do you mind if I ask you a personal question?

PIROVITCH:
  No—go ahead.

KRALIK (a little self-consciously):
  This is very confidential . . . Suppose a fellow like me wants to get married . . .

PIROVITCH (with delight):
  Well, that's wonderful! That's the best thing that could happen to you. Who's the girl?

KRALIK:
  Listen—what did I say? I said *suppose*—and I didn't say me, I said a fellow *like* me. Now, look . . . For instance, how much does it cost you to live? Just you and Mrs. Pirovitch, leaving out the children—

PIROVITCH:
  Why fool yourself?

KRALIK (embarrassed):
  Well, let's say—temporarily. How much does it cost?

PIROVITCH:
  It can be done—and very nicely. Naturally, you can't be extravagant.

KRALIK:

> Now—suppose such a fellow took a three-room apartment—dining room, living room, and bedroom.

PIROVITCH:

> What do you need three rooms for? You live in the bedroom.

KRALIK:

> Where do you eat?

PIROVITCH:

> In the kitchen—you get a nice, big kitchen.

KRALIK:

> Then where do you entertain?

PIROVITCH:

> Entertain! What are you, an ambassador? Who do you want to entertain? Listen, if someone is really your friend, he comes *after* dinner.

MED. SHOT

Klara enters and stops near Pirovitch.

KLARA:

> Good morning.

PIROVITCH (very friendly):

> Good morning, Klara.

KRALIK (barely tipping his hat; brusquely):

> Morning. (He opens his paper.)

KLARA (ignoring him):

> How's your wife, Mr. Pirovitch?

KRALIK (looking up):

> Yes—how is she?

PIROVITCH (suddenly worried):

> Oh, my goodness!

KLARA (alarmed):

> What's the matter?

PIROVITCH:

> I forgot to call Dr. Hegedus.

KRALIK:

Is there anything serious with Mrs. Pirovitch?

PIROVITCH:

No—she couldn't be better.

KRALIK:

Then what do you want to call the doctor for?

PIROVITCH:

If I don't call him, he'll *come*. Excuse me—I'd better telephone him right away. (Pirovitch hurries out.)

CLOSE SHOT   KLARA AND KRALIK

They are on opposite sides of the entrance, each leaning against a show window. Klara opens her book, which has a library cover. She starts to read. Kralik returns to his paper. They read for a moment, then:

KRALIK (uncomfortable, but trying to achieve an air of correctness):

Miss Novak.

KLARA (coldly):

Yes, Mr. Kralik?

KRALIK:

I noticed that you wore a yellow blouse with light green dots yesterday . . .

KLARA (interrupting):

No, Mr. Kralik—as usual, you're mistaken. It was a *green* blouse with light *yellow* dots—and *everybody* thought it was *very* becoming. (Kralik tries to get a word in, but Klara goes on.) And I don't remember that I ever remarked about your neckties—and believe me, Mr. Kralik, if you think I *couldn't* say anything about them, just ask Mr. Vadas. So please leave my blouse alone. It's none of your business! (She returns to her book.)

KRALIK (stiffly):

I'm sorry, but Mr. Matuschek seems to think it *is* my business.

KLARA (maliciously):

Oh yes, that's right—I'm working under you. Well, from now on, I'll telephone you every morning and describe just what I'm going to wear—and before I select my next season's wardrobe, my dressmaker will submit samples to you! Imagine you dictating what I should wear!

KRALIK:

For heaven's sake, I don't care what you wear. If you want to look like a pony in a circus, all right! But I have troubles of my own, without your blouse coming between Mr. Matuschek and me.

KLARA:

Listen, I sold as much goods yesterday as anybody in the place. Hundred ninety-seven pengo fifty isn't bad for a rainy Monday three weeks before Christmas. Did you tell *that* to Mr. Matuschek?

KRALIK:

I did!

KLARA:

What did he say?

KRALIK:

He said, "Tell her not to come in that blouse anymore."

KLARA:

Tell him I won't!

KRALIK:

I will!

Klara turns angrily back to her book; Kralik walks away. Camera pans with him. Pirovitch returns. During the following, we see in the background the arrival of Pepi, Ilona, and Flora.

PIROVITCH:

Well, I caught him just in time. Saves me five pengo, and that counts when you're married. (Relaxes; in a good mood.) Now come on—tell me, who is the girl?

KRALIK (in a lower voice, which brings Pirovitch closer to him):

You remember the girl I was corresponding with?

PIROVITCH:

Oh, yes—about the cultural subjects.

KRALIK:

Well—after a while, we came to the subject of love. Naturally, on a very cultural level.

PIROVITCH (dryly):

What else can you do in a letter?

KRALIK (intimately):

She's the most wonderful girl in the world . . .

PIROVITCH:
> Is she pretty?

KRALIK:
> She has such *ideals*, such a point of *view* on things . . . She's so far above the girls you meet today; there is simply no comparison.

PIROVITCH:
> So she's not so pretty.

KRALIK:
> Now don't say that!

PIROVITCH (quickly):
> I'm sorry! (Conciliatory.) The main thing is that you like her.

KRALIK:
> I *hope* I will.

PIROVITCH (puzzled):
> What do you mean? You love a girl, and don't know if you like her?

KRALIK:
> That's right, Pirovitch. That's just the question. You see, I haven't met her yet.

PIROVITCH:
> You haven't—

KRALIK:
> I postponed it again and again. I'm scared. Pirovitch, you see, this girl thinks I'm the most wonderful person in the world—and after all, there's a chance she might be disappointed.

PIROVITCH (a little dryly):
> Yes—there is a chance.

KRALIK (ardently):
> On the other hand—

PIROVITCH:
> *You* might be disappointed, too.

KRALIK:
> I don't dare think of it! . . . Pirovitch, did you ever get a bonus?

PIROVITCH:
> Yes—once.

KRALIK (in the clouds):
> The boss hands it to you in an envelope—and you don't want to open it. You wonder how much it is. As long as that envelope isn't opened, you're a millionaire. You keep postponing the moment . . . But you can't postpone it *forever* . . . (With excitement.) Pirovitch, I'm meeting her tonight—at eight thirty—in a cafe . . .

PIROVITCH (knowingly):
> A red carnation?

KRALIK:
> Yes! She's using one as a bookmark in a copy of Tolstoy's *Anna Karenina,* and I'm going to wear one in my lapel . . . I haven't slept for days . . .

PIROVITCH (warmly):
> I'm sure she'll be beautiful.

KRALIK:
> Not *too* beautiful . . . What chance would there be for a fellow like me?

PIROVITCH:
> What do you want—a homely girl?

KRALIK:
> No, Pirovitch. (Earnestly.) Knock wood—for just a lovely, average girl . . . That's all I want.

MED. SHOT   SHOOTING TOWARD OPPOSITE SIDE OF STREET
Pirovitch and Kralik in the foreground. They are interrupted by an arriving taxi. Pirovitch, thinking it is the boss, hurries and opens the taxi door. Not the boss but Vadas steps out. His fur-collared coat is in flashy contrast to the modest coats of the other two.

VADAS (to Pirovitch):
> Thank you, my good man.

Pirovitch angrily slams the door and goes out back to Kralik.

VADAS (loudly):
> Good morning, everybody.

CLOSE SHOT   VADAS AND TAXI DRIVER
Vadas takes a big bankroll out of his pocket, peels off a note.

VADAS:

Here, my good fellow. Keep the change—and send your boy through college.

DRIVER:

Thank you, sir.

The taxi goes. Camera pans with Vadas as he struts toward Kralik and Pirovitch, who are looking at him with great interest.

VADAS:

I can see by the expression on your underpaid faces that you wonder where I got all this money.

PIROVITCH (quietly):

No, Mr. Vadas, I don't wonder.

VADAS (sharply):

What do you mean?

PIROVITCH (with an innocent air):

I just mean I don't wonder.

Before the argument can develop, we hear another taxi arriving.

SHOOTING TOWARD STREET

Mr. Matuschek steps out of the taxi. He pays quickly; his expression is stern; his thoughts are elsewhere. Camera pans with him as he goes to the door. The men employees tip their hats; Matuschek ignores them. As Matuschek is about to open the door, he glances at one of the show windows.

MATUSCHEK:

This window looks terrible! There isn't a shop on the street that doesn't look better. It's a wonder we get *any* customers! Well, we'll have to stay after closing hour tonight and redecorate.

DOUBLE CLOSE-UP   KRALIK AND PIROVITCH

Kralik is shaken up. He makes a gesture of despair at the thought of missing his appointment tonight.

CLOSE-UP   KLARA

who also is upset. Camera pulls back to a double close shot of her and Ilona as they follow the others to the open door.

ILONA (angrily):

Redecorate windows—a fine way to spend your evenings! Well, my boy-friend will have to dine with his wife.

KLARA:

I'll have to get out of it *some* way.

ILONA:

Klara, you haven't got a chance.

KLARA:

I have a *very important* engagement at eight thirty. And I have to get home first—I have *so much* to do! (Forgetting her worries for a moment.) You see, I have to change . . . Tell me, Ilona, did you notice the blouse I wore yesterday—the green blouse—

ILONA:

With light yellow dots?

KLARA:

Yes.

ILONA:

Oh, I thought it was simply stunning!

KLARA:

Did you really? I'm so glad! (As they enter the shop.) You see, I'm planning to wear it tonight . . . (She closes the door behind her.)

DISSOLVE TO:

MATUSCHEK'S OFFICE   MED. CLOSE SHOT   MATUSCHEK AT HIS DESK
He holds several letters in his hand, but his mind is on something else; he is a deeply troubled man. The telephone rings.

MATUSCHEK (into telephone):

Hello— (We now can guess where his trouble comes from.) Yes, darling . . . Well, you were sleeping and I didn't want to disturb you. You came home late, and I thought you wanted to sleep a little longer . . . No, no—I'm not angry. Did you have a good time? Well, that's all that matters, isn't it? . . . What? A thousand pengos! Darling, I don't understand it. Only last Monday I gave you— No, I'm not complaining, but it's quite a bit of money . . . All right, all right—yes—certainly. I'll send it over as soon as possible . . . Goodbye . . .

On the telephone Matuschek has been controlled. Now he rises agitat-edly, moves around.

MED. SHOT OF OFFICE
Kralik enters, stopping just inside the door.

MATUSCHEK (annoyed):
    What is it?

Camera comes closer to both.

KRALIK:
    Mr. Matuschek, I'd like to talk to you for a moment.

MATUSCHEK (coldly):
    Is it important?

KRALIK:
    Well—it's—it's important to me.

MATUSCHEK:
    Is it important to Matuschek and Company?

KRALIK:
    No, not exactly. But—

MATUSCHEK:
    I'm pretty busy—you'll have to see me later.

He turns away, picks up the letters on the desk. Kralik, after taking a step toward the door, stops, decides to have a showdown.

KRALIK:
    Pardon me, Mr. Matuschek—

MATUSCHEK (looking up from the letter):
    Well, what is it now?

KRALIK:
    Well—for several days your attitude toward me seems to have changed . . .

MATUSCHEK:
    Has it?

KRALIK (with dignity):
    Yes, Mr. Matuschek, it has. And I'm completely at a loss to explain it. After all, I do my work—

MATUSCHEK:
    And you get paid for it?

KRALIK (taken aback):
    Yes, sir.

MATUSCHEK:
    Every month?

KRALIK:
    Yes, sir.

MATUSCHEK:
    So everything seems to be all right—doesn't it?

KRALIK (rendered helpless):
    Yes, Mr. Matuschek. (He goes out quietly.)

SHOP   MED. SHOT   OFFICE DOOR
Kralik enters the shop. He is depressed. Pirovitch comes over.

PIROVITCH:
    Did you see him?

KRALIK (in a low tone, but explosively):
    I'm not going to stand for this much longer! What does the man
    want? Why does he have to pick on *me?*

PIROVITCH:
    Well—you're his oldest employee—

KRALIK:
    That's a fine reason!

PIROVITCH (with the philosophy of the underdog):
    He picks on me, too. The other day he called me an idiot. What
    could I do? So I said, "Yes, Mr. Matuschek, I'm an idiot"—I'm no
    fool! Listen, maybe he has business worries—maybe trouble with
    his wife . . .

CLOSE SHOT   VADAS
standing on a small ladder nearby. He has been listening. Camera pans
with him as he hastens to Pirovitch.

VADAS:
    Is he having trouble with his wife?

PIROVITCH (scared to death):
    I don't know—it's none of *my* business! I'm talking to *Kralik.* What
    do you want? (Camera pans with Pirovitch as he takes Kralik a few

steps aside to be sure Vadas can't hear. With great concern.) Kralik—don't be impulsive—not at a time like this. Not when millions of people are out of work—

KRALIK:
I can get a job anywhere!

PIROVITCH:
Can you? Let's be honest.

KRALIK (brooding):
I'll take a chance. I'm not a coward—I'm not afraid.

PIROVITCH (with great simplicity):
I *am*, Kralik. I'm afraid of the boss. I'm afraid of the grocer, of the butcher—of the doctor. I have a family, Kralik.

KRALIK:
Well, I *haven't*—

Almost in the middle of the word he stops, reminded of his approaching romance.

PIROVITCH (responding to what he sees in Kralik):
Think it over . . . Those were nice letters, weren't they?

Camera pans with Kralik as he goes thoughtfully toward the stock room door.

MED. SHOT   STOCK ROOM
In the foreground we see Klara and Pepi. Pepi has just put several packages into a sort of canvas cover. Klara hands him the last package. Kralik enters. Paying no attention to them, he gets busy.

PEPI (as he grabs his bundle):
Mr. Kralik, do you think I have to work tonight, too? (In an unchildlike voice.) After all, I'm a child—

KRALIK:
No, you don't have to stay.

PEPI:
Do you *mean* it?

KRALIK:
I'll straighten it out with Mr. Matuschek.

PEPI (very happy):
   Thank you, Mr. Kralik! (He goes.)

CLOSE SHOT   KLARA
She has listened with great interest. It is possible for somebody to get
off tonight, and Kralik might be instrumental! Camera pans with her as
she approaches him with the sweetest smile. Kralik is busy putting
articles on a shelf.

KLARA (in a voice of honey):
   May I help you, Mr. Kralik?

KRALIK (busy with his own thoughts):
   No, thank you.

KLARA:
   No trouble at all! (As she hands him one of the articles.) I've put
   all the imported bags on the other shelf.

KRALIK (nods):
   Uh-huh.

KLARA:
   Is that the way you wanted it, Mr. Kralik?

KRALIK:
   Yes.

KLARA:
   I'm so glad you like it. If there's anything wrong, I'd appreciate it
   if you'd tell me.

KRALIK (stopping work; distrustfully):
   Since when are you so interested in my idea of what's wrong?

KLARA:
   Well, I like to please you, Mr. Kralik. After all, I'm working under
   you.

KRALIK:
   You don't have to keep harping on that! (He resumes his work.)

KLARA (persistently helping him):
   I don't mean it that way at all, Mr. Kralik. Regardless of what I
   think of you personally, I believe that anybody who works with
   you and doesn't get a great deal out of it is just plain dumb.

KRALIK (stopping again):
What do you mean, what you think of me personally?

KLARA (wriggling her way):
Well, since you ask, I would say, no matter what can be said against you, I think you're a *gentleman*.

KRALIK (not quite won over; gruffly):
Well, I try to be. (He continues work.)

KLARA:
And oh, Mr. Kralik, you don't realize what that *means* to a working girl. What a girl has to go *through* in some shops! For instance, when I worked at Foeldes Brothers and Sons. Well, the sons were all right—but the *brothers*, Mr. Kralik! . . . And that's why I like it here so much. When *you* say, "Miss Novak, let's go in the stock room and put some bags on the second shelf," you really *want* to put some bags on the second shelf. And that's my idea of a gentleman!

KRALIK:
Well, I just don't believe in mixing bags with . . . pleasure.

KLARA (feeling that she is gaining ground):
Mr. Kralik—

KRALIK:
Yes, Miss Novak.

KLARA:
About that blouse—

KRALIK (actually friendly):
Listen—I'm sorry, but I *had* to do that.

KLARA:
But I want to *thank* you. I'm so *glad* you did it. You know, in the bottom of my heart, after thinking it over—you're *so* right. That blouse was *awful*.

KRALIK:
I wouldn't say awful.

KLARA (charmingly):
Yes, it was! Of course, I didn't admit it at the time—but what woman would? We hate to admit we're wrong—that's why we're so feminine.

KRALIK (good-natured):
You know, this is the first time you've shown a little sense. There's a change in you.

KLARA (modest little girl):
I know it.

KRALIK (seeing her with new eyes):
And if you keep on like this, I think we'll be able to get along much better.

KLARA:
Thank you, Mr. Kralik.

KRALIK (back to work):
That's all right, Miss Novak.

KLARA (moving in for the kill):
I was actually planning to wear that awful blouse tonight. You see, I have a date—

KRALIK (staring at her):
Tonight? Didn't you hear what Mr. Matuschek said? We have to stay and decorate the windows.

KLARA (innocently):
Oh, I almost forgot! Would it be possible—do you think you could spare me tonight? Then maybe Mr. Matuschek would let me off?

This shocks Kralik.

KRALIK (furiously):
So! That's why I'm a gentleman! That's why you learned so much from me all of a sudden!

KLARA (stammering):
I don't—I don't know what you mean . . .

KRALIK:
So you want to get tonight off?

KLARA:
I *have* to, Mr. Kralik.

KRALIK:
Well, you're out of luck. Such an obvious trick—and I nearly fell for it!

KLARA (desperately):
Please, Mr. Kralik, I simply *have* to get off—it's *terribly important.*

KRALIK:
For six months you've done everything you could to antagonize me, and now you have the nerve—

KLARA (dropping all tactics; in open combat):
Well, you haven't been very nice to *me!*

During the following, Kralik pays no attention to her words. He goes to the counter, assembles some packages, then hands her one after another until she has a stack in her arms.

KLARA:
No matter what I do, it's wrong! If I wrap a package, that's not the right way. If I make a suggestion—and some of them are very good—you don't even listen. Everything has to be done exactly your way, and even then you don't like it! When I came into this shop I was full of life and enthusiasm, and now—I'm nothing. You've taken my *personality* away! You're a *dictator*—that's what you are! Well, let me tell you, Mr. Kralik—any day now I may be in a position where I won't have to work anymore. And then, Mr. Kralik, I'll *really* tell you what I think of you!

By now Kralik has a stack of boxes in his own arms too, and both are moving toward the door, apparently following a familiar work pattern.

KLARA:
And as for that blouse, I think it's *beautiful* and I'm going to wear it tonight, yes, *tonight!*

Kralik opens the door. As she passes him into the shop, Klara ineffectually concludes:

KLARA:
Mr. Kralik, I don't like you!

She goes into the shop. Kralik follows her.

MED. SHOT   COUNTER CLOSE TO STOCK ROOM DOOR
Klara and Kralik put their armloads down on the counter. Klara sees Mr. Matuschek, goes quickly to him.

CLOSE SHOT   MR. MATUSCHEK   ANOTHER PART OF THE SHOP

KLARA:

Mr. Matuschek, I wonder if I could see you for a moment?

MATUSCHEK (not exactly friendly but much more civil than with Kralik):
What is it?

KLARA:

Would it be possible, by any chance—do you think you could spare me tonight?

MATUSCHEK:

Well, let me see—we'll need three people to dress the A window—(Camera pans with him as he goes to Kralik.) Could you get along without Miss Novak?

KRALIK:

Well, Mr. Matuschek—I wonder if I could talk to you for a moment—

MATUSCHEK (with lightning speed):
You want to get off, too!

KRALIK:

Well, *yes*—Mr. Matuschek. I would appreciate it very much.

MATUSCHEK (violent and loud):
What is this? Does *everybody* want to leave? *Once a year* I ask you to stay here . . . !

As the scene goes on we see, in individual close shots, the effect on the whole shop: Klara is scared to death. She wouldn't dare to ask again for the evening off. She puts things back and forth, without sense. Everyone frantically acts busy. Vadas runs up and down the stepladder. Pirovitch, trembling, rearranges boxes under the counter. Flora and Ilona make a to-do in their places. Meantime:

KRALIK:

I'm sorry, Mr. Matuschek. If I had only known yesterday—

MATUSCHEK:

I *see*—you want a special invitation! Next time I'll send you an engraved announcement!

Pirovitch approaches with what for him is great courage.

PIROVITCH:

Mr. Matuschek—I've talked everything over with Mr. Kralik. I know his ideas, and I think Miss Novotni and I can manage the novelty window by ourselves.

MATUSCHEK:
Did I ask you for advice? What do you mean, Mr. Kralik and you have talked it over! *Whose shop is this?*

PIROVITCH (there is only one answer):
Yes, Mr. Matuschek. (Camera pans with him as he goes back and gets busy behind the counter.)

CLOSE SHOT   MATUSCHEK AND KRALIK

MATUSCHEK (a change of tone; icy and harsh):
So you want the evening off, Mr. Kralik? Very good. I think we can manage without you.

KRALIK (wounded):
This is the first time in *years* that I've asked a favor. If it weren't very important—

MATUSCHEK:
I *gave* you your evening—what more do you want? Do you want a brass band to see you off?

KRALIK (hanging on to his dignity):
Please, Mr. Matuschek, I think you're being unjust.

MATUSCHEK (exploding again):
I'm being unjust! *Once a year* I ask six ladies and gentlemen—*six*, mind you, when next door a shop *twice* as big as mine employs only *four*—

We hear the opening of the outside door. Matuschek changes completely, walks smilingly forward.

CLOSE SHOT   THE DOOR
A woman customer has entered. Matuschek approaches—the salesman, courteous and smiling.

MATUSCHEK:
Good morning, madame. Is there anything I can show you?

WOMAN:
Have you traveling bags for men—with a zipper?

MATUSCHEK:

    Oh, yes, madame. We have all types of men's traveling bags with zippers.

WOMAN:

    Thank you very much. I'm just doing a little window shopping for my husband. He'll be here tomorrow.

MATUSCHEK:

    We'll be delighted to serve your husband.

WOMAN:

    Thank you. Good morning.

MATUSCHEK:

    Good morning, madame. (He bows politely, closes the door after the lady, and instantly, without the slightest loss of momentum, resumes shouting as he moves back into the shop.) —*Six* ladies and gentlemen, who stand around here for days telling *jokes* and talking about *movies*, while *I* pay the *gas* and *rent* and *light* and *taxes* and their *salaries!* (The nearby telephone rings. Before Flora has a chance to answer, Matuschek takes the receiver. Very politely.) Good morning, Matuschek and Company. (His expression darkens. It is not a customer.) Just a moment. Mr. Pirovitch!

CLOSE SHOT   PIROVITCH

This is no time for him to get a personal call. He approaches like a lamb to slaughter.

CLOSE SHOT   CASHIER'S PLACE

Matuschek stands there sternly. Pirovitch takes the receiver.

PIROVITCH (thinking a mile a minute):

    Yes, Mama—I called you. Imagine, Mama, we're decorating the window after closing hour—so we don't have to have dinner with the Martons! Isn't that wonderful! (Getting rid of Mama quickly.) Yes, Mama, I knew you'd be glad—goodbye. (He scurries back to his counter.)

MATUSCHEK (the instant Pirovitch hangs up):

    Six people! I ask, one day in a year, to be so kind as to redecorate a window—and *you* have the nerve, Mr. Kralik—the *oldest employee* in the place, who should set an *example*—

KRALIK:

Mr. Matuschek, you spoke like this to me yesterday. What did I do yesterday? The whole week you've treated me like this, without any reason.

MATUSCHEK (barely restraining hatred):

Without any reason? Maybe I have more reason than you think.

KRALIK (quietly):

It's obvious that you're not satisfied with me.

MATUSCHEK (also quiet):

You can draw your own conclusions.

KRALIK:

In that case, there's only one thing to do. Maybe we'd better call it a day.

There is great tension. This has no resemblance to the charming little family quarrel of several months ago. Matuschek's answer is to walk away, camera panning with him. We see a suffering man. The telephone rings.

FLORA'S VOICE:

Matuschek and Company . . . Yes, Mrs. Matuschek, he's here.

Matuschek goes to the phone, takes it from Flora.

MATUSCHEK (very quietly):

Yes, Emma—no, I'm not coming home until—very late . . . Yes, that's all right . . . Oh, yes . . . Yes, yes—I'll send it right away. Goodbye. (To Flora.) Put a thousand pengos in an envelope and tell Pepi to take it over to Mrs. Matuschek.

FLORA:

Pepi is out—he has quite a few packages to deliver and I don't think he'll be back until after lunch.

Matuschek thinks for a moment.

CLOSE SHOT   PIROVITCH

He sees an opening to help his friend. Camera moves with him as he goes to Matuschek. (Kralik is in the middleground.)

PIROVITCH:

Mr. Kralik and I always have lunch at Farago's—it's only a few blocks from your home, Mr. Matuschek. We can deliver it. Isn't that right, Mr. Kralik?

KRALIK (deeply hurt but willing to make up):
Yes.

CLOSE SHOT   MATUSCHEK

MATUSCHEK:
No, thank you, Mr. Kralik. (Into the shop.) Mr. Vadas!

CLOSE SHOT   VADAS
He races toward Matuschek, camera with him.

VADAS:
Yes, sir!

MATUSCHEK:
I don't like to break in on your lunch hour—

VADAS:
That's perfectly all right, Mr. Matuschek!

MATUSCHEK:
Thank you.

LONG SHOT   THE SHOP
Matuschek walks quietly back to his office.

FADE OUT

SEQUENCE C

FADE IN
INT. OF SHOP   MED. SHOT AT ONE SHOW WINDOW   LATE AFTERNOON
Vadas and Ilona are decorating. Matuschek enters, watches. Camera pans with him as he goes to the other window. There we discover Kralik hanging little things on the branches of the Christmas tree, Klara handing them to him. The atmosphere is subdued and gloomy.

MATUSCHEK (very politely):
Mr. Kralik—will you come to my office? I'd like to talk to you.

KRALIK:
Yes, sir.

Matuschek, followed by Kralik, goes to the office.

208

CLOSE SHOT   OFFICE DOOR

Matuschek goes into the office. Kralik, before following, turns to the others with a smile, believing that Matuschek, as usual, wants to make up.

INT. OFFICE

Matuschek stands by the desk. Kralik comes in. Camera moves to a close shot on both.

MATUSCHEK (very quietly):
Mr. Kralik, I've been thinking about what you said this morning.

KRALIK (with a smile):
I'm very sorry, Mr. Matuschek. I'm afraid I lost my temper.

MATUSCHEK:
No, no—I think you were right. I really believe you'd be happier somewhere else.

KRALIK (stunned):
You think so, Mr. Matuschek?

MATUSCHEK:
Yes, I'm sure of it.

KRALIK (after a long pause; realizing that he has hit bottom):
Well—I guess there's nothing more to be said.

MATUSCHEK (businesslike, wallet in hand):
Now—let's see. Naturally you're entitled to a full month's salary— two hundred pengos. I believe that's correct.

KRALIK:
Yes.

MATUSCHEK:
Will you sign this receipt, please? (Dazed, Kralik signs.) And here's a letter which certainly won't handicap you in seeking employment.

KRALIK (takes it):
Thank you, Mr. Matuschek.

MATUSCHEK:
Well, we might as well say goodbye.

KRALIK (as they shake hands):
Goodbye, Mr. Matuschek.

MATUSCHEK:
Goodbye.

Kralik leaves quickly.

SHOP   CLOSE SHOT   DOOR OF OFFICE
Kralik comes out, shuts the door.

CLOSE SHOT   OTHER EMPLOYEES (KLARA IS NOT THERE)
who are looking at him—Pirovitch, Ilona, and Flora; Vadas in middle ground—in anticipation of his success.

CLOSER SHOT   KRALIK AT DOOR
Camera precedes him as he goes toward the others. His expression leaves no doubt. Pirovitch steps out.

PIROVITCH:
Well, what happened?

Kralik takes the letter out of the envelope in his hand, unfolds it. Camera pulls slowly back and they all group around Kralik as he reads the letter.

KRALIK:
"To Whom It May Concern: I wish to state that Mr. Alfred Kralik leaves my employ of his own accord. Mr. Kralik started with Matuschek and Company nine years ago as an apprentice. Through his diligence he advanced to the position of clerk, and for the last five years he has been our first salesman. We have found him reliable, efficient, and resourceful, and we can recommend him without reserve. He carries with him our best wishes for success in his future career. Signed, Hugo Matuschek."

All are deeply moved, except Vadas, who pretends to be even more deeply moved. After a moment Kralik turns, goes toward the locker room.

MED. SHOT   LOCKER ROOM
Kralik enters, goes to his locker, opens it with a key. Camera moves to a close-up. He takes his few belongings—a spare collar, a piece of soap,

a comb, a brush. Then, out of a glass of water, he lifts a carnation, puts it on a table.

He lifts the paper that lines the locker to see if he has forgotten anything. His hand reaches in and brings out a little package.

INSERT   A LITTLE PACKAGE
It is the bicarbonate of soda of several months ago.

MED. SHOT OF LOCKER ROOM
He moves to a table, takes wrapping paper, gathers his belongings. Pirovitch enters, heartbroken.

PIROVITCH:
  Kralik, I still can't believe it. There's no *reason* for it.

KRALIK (putting on hat and coat):
  Listen—the boss doesn't have to give you a reason. That's what's so wonderful about being a boss . . . Well, I wanted to get off to-night. I got off, all right.

He takes the carnation, looks at it a few seconds, then crushes it and throws it away. This shocks Pirovitch.

PIROVITCH:
  Kralik—you're not *going?*

KRALIK:
  I couldn't face her. This morning I had a position—a future. And now . . . You see, I'm afraid I exaggerated in my letters. I showed off a little. She's expecting to meet a pretty important man . . . (As they go into the shop.) And I'm not in the mood to act important tonight.

SHOP   MED. SHOT
The other employees have stopped working. They are almost in a group, except Klara, whom we don't see at the moment. Kralik and Pirovitch enter. Kralik stops near a counter. He faces the task of saying goodbye.

KRALIK:
  Well . . .

Nobody moves.

CLOSE SHOT   KRALIK

He remembers his sales book. He takes it, with great feeling, out of his pocket, along with two pencils and a key which belong to Matuschek and Company, and deposits them on the counter.

CLOSE SHOT   WHOLE GROUP

Everybody is touched. In the silence cuts Vadas's voice.

VADAS:

Well, my dear Kralik, I think I speak for all of us when I say that this is a shock and a surprise. We feel we are losing a splendid fellow worker, and we certainly wish you all the luck you so rightfully deserve.

The others watch uncomfortably as Vadas grabs Kralik's hand in a vigorous shake and, pretending to be overcome with emotion, goes out.

KRALIK:

Well, Ilona—I'm going to miss you.

ILONA:

I just don't understand it!

KRALIK:

That's nothing unusual. It happens every day . . . Someone gets fired . . . (Taking her hand.) Goodbye, Ilona.

ILONA:

Goodbye, Kralik.

Kralik now turns to Flora, who has tears in her eyes. He tries to play against sentiment.

KRALIK:

Flora, when you go through my sales book, you'll notice I canceled slip number five; but I deducted it from the total.

Flora nods, trying not to give way, but she starts sniffling as Kralik turns from her to his dear friend, Pirovitch.

PIROVITCH:

Now, Kralik—we're going to see each other. If you have an evening with nothing to do—you know where we live.

KRALIK:

Thanks, Pirovitch.

They shake hands, and camera pans with Kralik as he goes to the door. He looks around the shop, his eyes saying goodbye. As he nears the door the camera discloses Klara, waiting there.

KRALIK:

> Well, Miss Novak, if I had anything to do with your not getting the evening off—I'm very sorry.

KLARA (sincerely):

> And if it's my fault in any way that you got into this trouble— believe me, I'm sorry, too.

KRALIK:

> Oh, that's all right.

KLARA:

> It's true we didn't get along—I guess we fought a lot—but losing a job at a time like this is something you don't wish— (She catches herself.)

KRALIK:

> —on your worst enemy. I know.

KLARA (resentfully):

> I didn't say that, Mr. Kralik!

KRALIK:

> Let's not quarrel anymore. (He extends his hand.) Goodbye.

KLARA (shaking hands):

> Goodbye, Mr. Kralik.

Kralik leaves the shop.

LONG SHOT   SHOP
There is complete silence.

VADAS:

> Well—life has to go on!

He leaves quickly toward the window. All the others also gradually resume work.

DISSOLVE TO:

MATUSCHEK'S OFFICE   MED. SHOT OF DESK
Matuschek is standing at the desk. He is in tragic suspense. The telephone rings.

MATUSCHEK:

> Yes? . . . Oh . . . I see . . . You *have!* . . . (Very excited.) How long
> will it take you to get here? Well, then come right away. Very good.
> I'll be waiting . . . (He hangs up the receiver, stands a moment,
> thinking, then goes decisively out of the office.)

LONG SHOT   SHOP

Everybody is working. Matuschek appears in the doorway.

MATUSCHEK:

> You may all go home—we'll finish the windows tomorrow.

CLOSE SHOT   KLARA

She is thrilled. She races to the locker room, camera panning with her.

LOCKER ROOM   MED. SHOT

Klara enters. In a few seconds she has jammed her hat on and slipped
into her coat. She reaches into her locker.

INSERT   SHELF

We see a book. Her hand reaches in, takes out the book. It is Tolstoy's
Anna Karenina.

MED. SHOT   LOCKER ROOM

Klara leaves quickly. In the doorway she collides with the others as
they come in.

KLARA:

> Good night!

OTHERS:

> Good night!

SHOP   MED. SHOT   LOCKER ROOM DOOR

Klara comes out. Camera pans with her as she dashes to the door and
is gone.

MED. SHOT   LOCKER ROOM DOOR

Pirovitch emerges in hat and overcoat. Camera pans with him as he
goes quickly to telephone, moves to a close shot. He dials.

PIROVITCH:

> Hello . . . Is this Mrs. Hojas? This is Mr. Pirovitch, Mr. Kralik's

friend. I know he's not there yet, but when he comes, will you please tell him we are not working tonight and I'm coming over. Thank you.

As he hangs up:

CLOSE SHOT   MATUSCHEK
He has just come out of the office. He obviously has heard Pirovitch.

PIROVITCH (scared):
I hope you don't mind, Mr. Matuschek. He probably feels pretty low tonight and—

MED. SHOT   PIROVITCH AND MATUSCHEK

MATUSCHEK (coldly):
You don't have to explain. What you do after working hours is your own business.

PIROVITCH:
Thank you, sir. (Pause. He resolutely faces Matuschek.) You haven't changed your mind by any chance, Mr. Matuschek?

MATUSCHEK:
You've got the evening off, haven't you? Well, go home.

PIROVITCH (daringly for his friend):
He's the best man you had, Mr. Matuschek. Why did you let him go?

MATUSCHEK:
I warn you, Pirovitch—

PIROVITCH:
His whole life he lived in this shop. He was almost like a son to you. And you were so proud of him— You invited him to your home again and again—

The last words strike like a hot iron.

MATUSCHEK:
Mr. Pirovitch, you want to keep your job, don't you?

PIROVITCH (humbly):
Yes, Mr. Matuschek—I have to. I have a family—two children . . .

MATUSCHEK:

In that case, mind your own business and go home.

PIROVITCH:

Yes, Mr. Matuschek! (Camera pans with him as, defeated, he leaves.)

MED. SHOT   INCLUDING OFFICE AND LOCKER ROOM DOORS

Matuschek, in a strange mood, stands waiting for everyone to be gone. Ilona and Flora come out of the locker room.

ILONA AND FLORA:

Good night, Mr. Matuschek.

MATUSCHEK:

Good night, good night.

Vadas is last. He stops in front of Matuschek, clicks heels.

VADAS:

Good night, Mr. Matuschek.

MATUSCHEK:

Good night.

Vadas is about to go when he remembers something.

CLOSE SHOT   MATUSCHEK AND VADAS

VADAS:

Oh, Mr. Matuschek, I beg your pardon— I'm not quite certain if I delivered Mrs. Matuschek's message. She told me when I gave her the thousand pengos to remind you to call her in case you change your mind and don't work tonight.

MATUSCHEK (inscrutably):

Yes—you did. Thank you.

VADAS (still lingering):

You know, Mr. Matuschek, the last time I had the pleasure of being at your apartment was several months ago when you sent me after your briefcase. And today I had a chance to get a glimpse of your new dining room set— It's exquisite. I can imagine what it will look like with all the lights on at a dinner party. It must be simply stunning.

MATUSCHEK:
Thank you, Vadas.

VADAS:
Good night, Mr. Matuschek.

MATUSCHEK:
Good night, Vadas.

CLOSE SHOT   STREET DOOR
Vadas goes.

CLOSE SHOT   MATUSCHEK
He pauses, then goes to the street door.

CLOSE SHOT   STREET DOOR
Matuschek locks the door. Camera pans with him to the light switch. Most of the lights go off. He paces up and down, stops. He is a man completely off-guard, trembling with emotion. A knock on the door. He goes quickly, camera with him, opens the door. A middle-aged man enters, carrying a briefcase. He is a detective, looks like a bank clerk.

DETECTIVE:
Good evening, Mr. Matuschek.

MATUSCHEK:
Good evening. (They move together to a counter.) Please?

DETECTIVE:
Thank you. (He promptly opens the briefcase and brings out a report.)

MATUSCHEK:
So it's true?

DETECTIVE:
I'm afraid so, Mr. Matuschek. Now, here we have the complete record from our operatives, two of our most reliable men.

MATUSCHEK (nodding):
Um-hum.

DETECTIVE (reading):
"Report on Mrs. Emma Matuschek. On December sixth, Mrs. Matuschek left her residence at Balta Street, twenty-three, at eight

217

forty-five. She walked two blocks up to Karl Street, where she engaged a taxi. At nine three, the taxi stopped on the corner of Castle and Johann streets. There Mrs. Matuschek was joined by a young man." (Matuschek, who has been listening like a person to his death warrant, gets up abruptly and turns away. Detective gets up, too, giving Matuschek a moment to recover.) Well, Mr. Matuschek, your suspicion was right. It was one of your employees. Both our operatives identified him later as Mr. Vadas.

MATUSCHEK (turning; incredulously):
Vadas?

DETECTIVE (referring to his report):
Yes, Ferencz Vadas. Danube Place, fifty-six. There is such a man in your employ, isn't there?

Matuschek can hardly speak.

MATUSCHEK (in great confusion):
Yes . . . Um-hum . . . (He takes the report from the detective, tries to read it. After a few moments he stops. Half to himself.) Twenty-two years we've been married. Twenty-two years I was proud of my wife. Well—she didn't want to grow old with me . . . (To the detective.) If you'll send me your bill, I'll take care of it immediately.

DETECTIVE (respecting Matuschek's mood):
Thank you, Mr. Matuschek. Good night.

MATUSCHEK:
Good night. (Camera pans with the detective as he leaves the shop.)

SHOP   LONG SHOT   SHOOTING TOWARD OFFICE DOOR
For a few seconds Matuschek is unable to move. Then he slowly goes to the office, shutting the door behind him.

SHOP   MED. SHOT   TOWARD STREET DOOR
Pepi enters. He is surprised to see the shop deserted. The telephone rings. Pepi answers it.

CLOSE SHOT   PEPI AT TELEPHONE

PEPI:
Good evening . . . (Changing his voice to a ludicrous falsetto, a

218

malicious smile on his face.) No, Mrs. Matuschek, this is Flora speaking. Good evening! . . . Who? Pepi? No, Pepi isn't back yet . . . I see, Mrs. Matuschek, he did some errands for you . . . Oh, you *don't say*—he forgot to pick up a bottle of perfume at Chabot's . . . Isn't that *too bad!* . . . Yes, I'll give a *good scolding* to the little rascal . . . Have a good time, Mrs. Matuschek! Good night.

He hangs up, muttering in his own natural voice. He becomes aware again of the mystery of the deserted shop. He starts toward the stock room door.

STOCK ROOM   MED. SHOT AT DOOR
Pepi enters, sees it is deserted. Camera pans with him as he hurries to the locker room. Also empty. He goes toward the office door.

MED. SHOT   OFFICE DOOR
Pepi opens the door, and what he sees horrifies him. He runs into the office, leaving the door open.

PEPI (screaming):
    Mr. Matuschek, don't do that! No—no, no, Mr. Matuschek!

Pepi disappears as he dashes toward the unseen man. We hear sounds of a short struggle, then the sound of a shot, and we see glass of the ceiling lamp crash, struck by a deflected bullet. Next moment Pepi dashes into the picture, a revolver in hand, puts it on a table, dashes back.

MED. SHOT   MATUSCHEK
He stands by desk, dazed. Pepi returns.

                                                    DISSOLVE TO:

MED. SHOT   EXT. A CAFE
Camera moves with Kralik and Pirovitch as they approach sadly along the street and stop.

PIROVITCH:
    Why don't you go in? I really think you should go in and keep your date.

KRALIK (with patience, but with finality):
    Now, Pirovitch—just do me a favor and deliver my note.

PIROVITCH:
    All right.

KRALIK:

And, Pirovitch—I don't want to know what she looks like. If she's bad looking—well, I've had enough bad news today. And if she's lovely—it'll make it that much more difficult.

PIROVITCH:

I won't. Now, what's the name of that book?

KRALIK:

Anna Karenina—and a red carnation as a bookmark.

PIROVITCH:

Let me see . . . Just a minute . . .

Pirovitch is about to go in. But he pauses, and the camera pans with him as he goes to the corner of the window. The window is curtained only about shoulder-high, so he can survey the cafe. Kralik joins Pirovitch, and remembering his resolve he does not look, but he watches Pirovitch's face with intensity.

KRALIK:

See anything?

PIROVITCH (looking):

Not yet. Oh . . . There's a beautiful girl.

KRALIK (excitedly):

Really?

PIROVITCH:

Very beautiful. But no book. (Kralik reacts a little. Pirovitch is now on tiptoe, looking right down underneath where he stands.) Wait a minute—I think I see it . . . Right here under the window. Yes— *Anna Karenina*, by Tolstoy. *And* a carnation. (Kralik is listening with the suspense of a man hearing the round-by-round report of a prizefight, and Pirovitch is almost telling it like that.) I can't see her face. She's sitting behind a clothes rack. There's a cup of coffee on the table. She's taking a piece of cake . . . Kralik, she's dunking.

KRALIK (defending his girl):

Why shouldn't she?

PIROVITCH (philosophically):

All right. (Very excited.) She's leaning forward now, Kralik, she— (Abruptly he stops.)

KRALIK:
> *Can you see her?*

PIROVITCH (in a strange voice):
> Yes.

KRALIK (timidly):
> Is she . . . pretty?

PIROVITCH:
> *Very* pretty.

KRALIK (controlling his vast relief):
> She is, huh?

Pirovitch turns from the window to Kralik. It is difficult news he has to break.

PIROVITCH (stalling for time):
> I would say—she looks—she has a little of the coloring of—of Klara.

KRALIK (sourly):
> Klara? You mean Miss Novak of the shop?

PIROVITCH (trying to build a bridge):
> Now, Kralik, you must admit that Klara is a good-looking girl— and personally, I've always found her a very *likable* girl.

KRALIK (exasperated):
> This is a fine time to be talking about Miss Novak!

PIROVITCH (measuring his words):
> Well, if you don't like Miss Novak, I can tell you right now, you won't like this girl.

KRALIK:
> Why?

PIROVITCH:
> Because—it *is* Miss Novak.

This has the effect of a bombshell. Kralik is speechless. He simply can't believe it. With a tremendous effort of will, he goes to the window.

INT. CAFE   CLOSE SHOT   THROUGH WINDOW TOWARD OUTSIDE
We see Kralik looking in. He focuses directly beneath him.

CLOSE SHOT   TABLE BELOW

We see the book, *Anna Karenina*, the carnation in it. Camera pans up. There sits Klara. She opens her little jacket. Camera moves to a close shot of the blouse. It is indeed the blouse with the dots.

CLOSE-UP OF KRALIK THROUGH WINDOW
There is no more question in his mind.

EXT. CAFE   KRALIK AND PIROVITCH
Kralik turns away, crushed. Pirovitch realizes what a shock this is. But he is not entirely on Kralik's side.

PIROVITCH (bringing out the note):
Shall I give the note to the waiter?

KRALIK:
No! (He takes the note, tears it up, jams it into his pocket.)

PIROVITCH (impatiently):
What are you going to do? Let that poor girl *wait?*

KRALIK (bitterly):
Why *shouldn't* Miss Novak wait? For six months she *fought* with me *every day*—

PIROVITCH:
But still . . . She wrote those letters, my friend.

KRALIK:
That's my misfortune! . . . Well—goodbye, Pirovitch.

He turns abruptly and walks away. Pirovitch looks after him a moment, then goes off in another direction.

INT. CAFE   MED. SHOT AT KLARA'S TABLE
Klara, waiting, is looking nervously toward the door and around the cafe to be sure she has not missed a wonderful young man with a carnation. An elderly, good-natured waiter approaches.

WAITER:
Excuse me, miss—please—could I have this chair?

KLARA (quickly):
Oh, no, you can't! I'm expecting somebody. The party will be here any minute.

WAITER (in a hurry):
   That's all right.

He gives her a friendly look and is about to go when he notices:

INSERT   BOOK WITH CARNATION

CLOSE SHOT   KLARA AND WAITER
The waiter smiles at her. Klara looks back with some embarrassment.

WAITER:
   Carnation, huh? (Getting closer for a bit of friendly gossip.) A few
   nights ago we had a case with roses. Turned out very nice, very
   nice. But once, about three months ago, we had a very sad case—
   with gardenias. She waited all evening and nobody came—and
   when we cleaned the cafe, we found, underneath one of the
   tables, another gardenia. Well, you can imagine. The man must
   have come in, taken one look at her, said "Phooey," and threw
   away his gardenia.

Klara is shaken. This is a possibility she had not considered.

KLARA:
   Isn't your clock a little fast? My watch is only eight twenty-seven.

WAITER (sympathetically):
   Listen, you have nothing to worry about—a pretty girl like you. If
   he doesn't come, I'll put on a carnation myself.

A VOICE (off screen):
   Waiter!

The waiter hurries out. Klara remains in growing anxiety. Now outside
the window, above Klara, Kralik slowly returns, stopping for a cautious
look. He has apparently changed his mind. After a moment he makes
a decision, goes to the door.

MED. CLOSE SHOT AT DOOR   INSIDE CAFE
Kralik enters. Camera moves with him as he reaches Klara's table, pretends he sees her unexpectedly.

KRALIK (acting surprised):
   Well—Miss Novak!

Klara is dismayed. Of all people at this moment—to get Kralik.

KLARA:

Good evening, Mr. Kralik.

KRALIK:

Well—what a coincidence! You know, I had an appointment here—
you haven't seen Mr. Pirovitch, by any chance?

KLARA (coldly):

No, I haven't.

KRALIK (wanting to be invited):

Well, I guess I'll wait.

Pause. Klara wants him to disappear, evaporate, vamoose.

KRALIK:

Do you mind if I sit down?

KLARA (almost frantically):

Yes, I do! *Please*, Mr. Kralik, you know *I* have an appointment, too.

KRALIK (playacting):

Oh, yes! Of course! I remember now . . . (Seeming to size up the
situation.) Your friend seems to be a little late.

KLARA:

Now, please don't be sarcastic. I know you had a bad day, and you
probably feel very bitter—but still—

KRALIK (bragging):

Bitter—me? About leaving Matuschek and Company? When I came
home I sat down at the phone, and in five minutes I had what
amounts to two offers.

KLARA (in dismissal):

I congratulate you, and I wish you good luck.

KRALIK (oblivious):

I see you're reading Tolstoy's *Anna Karenina*.

KLARA:

Why, yes—do you mind?

KRALIK (trying to find a way to maneuver himself into that empty
chair):

No, no, no! But I never expected to meet you in a cafe with . . .
Tolstoy. It's quite a surprise. I didn't know you went in for high
literature.

KLARA:
There are *many* things you don't know about me, Mr. Kralik.

KRALIK (leaning closer):
Have you read *Crime and Punishment* by Dostoyevsky?

KLARA:
No, I haven't.

KRALIK:
I have! There are many things you don't know about *me*, Miss Novak. In fact, there might be a lot we don't know about each *other*. You know, people seldom go to the trouble of scratching the surface of things to find out the inner truth.

KLARA (very superior):
Mr. Kralik, I wouldn't care to scratch your surface, because I know exactly what I would find. A handbag instead of a heart, a suitcase instead of a soul, and instead of an intellect, a cigarette lighter— that doesn't work.

KRALIK (greatly impressed):
That's very well put! Comparing my intellect with a cigarette lighter that doesn't work is such an interesting mixture of poetry and—meanness—

KLARA (indignantly):
Meanness?

KRALIK (absentmindedly slipping into the chair):
Now, don't misunderstand me, Miss Novak— (As if unconsciously, he picks up the book and gestures with it.) I was only trying to pay you a compliment.

Panic-stricken, she grabs the book out of his hand, puts it back exactly where it was, carefully arranging the carnation. As she does:

KLARA:
Please, Mr. Kralik! I told you I was *expecting* somebody.

Kralik gets up but does not go.

KRALIK (he is actually trying to make a date):
Listen, if your party doesn't show up—would I—

KLARA:
Don't worry about *that*, Mr. Kralik. This party will show up. You don't have to entertain me.

Kralik doesn't know what to do, decides to go. He starts away, the camera with him. As he passes the adjoining table, the people are leaving. Instantly he sits down in a chair which is back to back with Klara's chair.

CLOSE SHOT   KLARA AND KRALIK
back to back.

KRALIK (over his shoulder):
> Have you read Zola's *Madame Bovary*?

KLARA (turning around):
> *Madame Bovary* is not by Zola. (Suddenly realizing what has happened, she turns more.) *Are you still here!* Now, Mr. Kralik, are you deliberately trying to ruin my evening? Why do you want to do me harm? Why do you *hate* me so?

KRALIK:
> I don't hate you.

KLARA (sarcastically):
> I suppose you love me!

KRALIK:
> No, why should I? What have you ever done to make me love you?

KLARA (angry):
> I don't *want* you to love me.

KRALIK (just as angry):
> Well, I *don't!*

Both turn, and they are again back to back.

CLOSE SHOT   ON ORCHESTRA
It starts to play "Otchi Tchornya."

CLOSE SHOT   KRALIK AND KLARA
They react. The song has different meanings to each.

KRALIK (turning again; in a warm, friendly tone):
> You know what that song reminds me of?

KLARA:
> Yes, thank you—two dozen unsold cigarette boxes.

KRALIK:

Wrong. It reminds me of a girl who was out of a job—and a very nice girl, I thought.

KLARA:

You thought that? How you can lie!

KRALIK:

Of course, that was before you began to make fun of me—giving imitations of me in the locker room. And I want to take this opportunity, Miss Novak, to inform you that I don't walk like a duck—and I am not bowlegged.

KLARA (calmly):

Aren't you?

KRALIK (furiously):

No, I'm not!

KLARA (smugly):

I have information to the contrary. Mr. Vadas assured me that you have your trousers specially made.

KRALIK:

That's a lie! Mr. *Vadas* . . . ! That's the kind of man you trust, huh? I've never been to a tailor in my life! (He gets up and steps over to her chair.) And if you think I'm bowlegged, you come out on the sidewalk with me and I'll pull up my trousers!

Klara is so irritated by his preposterous invitation that for the moment she does not realize he has sat down again at her table.

KRALIK:

How would you like it if I made remarks about your hands being red?

KLARA:

That's exactly what you did!

KRALIK:

Yes, but only after you made fun of my legs.

KLARA:

And they aren't red at all!

227

KRALIK:

Not anymore—after I called your attention to them. Let me tell you something, Miss Novak, you may have beautiful thoughts, but you certainly hide them. So far as your actions are concerned, you're cold and snippy like an old maid—and you'll have a tough time to make *any* man fall in love with you.

KLARA (with queenly superiority):

I, an old maid? No man will fall in love with me? Mr. Kralik, you're getting funnier every minute. I could show you letters that would open your eyes— No, you probably wouldn't understand what's in them! They're written by a type of man so far above you that it's ridiculous. Ha! I have to laugh when I think of *you* calling *me* an old maid—you—*you little, insignificant clerk!*

Kralik is stung by this proof that he has failed to make the slightest impression on Klara and, still worse, that she is expecting a man completely the opposite of what she thinks Kralik is. He gets up.

KRALIK (with bravado):

Goodbye, Miss Novak! (Camera pans with him as he hastens out of the cafe.)

CLOSE SHOT AT TABLE

Klara quickly reaches to the empty chair and tips it against the table. It is clear that the chair is reserved.

FADE OUT

SEQUENCE D

CORRIDOR IN A HOSPITAL   EARLY MORNING

We fade in on an insert of a card in a frame on the door of a hospital room. We read:

MR. H. MATUSCHEK

Camera pulls back to a medium shot of the door. A doctor comes out, followed by Pepi in his Sunday suit. The doctor is middle-aged, slightly pompous. The two walk toward the elevator, camera with them.

PEPI (with the air of a colleague):

Well, Doctor, I'd say it's a nervous breakdown. What do *you* think?

DOCTOR (taking Pepi straight, full of medical dignity):

It's a mixture of an acute epiledtoid manifestation in a panphobic melancholiae with some indications of a neurasthenia cortis.

PEPI:

Is that more expensive than a nervous breakdown?

DOCTOR:

Pardon me, Mr. Katona—are you related to the patient?

PEPI:

No, I'm a business associate of Mr. Matuschek's. Now, look here, Doctor, let's cut out this high-priced Latin and get down to business . . . You think our patient has to stay here?

DOCTOR:

I would say he shouldn't leave too soon—to be sure he doesn't have a relapse.

PEPI (grand manner):

Doctor, I leave that to you. You know best. And if you want to be *positive* he doesn't have a relapse, don't make the bill too high.

By now, they have reached the elevator.

DOCTOR (irritated):

Pardon me, Mr. Katona, but precisely what position do you hold with Matuschek and Company?

PEPI:

Well, I would describe myself as a contact man. I keep contact between Matuschek and Company and the customers—on a bicycle.

DOCTOR:

You mean—an errand boy?

PEPI (undismayed):

Doctor—did I call you a pill-peddler?

The elevator door opens. Doctor goes in; Kralik emerges. Pepi keeps up his grand manner before the new audience of Kralik.

PEPI:

Morning, Mr. Kralik! (Patting Kralik on the shoulder.) I want to thank you for your splendid reaction to my telephone call. I knew you wouldn't fail us.

KRALIK (getting to the point):

Is it serious?

PEPI:

Naturally, it was a terrible shock—but I have to get over it. Now, this whole thing must be in strictest confidence. What I told you

over the telephone is between the three of us—me, Mr. Matuschek, and you.

They are in front of Matuschek's room. Kralik, who has paid no attention to Pepi's jabbering, enters carefully. Pepi remains outside.

MATUSCHEK'S HOSPITAL ROOM   CLOSE SHOT AT DOOR
Kralik enters, shuts the door carefully. Camera pans with him to Matuschek's bed. Now we see Matuschek, grief-stricken, haggard, lying
very still. His eyes welcome Kralik. He lifts himself with some difficulty, extends his hand. There is a silent handshake.

MATUSCHEK (in a weak voice):
Thank you for coming, Kralik, thank you. Sit down.

Kralik sits.

CLOSE SHOT   BOTH

MATUSCHEK:
Do you remember, when you were at my house for dinner the last
time, I told you if things go well, I might take it easier—and,
maybe by Christmas, make you manager of the shop? (With a sad
smile.) Now, I *have* to take it easier . . . Would you care to work for
me again, after what I . . .

KRALIK:
Please, don't even think about it.

MATUSCHEK:
Is it possible that I ever distrusted you, Kralik? I hated you—I
couldn't stand your presence anymore. That's how far jealousy can
drive a man.

KRALIK:
Well, it's all over now, Mr. Matuschek.

MATUSCHEK:
When I first got that anonymous letter, I laughed at it. My wife
having secret rendezvous with one of my employees! . . . *My wife?*
That's impossible! But you can't throw a letter like that away. It
stays with you—every word. The first day you say it *can't* be true—
and the next day you say, I *hope* it isn't true.

KRALIK:
But how could you suspect *me?*

MATUSCHEK:
> You were the only one from the shop who came to my home. You sent flowers to my wife.

KRALIK:
> It was only—

MATUSCHEK:
> You don't have to tell me! But if this poison once gets into your mind . . . Please try to understand.

KRALIK:
> I understand.

Matuschek takes a ring of old-fashioned keys from the night table and hands them to Kralik.

MATUSCHEK (with great feeling):
> Here are the keys to Matuschek and Company!

KRALIK (aware of the significance of this moment):
> Thank you, sir! (He rises. He feels uncomfortable that he has to bring up the subject.) What shall I do about Mr.—

MATUSCHEK (his face showing pain):
> Vadas? . . . I want him dismissed as quietly as possible—no scandal. Don't even mention the subject to him. We shouldn't lower ourselves.

KRALIK:
> Very good, sir. (With vigor and high resolve.) Well, we're going to make this the biggest Christmas in the history of Matuschek and Company.

MATUSCHEK:
> I know you will!

They shake hands. Kralik goes. Camera pans with him.

MATUSCHEK'S VOICE:
> And, Kralik . . .

KRALIK (turns):
> Yes, sir?

CLOSE SHOT   MATUSCHEK

MATUSCHEK (with a benevolent smile):
> Now that you're the boss—if you want to give yourself a raise . . .

CLOSE SHOT   KRALIK AT DOOR

KRALIK (with a shy grin):
> Well, I think I'll talk to myself—and if I don't ask for too much, I'll give it to myself. Thank you, Mr. Matuschek!

He goes. The door stays closed an instant; then Pepi opens it, peeks in, enters.

MED. SHOT OF ROOM
Pepi takes his coat and hat from an armchair, and approaches the bed.

CLOSE SHOT   MATUSCHEK AND PEPI

PEPI:
> Well, goodbye, Mr. Matuschek.

MATUSCHEK (warm and grateful):
> Pepi, I don't know how to thank you. You saved my life.

PEPI:
> Don't mention it. It was a pleasure. Now, if you want anything else—you know where to reach me. (Pretending to joke, but meaning it plenty.) I'm still nothing but an errand boy at Matuschek and Company.

MATUSCHEK (with a smile):
> In other words, you'd like to be a clerk.

PEPI:
> I wouldn't put it that crudely.

MATUSCHEK (a little tired):
> Well—after I get better . . .

PEPI (relentless):
> Then you might change your mind. And besides, who knows how long you'll have to stay here? . . . You're a pretty sick man, Mr. Matuschek. This isn't just an ordinary breakdown.

MATUSCHEK (exhausted and annoyed):
> All right, you're a clerk! Now get out! (He sinks back.)

PEPI (jubilantly):
> Thanks, Mr. Matuschek! (Camera pans with him as he jauntily goes.)
> > DISSOLVE TO:

INT. SHOP   MED. CLOSE SHOT   ENTRANCE DOOR   EARLY MORNING
Through the door we see Kralik turning the key. With him are Ilona, Flora, Pirovitch, and Vadas, all congratulating him as they proceed into the shop.

KRALIK (shyly):
Thank you—thank you so much.

VADAS (getting set for a speech):
Well, old fellow, I think I speak for everybody as well as myself— (The rest move away while Vadas, pulling the glove off his right hand, grabs Kralik's unwilling hand and keeps shaking it.) Heartiest congratulations! And what a load off my mind! Now we're all one happy little family again.

KRALIK:
Yes—ah—yes.

He starts toward the office door. Vadas follows him, puts his arm around Kralik's shoulder.

VADAS:
And, Kralik, you can be assured of my personal cooperation to the fullest extent. I want you to be a real success and—

They reach the office door, and Vadas realizes that Kralik is not going to the locker room anymore.

VADAS (with a sour-sweet smile):
Oh, that's right, you're going into the office now . . . Ha, ha, ha . . . Well, if anybody deserves it, it's you!

He has taken off his left glove, and he holds his hand out admiringly.

INSERT   OF HAND
On the little finger we see a diamond ring.

CLOSE SHOT   VADAS AND KRALIK

VADAS:
Nice, isn't it? *I* had a little luck last night, too. Real diamond.

KRALIK (controlling his loathing; mutters):
Um-hum . . .

VADAS:
My grandma gave it to me. That's what you get for being a good

boy! Some boys get red apples—and I get diamonds . . . (Switching; businesslike.) By the way, Kralik, I have several very unusual ideas for that window display—and—

KRALIK (interrupting):
Thank you, Vadas. But I think the rest of us can take care of the windows. (Killing him with politeness.) Just at the moment, I wish you'd go right into the stock room. You know those big suitcases on the top shelf?

VADAS:
Yes—the black suitcases.

KRALIK:
And then there are the big *brown* suitcases—

VADAS:
On the *bottom* shelf.

KRALIK:
Correct. Now, I want you to take all the big *black* suitcases from the *top* shelf and put them on the *bottom* shelf—and I want all the big *brown* suitcases on the *bottom* shelf put on the—*top* shelf.

VADAS (knowing definitely that he is being insulted):
But, Kralik—

KRALIK:
Well, if you don't *want* to do it—

VADAS:
I didn't say anything like that! Certainly, I'll do it. I'm a good soldier!

KRALIK:
Then do it right away!

He goes into the office, slams the door. Vadas gives the door a furious look and turns toward the stock room.

WIPE TO:

SHOP NEXT DOOR TO MATUSCHEK'S
It is a haberdashery. Pepi comes out, in all the splendor of a newly purchased derby hat and cane. It makes a remarkable difference in his appearance. He smokes a cigarette with a rakish air. Camera pans with him as he strolls into Matuschek and Company.

INT. SHOP   MED. LONG SHOT

Flora, Pirovitch, and Ilona have just come out of the stock room and are into their morning preparations. Pepi enters. All three are aghast at his transfiguration. Ignoring them, Pepi steps briskly to the telephone. Pirovitch, Ilona, and Flora watch with astonishment and gradually come closer, and the camera, with them, moves to a close shot of the whole group as:

PEPI (into the telephone):
> Three, one, one, two, eight . . . Atlas Employment Agency? This is Mr. Katona of Matuschek and Company speaking . . . We have an opening for a new errand boy. Now, see here—I want an educated, healthy boy of good family and no bad habits. Send me four or five—I'll look them over—and right away, if you please. Tell them to ask for Mr. Katona of the sales department . . . All right! (Haughtily to the dumbstruck others.) What's the matter—didn't you ever see a clerk in your life before?

FLORA:
> Who made *you* a clerk?

PIROVITCH:
> Yes—who did this dreadful thing?

PEPI (patronizingly):
> Listen, folks, I can't give you the whole story. I'm tied up with my word of honor. But, if it hadn't been for me, this shop would be closed on account of suicide, and you all would be out of a job.

The telephone rings. Flora takes it.

FLORA:
> Matuschek and Company . . . Oh, yes, Mrs. Matuschek—

Pepi grabs the receiver from Flora.

PEPI (hand over the mouthpiece):
> Don't miss this, folks. (Into telephone; with nasty politeness.) Hel-*lo*, Mrs. Matuschek . . . Yes, this is Pepi speaking. That's *right*—I *didn't* bring you that bottle of perfume—and you're *never* going to get it, what do you think of that? Your perfume days are over, Mrs. M! . . . Yes, *this is* Pepi speaking. Oh, you want to talk to *Mr.* Matuschek? That's too bad. Just at the moment, he's up in a balloon with two blondes! (To the other three clerks.) Now watch this. (Into the telephone.) You wouldn't like to talk, by any chance,

to Mr. Vadas, ha, ha, ha! (He hangs up.) *That* got her! (As he strolls out of the picture.) Draw your own conclusions!

Pirovitch, Ilona, and Flora have listened, spellbound. Finally they have caught a glimpse of what must have happened.

DISSOLVE TO:

MED. SHOT   OFFICE INT.
Kralik walks up and down, waiting. Vadas enters—big smile, invincibly eager to please. Camera moves up to a double close shot.

VADAS:
You sent for me, chief?

KRALIK (determined to delay no longer, yet respecting the boss's desire for "no scandal"):
Vadas, I'm a little worried about you. Do you think you'll be comfortable under a former fellow clerk—working under a younger man?

VADAS:
Kralik, this is the age of youth. I always ride with the times. You're a very smart young man, and I take my hat off to you.

KRALIK (a little bored with his own diplomacy):
Oh, let's stop beating around the bush. You and I never got along.

VADAS (a phony, puzzled expression):
You think so?

KRALIK:
Come on, admit it—you don't like me.

VADAS (fighting, drawing from a bottomless bag of tricks):
I don't like you? Kralik, you're the boss—that's right—but I refuse to be a yes-man! You know what I'm going to do? I'm going to contradict you. *I do like you.* Anything else bothering you?

KRALIK:
Yes. *I* don't like *you!*

VADAS:
That's every man's privilege—and I *thank* you for being so frank. Now at least I know my problem! It's up to me to make you change your mind—and I don't think that will be so hard. (Shifting clumsily in desperation; breaking into hollow laughter.) Kralik, I heard the funniest joke—want to hear it?

KRALIK:
> No!

The telephone rings.

KRALIK (answering):
> Hello . . . Yes, this is Matuschek and Company . . . Who is this—
> Johanna? Oh, you're calling for Miss Novak . . . (In swift anxiety,
> Vadas forgotten.) What's the matter with her? . . . I hope it's noth-
> ing serious . . . Fine, I'm glad to hear it. Just tell her not to worry,
> and unless she's *absolutely all right*, tell her not to come today.
> There's *no* hurry at *all*. Be *sure* and tell her to take *good care of herself.*
> (He hangs up, his thoughts still on Klara.)

VADAS:
> Really, Kralik, that's a wonderful attitude.

KRALIK (coming to):
> What's so wonderful about it?

VADAS:
> After all, I've been around here, you know. My eyes are open; and
> if anybody *didn't* get along with you—it was nobody else *but* Miss
> Novak.

KRALIK:
> *Leave Miss Novak out of this!*

VADAS:
> All right, Kralik. *I* have nothing against Miss Novak. *I* always
> thought she was a very nice girl. But *once in a while*, perhaps, she
> went a *little* too far.

KRALIK (losing control):
> Now, look here—I don't want another word about Miss Novak!
> She's a fine girl! She's working hard! She's a very good salesgirl—
> *and you shut up!*

VADAS:
> Now, Kralik, what have I said? As a matter of fact, I was *agreeing*
> with you.

KRALIK (exploding; he has reached his limit):
> I don't *want* you to agree with me! *You're fired!*

Kralik dashes to the door, yanks it open.

VADAS (stiffening—a final stance):
> Oh, so I'm fired!

KRALIK:
> Get out of here—and quick! You two-faced, double-crossing two-timer—*get out of here!*

Vadas struts out.

MED. SHOT SHOP
Vadas appears, followed by Kralik. By now everybody knows what is happening.

VADAS (defiant):
> Folks, did you hear what he called me? I want you to remember on the witness stand—he called me a double-crossing two-timer.

KRALIK (pushing him):
> *Get out!*

VADAS:
> Don't you push! What right have *you* got to fire me, anyway? Does Mr. Matuschek know about this?

KRALIK:
> No—what do you think of that? Mr. Matuschek has nothing to do with it. I'm the manager, and you don't work here anymore!

VADAS:
> So you're the manager! How do I *know* you're the manager? *Anybody* can say that. Prove it! Show it to me in black and white!

KRALIK:
> You want it in black and white? Well, you're going to get it in black and *blue!*

He shoves Vadas. Vadas falls against a table stacked with the musical cigarette boxes, which spill over the floor. Some begin playing "Otchi Tchornya," but not in unison. Meantime Pepi, the practical man, hastens into the locker room for Vadas's belongings. Vadas gets up, straightens his clothes.

VADAS (equal to any occasion):
> Well—this is a very nice little case of assault and battery! You'll hear from my lawyer . . . And what about my salary?

Flora instantly hands him an envelope; she also has been thinking fast.

FLORA:
Here it is, Mr. Vadas.

Vadas opens it and counts; Pepi appears with hat and coat.

PEPI (with mock servility):
Pardon me, sir—your garments.

As Vadas is about to put coat on, Pepi drops coat and hat to floor and Vadas has to pick them up.

VADAS (quickly picking them up, scornful of Pepi):
And, by the way, I'm entitled to a letter of reference.

KRALIK:
Right. Flora, take a letter! (Flora grabs notebook and pencil. All watch, anticipating fun.) "To Whom It May Concern: Mr. Vadas has been in the employ of Matuschek and Company for two years, during which period he has been very efficient as a stool pigeon, troublemaker, and—rat . . ." (By now Vadas is out of the shop. Kralik, in doorway, shouts after him.) "Yours truly, Alfred Kralik, Manager, Matuschek and Company!" (Then he turns back and closes the door.)

DISSOLVE TO:

INT. POST OFFICE   MED. SHOT
We see two or three windows. Through the windows we see customers buying stamps. At each window sits a uniformed employee. Camera pans around a corner and stops, showing a wall of postboxes. On the postmaster's side, the boxes naturally are open. Camera moves to a close shot.

CLOSE SHOT   BOX 237
It is empty. Now it is being opened from the outside. The box is below face level; therefore we cannot see Klara's face. Her hand comes in, stops timidly, afraid to find the box empty, then goes in and feels to the far edges. Finally the hand knows there is no letter and withdraws. Then Klara apparently bends down; we see her face framed by the postbox. She looks in with great disappointment. The empty box is closed.

MED. CLOSE   SHOP   SHOOTING TOWARD ENTRANCE DOOR
The morning trade has begun. Every clerk is waiting on a customer. Klara enters. She is in a grievous state and, on top of that, she has to face the boss for being late. She hastens directly to the office, hardly

noticed by the busy clerks. She knocks on the door, opens it carefully, goes into the office.

MED. SHOT OFFICE
Instead of Mr. Matuschek, Klara sees Kralik. He is standing by the desk, reading some papers. Klara is puzzled. Kralik looks up, goes toward her. Camera moves to a double close shot on them.

KLARA:
Oh—good morning!

KRALIK:
Good morning! (In a very friendly tone.) I guess you're surprised to see me back?

KLARA (dazed):
Naturally—I'm glad you have your job again. I congratulate you.

KRALIK:
I hear you weren't feeling well.

KLARA (nervously):
That's all right—thank you—I'm looking for Mr. Matuschek.

KRALIK (enjoying himself):
Well, here he is—*I* am Mr. Matuschek.

KLARA (almost frantic; trying to hide her heartbreak):
Mr. Kralik, don't make any jokes—not today! And *please* if you *have* to pick on me, make it some *other* time! I want to talk to Mr. Matuschek.

KRALIK (understanding her; quite simply):
Miss Novak—I don't know what to say to you. I'm trying to tell you that Mr. Matuschek is not here—and I *am* the manager.

KLARA:
Haven't you any heart at all? Can't you see I am *not well?* I can hardly see straight! The room, everything is turning around . . . and in this state of mind I ask you a simple question . . . and, instead of having any *consideration* for me, you *deliberately* try to *frighten* me!

The telephone rings. Camera pans with Kralik as he sinks into the boss's chair and picks up receiver.

CLOSE SHOT KLARA
She is bewildered.

CLOSE SHOT   FROM BEHIND DESK
Klara in background and Kralik in foreground.

KRALIK:
Hello . . . Mr. Foeldes? . . . *Hello*, Mr. Foeldes! Thank you, *thank* you! . . . Well—it happened this very morning . . . (Klara gets tense.) Yes, Mr. Matuschek won't be with us for a while . . . Thank you—thank you very much! . . . (Klara can hardly believe what she hears.) No, please, no, no! Look here, Mr. Foeldes, I don't *own* the shop yet. I'm just the *manager*. (At the word "manager," Klara faints behind the desk.)

CLOSE SHOT   KRALIK

KRALIK (quickly into telephone):
Goodbye!

He hangs up, rushes out of picture to Klara. We hear his voice—"Miss Novak, Miss Novak!"

CLOSE SHOT   KRALIK AND KLARA
He lifts her, holds her in his arms.

KRALIK (tenderly; using her first name for the first time):
Klara . . . !

Camera pans with him as he carries her and eases her down on couch, raises her feet, lowers her head.

KLARA (coming out of it):
What happened?

KRALIK:
You fainted . . . Miss Novak.

FADE OUT

SEQUENCE E

FADE IN
KLARA'S BEDROOM
Evening, same day. A small bedroom in a lower-middle-class family apartment. Shot on door as it is opened by Klara's grandmother—a kindly old lady. Kralik enters as in a sickroom. He is in topcoat, hat in hand. The grandmother closes the door. Camera pans with Kralik, disclosing Klara in a frilly little bed jacket, sitting up in bed.

KRALIK (tenderly):
Good evening, Miss Novak.

KLARA (in the voice of an ailing but brave person):
Good evening.

KRALIK:
I hope you'll forgive the intrusion, but being in charge of the shop, I feel—well, like the father of our little family—and—anyway, how are you, young lady?

KLARA:
I'm all right, Mr. Kralik. Please sit down.

KRALIK (sits; addressing her in fatherly tones):
You know, Christmas is coming soon, and we'll all miss a good worker like you in the shop. So—you'd better get well!

KLARA:
I'm sure I'll be all right in a day or two.

KRALIK:
—But that doesn't mean you should *neglect* yourself. Now I'm *very serious*—you see, I feel responsible for the whole thing.

KLARA:
You? Oh, *no*, Mr. Kralik. I think I can relieve your mind. It wasn't *your* fault at all. (Tragically.) There's a much *bigger* reason, unfortunately.

KRALIK (worried by this):
Don't you think you should call a doctor?

KLARA:
Oh, I don't need a *doctor.* My trouble is what one might call psychological . . . (Bravely.) Well, it's my personal problem—and I'll come out of it.

KRALIK:
I'm so sorry. It's really a shame that you have to go through all this. But if it's only psychological—

KLARA (with scorn):
Only psychological! (Again the Klara of the love letters.) Mr. Kralik, it's true we're in the same room—but we're not on the same planet.

KRALIK (with critical appreciation):
Miss Novak, although I'm the victim of your remark, I must admire your exquisite way of expressing yourself. You certainly know how to put a man in his planet.

MED. SHOT   WHOLE ROOM
The grandmother opens the door.

GRANDMOTHER:
Aunt Anna has something for you.

KLARA (instantly alive; impatient):
She has? . . . Well, why doesn't she come in? *Come in, Aunt Anna!* (As Aunt Anna comes in with a letter and the postbox key; almost grabbing letter and key from her hand.) This is Mr. Kralik, of Matuschek and Company. This is my aunt Anna.

KRALIK:
Glad to meet you.

AUNT ANNA:
How do you do?

GRANDMOTHER (from the doorway):
I hope it's good news.

KLARA (wild to get at the letter; dismissing them):
I'll tell you later . . . (The two women go.)

CLOSE SHOT   KLARA AND KRALIK

KLARA (giving Kralik a hint):
Well, Mr. Kralik, it certainly was kind of you to drop in, but I don't want to spoil your evening . . .

KRALIK (stalling; dying to see the effect of his letter):
Oh, no, I have lots of time. Go right ahead—read your letter. Pay no attention to me.

KLARA (she cannot spare another second):
If you don't mind?

KRALIK:
Oh, no. Certainly not.

Camera pans with him as he goes to the window, watching her sidewise, not wanting to miss her change to happiness.

CLOSE-UP   KLARA IN BED

She studies the envelope, tantalizing herself by delaying what has to be great news.

INSERT   ENVELOPE

It is addressed to "Dear Friend, Postbox 237" and marked "Special Delivery Rush."

CLOSE-UP   KLARA

She reads the letter, scanning, turning pages swiftly. Her expression escalates to bliss.

CLOSE-UP   KRALIK WATCHING HER

CLOSE-UP   KLARA

She has the gist of the letter. Her face is bright with tears of joy.

MED. SHOT   KLARA AND KRALIK

Kralik comes nearer the bed. Camera moves to a close shot.

KRALIK:

Good news?

KLARA (vibrant, full of bounce):

Very good news. Mr. Kralik, I'm sure I'll be back to the shop tomorrow, and I can promise you I'll be on my toes. I'll sell more goods than I ever sold before!

KRALIK:

There's certainly a big change in you. It's amazing what one letter can do.

KLARA (with playful reprimand):

You know, if I weren't feeling so wonderful right now, I'd be very sore at you.

KRALIK:

At *me*? Why?

KLARA:

You really spoiled my date last night. I wasn't so wrong when I asked you not to sit down at my table. You see, this gentleman came to the cafe, looked into the window, saw us together—and he *misunderstood*.

KRALIK:

You mean he thought you and I were—*friends*?

KLARA:

He *must* have. (She picks up the letter, finds the place.) "Tell me,
and be frank—I think you owe it to me. Who is this very attractive
young man?" (Kralik looks both shy and smug.) "He's just the type
women fall for and—" (She can't control her amusement any
longer and bursts into giggles.) Ha, ha, ha—!

Kralik is dismayed by the unmistakable meaning of the giggles: how
absurd for anyone to consider *him* attractive.

KRALIK (echoing her laughter feebly):

Ha, ha, ha—I'm sorry I caused you so much trouble.

KLARA:

Well, I'll straighten *that* out. (Coquettishly.) Let him *be* a little jealous! Won't hurt him!

KRALIK (just a bit irritated):

Doesn't seem to be much of a man, this friend of yours. He walks
away. Afraid to come to a table because another man sits there!

KLARA (explaining as to a child):

Mr. Kralik, he was not afraid, I can assure you! He's *tactful*, he's
sensitive. He's not the kind of man—who would sit at a table *unin-
vited* . . . It's difficult to explain a man like him to a man like you.
(Rising to heights of eloquence.) Where you would say *black*, he
would say *white*. Where you would say *ugly*, he says *beautiful*. And
where you would say *old maid*, he says . . . (She picks up the letter.) "Eyes that sparkle with fire and mystery" . . . (she mumbles
a few lines) "vivacious" . . . (mumbling a few more lines) "fasci-
nating" . . . (Embarrassed at the compliments to herself, she
laughs.) Ha, ha, ha, I make him think of *gypsy music* . . .

Kralik now is fully enjoying the effects of his letter.

KLARA:

Speaking of gypsy music—we're still having some difficulty selling
those "Otchi Tchornya" boxes, aren't we?

KRALIK:

Well, that doesn't matter.

KLARA:

Mr. Kralik, consider one box definitely sold. I just got an inspiration. I'm going to give it to my friend for Christmas!

KRALIK (terrified):

Miss Novak, you're taking an awful chance. Look—why don't you give him a wallet? A wallet is a practical thing—and we have those new imported pigskins. He'll be crazy about them—any man would.

KLARA:

No, no, not interested.

KRALIK:

I'll make you a special price.

KLARA:

No, I'm sorry.

KRALIK (this is a matter of life or death):

A wallet is not only practical—it's romantic. On one side he carries your last letter. On the other side, your picture. And when he opens it, he finds *you*—and that's all the music he wants.

KLARA (seeing a new Kralik):

Why, Mr. Kralik, you surprise me! That's very well expressed. Yes, I must admit—that's very nice. (Kralik swells up.) But just the same, he's going to get the cigarette box. (Kralik swells down.)

KRALIK:

Well, I suppose there's nothing left for me to say—except—that I wish you a very merry Christmas—both of you.

KLARA (happily):

Thank you!

KRALIK (as they shake hands):

Good night, Miss Novak.

KLARA:

Good night, Mr. Kralik. (Kralik turns and goes.)

FADE OUT

SEQUENCE F

FADE IN

EXT STREET   MED. SHOT IN FRONT OF SHOP

It is morning on the twenty-fourth of December—Christmas Eve. The snow is beginning to melt. Rudy, the new errand boy, is piling packages into the box on his bicycle. He is seventeen, taller than Pepi, also more naive. Pepi comes out of the shop. He is a clerk to the hilt. A handkerchief flares out of his pocket; a pencil is jauntily behind his ear. Camera moves to a close shot of the two.

PEPI (completely the boss):
> Rudy!

RUDY (respectfully):
> Yes, Mr. Katona?

PEPI:
> You know what time it is?

RUDY:
> A few minutes after eight.

PEPI:
> And you're still here?

RUDY:
> Well, I—

PEPI:
> Don't contradict me—just listen!

RUDY:
> Yes, Mr. Katona.

PEPI:
> You have to be faster, especially on a day like this. It's Christmas Eve, young man. Am I asking too much?

RUDY:
> No, Mr. Katona. (Pepi goes quickly back into the shop.)

INT. SHOP   MED. SHOT
Pepi enters. Everybody is going through the daily morning routine. Klara is not there. Kralik emerges from the office. In high spirits, he addresses them.

KRALIK:
> I have great news for you. I've just talked to the hospital. Mr. Matuschek is much better.

All come toward Kralik, delighted. Camera moves up to a close shot of the group.

PIROVITCH:
> Well! Can we visit him?

FLORA:

Let's get together and buy him a nice Christmas present.

ILONA:

I have a suggestion—let's get him a cute little Christmas tree for his hospital room.

KRALIK (with the larger vision of a boss):

That's all very nice. But the biggest Christmas present you can give him tonight is an empty shop without a thing in it—but money in the cash register! Now, boys and girls, let's make this the biggest Christmas Eve in the history of Matuschek and Company! (Looking around.) Where's Klara? (He goes toward the rear.) Klara! Miss Novak!

KLARA (emerging from the locker room):

Coming! . . . Yes, Mr. Kralik—what is it?

CLOSE SHOT   BOTH

Klara approaches him eagerly, thinking he has something important for her to do.

KRALIK (forgetting business; gently):

How are you today?

KLARA (perplexed):

Fine!

KRALIK:

Good! . . . Now, look here, we're expecting a terrific business to-day—it's going to be very tough . . . But don't overdo it!

Camera pans with him as he goes with a busy air into the office, closing the office door behind him.

MED. CLOSE   KLARA

She is somewhat confused by Kralik's solicitude. She turns toward the counter and starts to prepare for the day. Pirovitch joins her. As he helps her:

PIROVITCH:

Klara, I wonder if I could ask a little favor of you.

KLARA:

With pleasure, Mr. Pirovitch.

248

PIROVITCH:

I wanted to buy one of those "Otchi Tchornya" boxes—and Kralik tells me you took the only one that really works.

KLARA:

That's right—I bought it for my friend.

PIROVITCH (cryptically):

Oh. Ah-ha.

KLARA (proudly):

Yes, he's coming tonight. We're celebrating Christmas Eve . . . Mr. Pirovitch, can you keep a secret?

PIROVITCH:

On my word of honor.

KLARA:

I might come back Monday with a ring on my finger. Maybe . . . You never know.

PIROVITCH (acting thrilled):

Well, Klara!

KLARA (complacently):

Um-hum.

PIROVITCH:

That's wonderful! And that's the young man who gets the cigarette box?

KLARA:

Yes.

PIROVITCH:

Then let's drop the whole thing. You see, I thought of giving it to my wife's uncle for Christmas.

KLARA:

Oh, I'm sorry. Can't you get him something else?

PIROVITCH:

Well, it's not so easy. You see, I don't like him—I hate to spend a nickel on him, and yet I must give him a present. So I thought if I *have* to give him a present—at least give him something he won't enjoy. (Klara looks worried.) The box costs two twenty-nine. That's money—but it's worth it to ruin my wife's uncle's Christmas . . .

(Suddenly pretending embarrassment.) Oh, excuse me, Klara! I forgot. You always liked those—

KLARA:
No, no, please, Mr. Pirovitch, speak freely. Tell me—if you were in my place, what would you give him?

PIROVITCH:
Well, it's hard to say.

KLARA:
What do you think of the idea, of—maybe—let's say, a wallet?

PIROVITCH:
A wallet! Klara, that's an inspiration! You mean one of those imported pigskins?

KLARA:
That's what I thought.

PIROVITCH:
You can't miss! If I'd get such a wallet, I'd be the happiest man in the world. On one side— (He takes out his own wallet.) Here, I'll show you: On one side I put my wife's picture, and on the other side my baby. And when I open it, it says, "Papa," and not "Otchi Tchornya."

KLARA (happy that she has averted a catastrophe):
Thanks, Pirovitch; I'll think it over.

She goes. Pirovitch looks after her a moment, then quickly he goes toward the office.

INT. OFFICE   MED. SHOT
Kralik is at the desk. Pirovitch opens the door.

PIROVITCH:
Kralik, you get the wallet! (He disappears; door shuts.)

DISSOLVE TO:

STREET IN FRONT OF SHOP
It is Christmas Eve—late afternoon. Lights are burning. The street is crowded. Peddlers are selling toys and Christmas novelties. As camera moves closer to the shop we see that Matuschek and Company is doing a terrific business.

INT. SHOP
It is packed, seething.

CLOSE SHOT   NEAR ONE OF THE WINDOWS   SHOOTING FROM DIRECTION OF STREET
TOWARD BACK OF SHOP
Pepi approaches the window. He is waiting on a stout, unpleasant-looking woman.
As he bends into the window to take a folding leather frame, he suddenly stops
because he sees:

SHOW WINDOW   SHOOTING FROM INSIDE INTO STREET
Behind the glass is Mr. Matuschek, his winter coat buttoned up, his
face pale. He is smiling, an invalid out for the first time, viewing his
own domain. Others also are looking into the window and, behind
him, are going into and out of the shop.

CLOSE SHOT   MATUSCHEK IN FRONT OF SHOP
He moves closer to the entrance. Our old friend the policeman joins
him.

POLICEMAN:
    Well, Mr. Matuschek! What are you doing here? Since when have
    you been back?

MATUSCHEK:
    I'm *not* here. I'm supposed to be a pretty sick man—that's what
    the doctor tells me. But it's Christmas Eve and—I just couldn't stand
    it anymore. Imagine me, for more than a week in a hospital with-
    out seeing a single customer. The only piece of leather goods in
    the place was my nurse's handbag—and do you know where she
    got it? Blasek and Company. And then they expect me to get well!
    By the way, did you happen to pass by Blasek's?

POLICEMAN:
    Oh, yes.

MATUSCHEK:
    What kind of business are they doing?

POLICEMAN:
    Pretty busy—but no comparison with this.

MATUSCHEK:
    Good! We're all right, are we?

POLICEMAN:
    Now, Mr. Matuschek—take it easy—don't overdo.

MATUSCHEK:
    Me? Don't worry—I'm no fool. I just wanted to look around and
    see—if the shop is still here. Ha, ha, ha! . . . That's all. And then
    I'll go.

POLICEMAN:
    Well, merry Christmas, Mr. Matuschek.

MATUSCHEK:
    Same to you.

They shake hands. As the policeman leaves, we hear two women behind Matuschek at the window.

FIRST WOMAN:
    You think Eric would like that briefcase? (Matuschek turns around
    and listens.)

SECOND WOMAN:
    Well, I don't know—I'm not so sure.

MATUSCHEK (pretending to be a stranger):
    Pardon me, I can't see very well without my glasses. Can you tell
    me how much that briefcase is?

FIRST WOMAN:
    Twenty-four fifty.

MATUSCHEK:
    Twenty-four fifty! You certainly get exceptional values here. I won-
    der how Matuschek and Company does it.

SECOND WOMAN (amused):
    Well, if you don't know, Mr. Matuschek—who should?

They depart. Matuschek looks after them, dumbfounded.

MED. SHOT   INT. SHOP
Cashier's booth in foreground. Matuschek, *sans* topcoat and hat, is
happy and healthy. The shop looks as it should after a terrifically busy
day. The employees are grouped around Flora, who is totaling the re-
ceipts. Great suspense.

CLOSE SHOT ON THE GROUP

MATUSCHEK:
Well, how much is it?

FLORA:
Nine thousand, six hundred fifty-four—and seventy-five. (The result is received triumphantly.)

MATUSCHEK (making a speech):
My friends—that's the biggest day since twenty-eight. You should be very proud. And I want to thank you from the bottom of my heart. (They listen with feeling and devotion.) I walked in here a sick man two hours ago. But you, Kralik, and you, Pirovitch, you are the best doctors. And you, Klara, and Flora, and Ilona—you are wonderful nurses. (Pepi pushes himself a little forward.) And, Pepi— (Pats him on the shoulder.) You know how I feel about you.

PEPI:
Yes, sir.

MATUSCHEK (returning to his speech):
When I got that little Christmas tree you all sent this morning, I was deeply moved. I read your little note over and over. I'm glad to know you missed me and hoped I would come back home again. You're right—this is my home. This is where I really spent my life. One makes acquaintances, one has relations—nephews, cousins—

PEPI (interrupting with comment):
No good!

MATUSCHEK:
Well, Pepi, I wouldn't go that far . . . What I want to say is this: Only too seldom one realizes that the people one works with are one's real friends. Well, there's no Christmas without a bonus. Am I right? (Everybody gets a little excited—particularly Pirovitch. Matuschek takes a stack of envelopes from his pocket. Handing them out.) Kralik . . .

KRALIK:
Thank you, Mr. Matuschek.

During this, Pirovitch gets more and more uneasy as his name doesn't come up.

MATUSCHEK:
> Klara . . .

KLARA (thrilled at getting a bonus at all):
> Oh! Mr. Matuschek!

MATUSCHEK:
> Pepi . . .

PEPI:
> Yes, sir, thank you, sir.

MATUSCHEK:
> Flora . . .

Flora, tears in her eyes, can't answer as she takes the envelope.

MATUSCHEK:
> Ilona . . .

ILONA:
> Thank you.

MATUSCHEK (to Pirovitch, who by now is sure there is no bonus for him):
> And, Pirovitch . . . there were a few times when I called you names. But when you see the bonus, you'll know I didn't mean it.

PIROVITCH (overwhelmed):
> Thank you, Mr. Matuschek!

MATUSCHEK:
> Well, that's about all. (Suddenly he realizes he has completely forgotten Rudy, who stands gawky and wistful.) Oh—what's your name?

RUDY:
> Rudy.

PEPI (boosting Rudy to the boss):
> Good boy!

Matuschek takes a bill from his wallet and hands it to Rudy.

RUDY (dazed at the size of the bill):
Thank you, Mr. Matuschek!

CLOSE SHOT   RUDY AND PEPI
Before Rudy has a chance to put it in his pocket, Pepi snatches the bill, has a look.

PEPI (returning it; *sotto voce*):
Too much.

MED. SHOT   THE WHOLE GROUP

MATUSCHEK:
Now I want you all to go home and have a very merry Christmas.

EVERYBODY:
Thank you, Mr. Matuschek. Merry Christmas!

MATUSCHEK (as most of them start for the locker room):
Well, Kralik . . . Nine, six, five, four, and seventy-five . . . Wonderful, wonderful! (To Flora, who hands him his hat, topcoat, and cane.) Thank you, Flora. (As Flora goes and Kralik helps him into coat.) Well, I think I'll have a little dinner, celebrate Christmas. Tell me, Kralik, have you ever eaten at Biro's?

KRALIK:
No, I'm afraid that's over my head.

MATUSCHEK:
Well—Christmas comes only once a year. How about joining me? We'll break a bottle of champagne.

KRALIK (embarrassed):
Mr. Matuschek—there's nothing I would love more—but—

MATUSCHEK (quickly):
You have another engagement.

KRALIK:
Well, I—

MATUSCHEK:
Shh! Not a word! I just wanted to be sure you were not alone. Good night; have a wonderful time. (With great feeling.) Merry Christmas.

KRALIK (as they shake hands):
Same to you, Mr. Matuschek.

Matuschek moves reluctantly toward door. He has no destination. Pirovitch comes along, in hat and overcoat. He is beaming. He opens the door.

PIROVITCH (as they leave together):
Thank you again, Mr. Matuschek. You were right about that bonus!

SHOT   DOOR OUTSIDE
There is a snowy Christmas Eve atmosphere as people all hurry to destinations.

MATUSCHEK (as the two come out):
Well, Pirovitch, I imagine you'll have a nice Christmas party tonight.

PIROVITCH (happily):
I should say so!

MATUSCHEK:
You'll probably have some guests?

PIROVITCH:
Oh, no, Mr. Matuschek. Just my wife, our boy, our little baby, and myself. That's all we want—and we are very happy.

MATUSCHEK:
Well, merry Christmas.

PIROVITCH:
Merry Christmas, Mr. Matuschek. (He goes, leaving Matuschek alone at the door.)

FLORA (coming out, full of Christmas hurry):
Merry Christmas, Mr. Matuschek.

MATUSCHEK:
Merry Christmas, Flora. My regards to your mother.

FLORA:
Thank you, Mr. Matuschek. (She goes. Pepi now comes out in all his swank.)

PEPI:

Still hanging around the shop, eh, Mr. Matuschek? Can't get away from here, huh?

MATUSCHEK:

Well, son, I guess you're going to celebrate Christmas with your father and mother . . . (Hoping against hope.) Or am I wrong?

PEPI (cold-bloodedly):

Yes, Mr. Matuschek . . . See that girl on the corner? I'm her Santa Claus. Good night, Mr. Matuschek. (Pepi goes. Rudy comes out, stops at sight of the boss.)

RUDY:

Mr. Matuschek, I don't know how to thank you for that marvelous present. After all, I'm only here a week.

MATUSCHEK:

That's all right—what was your name?

RUDY:

Rudy.

MATUSCHEK:

Um-hum—how old are you, Rudy?

RUDY:

Seventeen.

MATUSCHEK:

Wonderful age. You have your whole life before you. And it's all up to you, what you make of it.

RUDY:

Yes, sir.

MATUSCHEK:

Now, don't squander that money. Go right home and give it to your mother.

RUDY:

My people don't live here in town.

MATUSCHEK (this may be his chance):

Umm. Is that so? Have you any other relations here?

RUDY:
> No, Mr. Matuschek.

MATUSCHEK:
> You mean you're all by yourself in Budapest on Christmas Eve?

RUDY:
> That's right.

MATUSCHEK (with a bright smile):
> Rudy—do you like chicken noodle soup?

RUDY:
> I certainly do, Mr. Matuschek.

MATUSCHEK:
> And what would you think of roast goose, stuffed with baked apples, and fresh boiled potatoes with butter, and a little bit of red cabbage on the side?

RUDY (his mouth watering):
> I'd love it.

MATUSCHEK:
> And then a cucumber salad with sour cream?

RUDY:
> Oh, Mr. Matuschek!

MATUSCHEK:
> And *then* a double portion of apple strudel with vanilla sauce?

RUDY:
> Sounds wonderful!

MATUSCHEK (his Christmas is saved):
> Well, you're going to have it tonight. Come, Rudy. (He takes Rudy's arm. They go. We hear him calling.) Taxi!

LOCKER ROOM   MED. SHOT
Klara has unwrapped the wallet and is showing it to Ilona who, hat and coat on, is ready to leave.

ILONA:
> That's lovely. I'm sure he'll like it.

KLARA:

I think so, too.

ILONA:

Well, merry Christmas, Klara. And I hope everything turns out just as you want it to.

KLARA:

Thanks, Ilona. Merry Christmas.

They kiss. Ilona goes. Klara moves quickly to a little table, starts wrapping the wallet. Kralik appears, in hat and overcoat.

KLARA:

Oh, I'm sorry to keep you waiting. I'll be through in a second.

KRALIK:

That's all right—no hurry. (Sees the wallet.) Oh.

KLARA (a little embarrassed):

I followed your advice after all.

KRALIK:

Want to see something? (He takes a small jewel case out of his pocket, opens it—a gold locket with stones.)

KLARA (terribly impressed):

Oh, it's beautiful!

KRALIK:

Why don't you try it on? . . . I'd like to see how it looks on a girl. (Klara hesitates. Then she puts it on. Camera pans with both as they go to the mirror.)

KLARA:

Are they real diamonds?

KRALIK:

Pretty near.

KLARA:

Oh, my! . . .

During the following, Klara takes off the locket and returns it to Kralik; they wrap their respective gifts at the table; Kralik helps her into her coat, et cetera.

KLARA:

I didn't know you had a girlfriend.

KRALIK:

Yes—it's probably not easy for you to imagine that somebody should like a man of my type.

KLARA:

Now, Mr. Kralik, don't let's start all over again. It's Christmas, and I'd like to be friends with you—and besides, you're wrong. . . . Do you mind if I tell you something?

KRALIK:

Not at all.

KLARA:

When I started to work here, something very strange happened to me. I got psychologically mixed up.

KRALIK:

You don't say.

KLARA:

Yes, I found myself looking at you again and again. I just couldn't take my eyes off you.

KRALIK (astonished and hopeful):

Oh? . . .

KLARA:

Um-hum. And all the time I was saying to myself: "Klara Novak, what's the *matter* with you? This Kralik is not a particularly attractive man." (Kralik's face drops.) I hope you don't mind.

KRALIK:

Oh, no, no. Not at all.

KLARA:

And now comes the paradox. I caught myself falling for you!

KRALIK (up again):

I can't believe it.

KLARA:

Yes, Mr. Kralik—and very much so!

KRALIK:

You certainly didn't show it.

KLARA:

In those first few weeks—well, I know you won't misconstrue what I'm going to tell you. After all, I'm very happily engaged. At least it looks that way . . .

KRALIK:

Please go ahead.

KLARA:

Well—in those first few weeks—there were moments in the stock room when you could have swept me off my feet.

KRALIK:

Now, *I'm* getting psychologically mixed up.

KLARA:

You see I was a different girl then. I was rather naive. All my knowledge came from books. And at that time I had just read a novel about a glamorous French actress of the Comedie Fran-çaise—that's a theater in France—and when she wanted to rouse a man's interest, she treated him like a dog.

KRALIK:

That's true—you treated me like a dog.

KLARA:

Yes, but instead of licking my hand, you barked. You see, my mistake was I didn't realize that the difference between this glamorous lady and me was . . . that she was with the Comedie Française and I was . . . with Matuschek and Company.

KRALIK (very happy at this news):

Well, that's all forgotten now.

KLARA:

And now you go to your girlfriend and—by the way, is it serious?

KRALIK:

Oh, yes—very.

KLARA (giggling):

We might both be engaged Monday morning!

KRALIK:
> I think we will.

KLARA:
> I don't want you to misunderstand—in *my* case, I just say it *might* happen.

KRALIK:
> As a matter of fact, I can tell you it *will* happen.

KLARA (caught by something in his voice):
> How do you know?

KRALIK (as both are ready to leave the locker room):
> Let's not go into that.

He leaves the room, Klara anxiously behind him. He turns off the light, and they enter the shop.

SHOP   CLOSE SHOT AT STOCK ROOM DOOR
During the following, camera going with them, they move to front of shop; Kralik turns off the main switch and several other lights, picks up odds and ends.

KLARA:
> Mr. Kralik, do you mean you *know?*

KRALIK:
> Well, I might just as well tell you. He came to see me.

KLARA:
> Who?

KRALIK:
> Your fiancé. He came last night. You shouldn't have told him who I am. I spent a very uncomfortable hour. He apparently didn't believe it when you wrote him I meant nothing to you.

KLARA (stunned):
> I can't get it into my head. Coming to see you—it doesn't sound like him at all!

KRALIK:
> Listen, I straightened everything out. Don't you worry. In a little while you'll be Mrs. Popkin.

KLARA (off-guard):
Popkin!

KRALIK:
That's his name, isn't it? That's what he told me.

KLARA (shaken; recovering fast):
Yes, Popkin. That's right. Popkin.

KRALIK:
Nice fellow. I congratulate you.

KLARA (pulling herself together):
Thank you. (Desperately needing to know more.) I think he's a very attractive man—don't you?

KRALIK:
Oh, yes. For his type—I would say—yes.

KLARA:
Would you . . . classify him as a definite type?

KRALIK:
Absolutely. And don't you try to change him. Don't you put him on a diet!

KLARA (frightened; keeping her tone casual):
Would you call him fat?

KRALIK:
I wouldn't. But that's a matter of opinion. Personally, I think that little tummy of his gives him a nice homey quality. And that's what you want in a husband, isn't it?

KLARA (stuck with Popkin):
Yes, that's what I want.

KRALIK (cheerfully):
I thought so. And you're *right*. (Earnestly.) If I were a girl, and I had to choose between a young good-for-nothing with lots of hair and a fine, solid, mature citizen—I'd pick Mathias Popkin every time.

KLARA (realizing that there is no hope for his body):
But he has a fine mind, don't you think? Didn't he impress you as being rather witty?

KRALIK:

Well, he struck me as somewhat depressed—but it's unfair to judge a man when he is out of a job.

KLARA (shocked):

Out of a job! Why, he never told me!

KRALIK:

Shows how sensitive he is. But you have nothing to worry about. At least, he feels you both can live very nicely on your salary.

KLARA (now Popkin's inner quality is crumbling, too):

Did you tell him how much I *make?*

KRALIK:

Well, he's your fiancé, and he asked me. When I told him you make two hundred and fifty a month, he was a little worried. Then I assured him that you're going to get a raise, and he was greatly relieved. And let me tell you, mentioning that *bonus* didn't do you any harm.

KLARA:

That's terrible! I'm outraged! I never dreamed he was materialistic like this! If you read his letters—such ideals—such a lofty point of view! I could quote you passages . . .

KRALIK:

What, for instance?

KLARA (thinks a moment, then quotes):

"To love is to be two and yet one—a man and a—"

KRALIK (completing the quotation):

"And a woman, blended as an angel—Heaven itself!" That's by Victor Hugo. Popkin stole it.

KLARA (heartbroken, sits on an empty box):

I thought I was the inspiration of all those beautiful thoughts—and now I find he was just copying words out of a book! And he probably didn't mean a single one of them!

KRALIK (very sympathetic, sitting beside her):

I'm sorry you feel this way. I hate to think I spoiled your Christmas.

KLARA:

I built up such an *illusion* about him. I thought he was so *perfect*.

KRALIK:

And I had to be the one to destroy it.

KLARA:

That's all right. I—I really ought to thank you. (She gets up.)

KRALIK (getting up, too):

Klara, if I had known in the beginning how you really felt about me, things would have been different. We wouldn't have been fighting all this time. If we did quarrel, it wouldn't have been over handbags and suitcases, but something like—should your grandmother and your aunt live with us or not.

KLARA (wrecked but brave):

It's very sweet of you to try to cheer me up like this, but I think we'd better say good night. You have an engagement—and so have I. And we shouldn't be late. (She gives him her hand.)

KRALIK (taking her hand and holding it):

You know what I wish would happen? When your bell rings at eight thirty tonight and you open the door—instead of Popkin, *I* come in.

KLARA (suffering):

Please—you're only making it more difficult for me.

KRALIK (ardently beginning to embrace her):

And I would say to you, Klara, darling—

KLARA (fighting it):

Please don't!

KRALIK:

Dearest, sweetheart, Klara—I can't stand it any longer. Please get your key. Open postbox two thirty-seven. Take me out of my envelope—and kiss me.

KLARA (struggling):

No, Mr. Kralik, you mustn't—

She suddenly realizes that he knows about the postbox—the exact number. And he has quoted from one of her letters. She stares at him as at a ghost. Kralik takes a carnation out of his pocket and puts it in his buttonhole.

KRALIK (in a trembling voice):
Dear Friend! (She leans back against the counter, looking at him again and again.)

KLARA (trying to get it into her head):
You—Dear Friend?

KRALIK (not too sure of himself):
Are you disappointed?

KLARA:
Psychologically I'm very confused—but personally I don't feel bad at all! . . . Tell me—when you came to the cafe that night, I was pretty rude to you—

KRALIK (dismissing it):
Aw—

KLARA:
Yes, I was. Don't you remember? Why, I called you bowlegged!

KRALIK (laughing it off):
Yes—and I wanted to prove that I wasn't. I was going to go out on the street and pull up my trousers.

KLARA:
Yes . . . Well . . . Would you mind very much if I asked you to pull them up now?

Kralik, knowing he has nothing to fear, steps back and pulls up his trousers to the knees, proving forever that he is not bowlegged. With a sigh of relief, Klara goes to him and they embrace, as we

FADE OUT

THE END

Production Credits

Produced and directed by	Ernst Lubitsch
Screenplay by	Samson Raphaelson
Based on the play	
Illatszertar, by	Miklos Laszlo
Photography by	William Daniels
Art Director	Cedric Gibbons
Associate	Wade B. Rubottom
Set Decorations by	Edwin B. Willis
Edited by	Gene Ruggiero
Music by	Werner R. Heymann
Recording Director	Douglas Shearer
Hairstyles for Miss Sullavan by	Sydney Guilaroff
Assistant Director	Horace Hough

Studio: Metro-Goldwyn-Mayer
Shooting: November 1939; completed in 28 days
Running Time: 97 minutes
New York Premiere: January 25, 1940
Cost: Less than $500,000

Cast

Klara Novak	Margaret Sullavan
Alfred Kralik	James Stewart
Hugo Matuschek	Frank Morgan
Ferencz Vadas	Joseph Schildkraut
Flora	Sara Haden
Pirovitch	Felix Bressart
Pepi Katona	William Tracy
Ilona Novotni	Inez Courtney
Rudy	Charles Smith
Detective	Charles Halton
Doctor	Edwin Maxwell
Aunt Anna	Mabel Colcord
Grandmother	Mary Carr
Woman Customer	Sarah Edwards
Plump Woman	Grace Hayle
Policeman	Charlie Arnt
Woman Customer	Gertrude Simpson
Waiter	William Edmunds
Customers	Renie Riano, Claire Debrey, Ruth Warren, Joan Blair, Mira McKinney

Author's Notes

Lubitsch came to me one day in 1938 as an independent producer. He had broken with Paramount and was going to do *The Shop around the Corner* with private capital. It was a big adventure. His share would be divided: two-thirds to him, one-third to me. I accepted at once. I loved the possibilities in the Hungarian play by Miklos Laszlo as Lubitsch outlined it, and I fantasized a total of millions of dollars, of which at least one million would be mine and for good work. Alas, it all ended with Lubitsch succumbing to the vast resources of M-G-M, where he transposed his independence and made a two-picture deal—our picture starring James Stewart and Margaret Sullavan; *Ninotchka* starring Greta Garbo—and I emerged with a little less than if I had worked at my usual salary.

The assignment was very attractive. Lubitsch had respected the nature of the material, and for the first time there were no "Lubitsch touches"; the scenes were explored in *language*. This once, Lubitsch and I reached back into our own youth, emotion was present, and there was no call for film wizardry. The solid Laszlo opus flowered into a brand new screenplay; it begot the music box and its ramifications, the crusty, scolding, and later touching and sad Frank Morgan, the rambunctious Pepi, the inspired cravenness of Pirovitch, and the scenes between Stewart and Sullavan were all new-born, notably those in the cafe, in her little room, and the last ones in the shop.

On the screen, *Shop around the Corner* glows; it is Lubitsch in top form with actors coming alive as the very stuff of film. The performances—all, without exception—are so extraordinary that one has to think about them to be aware of them. We are caught in a tangle of real people—and our delight flows along with them, uninterrupted by audience wonder. But stop and contemplate the lanky, drawling young American playing a Hungarian clerk so flawlessly that no one seems to realize it is one of the great performances in cinema history. If you saw the picture ten times, and studied it, you would get a glimmer of the fine sense of detail, the capacity for controlled artistry that resides in Stewart and that Lubitsch delivered to us all. Similarly at their supreme best are Margaret Sullavan, Frank Morgan, Joseph Schildkraut, and every other actor in the film, including the new errand boy.

There are several added bits on the screen that I cannot account for and that make me shudder a little. Like the business of Pirovitch scuttling out of sight when the boss calls for "an honest opinion." It is repeated too often, "milked," and even the cue demand for an honest opinion becomes forced. Thus, and for one or two other added bits that may catch a finicky reader's eye, here or in the other two scripts, I must ease any impression of Lubitsch's infallibility I may have given elsewhere.

An oddity in this script and in *Heaven Can Wait* is that laughter is often spelled out as actual dialogue, thus: "ha-ha-ha!" or "tee-hee!" That is not my style nor could it have been Lubitsch's. Some script girl during a rehearsal, duty-bound to record every utterance, may have done this. I accept the anonymous contribution. Let it be.

Heaven Can Wait

Heaven Can Wait

FADE IN ON TITLE:

> As Henry Van Cleve's soul passed over the great divide, he realized that it was extremely unlikely that the next stop would be Heaven, and so, philosophically, he presented himself where quite a few people had often told him to go.

FADE IN

FRONT OF SWANK NEW YORK FUNERAL PARLOR   LONG SHOT   EARLY AFTERNOON LIGHT DRIZZLING RAIN

A small crowd has gathered. Limousines draw up. We hear organ music from inside. Camera moves up to the doors.

> DISSOLVE

INSERT   A PAGE IN NEW YORK TIMES

A large picture of a charming old gentleman, about seventy, dressed in the conservative style of a rich old family. The caption reads: HENRY VAN CLEVE FUNERAL HELD TODAY.

> DISSOLVE

HIS EXCELLENCY'S WAITING ROOM   CLOSE SHOT (LEANING AGAINST THE WALL) OF THE DECEASED HENRY VAN CLEVE

dressed exactly as in the insert. He is reading his own obituary in the *Times*.

CLOSE SHOT AT ELEGANT DOOR TO MODERNIST OFFICE

Engraved on the door, we read: His Excellency. Near the door sits a secretary behind a desk. The door opens. An attendant comes. As we pan with the attendant the camera discloses the background, a modern conception in gray and red: empty anterooms and a red-carpeted stairway rising from a long red-carpeted corridor. Coming down the stairs at the attendant's signal is Henry, an old man, elegant in cutaway and striped trousers. He moves solemnly to the door of His Excellency's office and goes in.

INT. EXCELLENCY'S OFFICE   LONG SHOT

Extreme elegance. His Excellency is a large man in striped trousers and black coat, diamond ring on finger, pearl in cravat. As Henry enters,

His Excellency steps from behind the desk and we see that he is limping slightly, owing to a clubfoot. His manner is elaborately courteous.

EXCELLENCY:
How do you do, Mr. Van Cleve?

HENRY:
Good afternoon, Your Excellency. It's very kind of you to receive me.

EXCELLENCY:
Not at all. Please sit down.

HENRY:
Thank you.

CLOSE SHOT   EXCELLENCY AND HENRY AT DESK
Both sit. Camera moves close.

EXCELLENCY:
I hope you will forgive me, but we're so busy down here. Sometimes it looks as if the whole world is coming to Hell . . . Frankly, I haven't had an opportunity to familiarize myself with your case. When did it happen, Mr. Van Cleve?

HENRY:
Tuesday. To be exact, I died at nine thirty-six in the evening.

EXCELLENCY:
I trust you didn't suffer much.

HENRY (as if talking about a charming social affair):
Oh, no, no—not in the least. I had finished my dinner—

EXCELLENCY:
A good one, I hope.

HENRY:
Excellent—I ate everything the doctor forbade. And then—well, to make a long story short, shall we say I fell asleep without realizing it. And when I awakened, there were my relatives, speaking in low tones, saying nothing but the kindest things about me. Then I knew I was dead.

EXCELLENCY:
And your funeral—was it satisfactory?

HENRY:

Well, there was a lot of crying, so I believe everybody had a good time. It would have been an ideal funeral if Mrs. Cooper-Cooper, a friend of the family, hadn't volunteered to sing "The End of a Perfect Day." You see, all my life I have succeeded in avoiding Mrs. Cooper-Cooper's coloratura, and this undoubtedly was her revenge.

EXCELLENCY:

Mr. Van Cleve, I can see that you have a sensitive, cultivated ear.

HENRY:

Thank you.

EXCELLENCY (standing; his voice becomes a little threatening):

Then let me warn you—the music down here is anything but pleasant ‡Beethoven, Bach, and Mozart—you hear *them* only above.‡

HENRY (getting up slowly):

I know . . . ‡It won't be easy not to hear the old masters again.‡ And— (with real feeling; pointing toward Heaven) there are several people up there I would love to see, particularly one—a very dear one. But I haven't a chance.

EXCELLENCY (sympathetic again):

Have you tried?

HENRY:

No, Your Excellency. I have no illusions. I know the life I lived. I know where I belong. I'd like to get it over as quickly as possible.

EXCELLENCY:

Very well. If you meet our requirements, we'll be only too glad to accommodate you. Would you be kind enough to mention, for instance, some outstanding crime you've committed?

HENRY:

Crime—crime . . . Well, I'm afraid I can't think of any. But I can safely say that my whole life has been one continuous misdemeanor.

EXCELLENCY:

My dear Mr. Van Cleve, a passport to Hell is not issued on generalities. (Returns to the desk.) No, I'm afraid you'll have to wait till I have time to study your records.

275

CLOSE SHOT   HENRY
Camera pans with him as he moves toward the desk.

HENRY:
 Your Excellency, if you'll only give me five minutes . . .

Suddenly both men look up; we hear from outside a woman's voice.

MRS. CRAIG'S VOICE:
 Now, see here, I have to see His Excellency, and no office boy's going to stop me!

SHOT   AT DOOR
Mrs. Craig pushes the secretary away and forces herself into the office. She is a woman of sixty, flashily dressed, bejeweled.

MRS. CRAIG:
 I beg your pardon, Your Excellency—

EXCELLENCY:
 Just a moment—

MRS. CRAIG:
 I am Edna Craig.

EXCELLENCY:
 Oh, yes. I have your record here. You'll be taken care of.

MRS. CRAIG (not even the devil can stop her):
 That's exactly what I want to see you about—my record. It just occurred to me there's one little point which would make all the difference in the world. Whatever I did, remember I had a lame sister to take care of. (To Henry.) I guess I'm just a sentimental family girl. (To Excellency.) Really, I don't want to seem rude—but I don't think I belong here.

EXCELLENCY:
 Just a *moment* . . .

MRS. CRAIG:
 Don't misunderstand me; I think it's a charming place. (To Henry.) Isn't it? (Suddenly recognizing him.) Henry Van Cleve!

EXCELLENCY (pleased; this may help classify Henry):
 You know Edna Craig?

HENRY:
 I'm sorry, madame—but I seem to be at a loss.

MRS. CRAIG:

> Henry! Think back—many, many years. The little brownstone house around the corner from the old Waldorf?

HENRY (it all comes at once):

> *Marmaduke Harrison's party!* . . . We were dressed as children . . .

MRS. CRAIG:

> You came as Little Lord Fauntleroy . . .

HENRY:

> And they wheeled you in in a baby carriage—*Little Constantinople!*

MRS. CRAIG:

> That's what they called me!

HENRY:

> And after the party I pushed that baby carriage down Fifth Avenue—

MRS. CRAIG:

> Right up to the desk of the Waldorf.

HENRY:

> And the manager said, "You kiddies can't get a room here—you'd better go home." And we did.

MRS. CRAIG (nostalgically):

> Oh, Henry!

HENRY:

> No girl in New York walked on two more beautiful legs than you. Little Constantinople!

MRS. CRAIG (coquettish to the end):

> Well, Henry, I still walk—and on the same two legs.

HENRY:

> And I'm sure they're still beautiful.

MRS. CRAIG:

> Tee-hee! Tee-hee! I'll let you be the judge, Henry!

CLOSE SHOT   EXCELLENCY

As Mrs. Craig lifts her skirt he leans over desk to see for himself. He does not seem impressed.

INSERT   BUTTON UNDERNEATH DESK
Excellency's hand pushes the button.

SHOT   THE GROUP
A trap door in the floor opens and Mrs. Craig, screaming, disappears in a billow of smoke and hellish sounds. The trap door closes. Henry is startled as he gets his first taste of Hell.

EXCELLENCY (comfortingly):
Those things are better left to memory. But I must say you're beginning to interest me. I think I can spare the time to listen to your story. Sit down, Mr. Van Cleve.

HENRY:
Thank you, Your Excellency. (Camera pans with them as they move to the couch and sit.) Perhaps the best way to tell you the story of my life is to tell you about the women in my life. Let's start with the first woman—my mother . . .

DISSOLVE

A FASHIONABLE NEW YORK FIFTH AVENUE HOME 1872
INT. HENRY'S NURSERY
A typical respectable society lady of the period enters the room, goes to the cradle, and takes baby Henry into her arms, a doting mother.

HENRY'S VOICE:
—a lovely lady, but prejudiced.

CLOSE-UP   BABY AND MOTHER
Mother gives baby adoring smile.

HENRY'S VOICE:
She thought I was wonderful—she was the first woman I ever fooled. Then there was my grandmother—just as prejudiced as my mother.

CLOSE SHOT   AT DOOR
Grandmother enters, joins Mother in adoring the baby.

GRANDMOTHER:
How is the little darling? Let me hold him.

BERTHA:
No, please, Mother Van Cleve—let the baby rest.

GRANDMOTHER:
> You're just jealous, Bertha.

BERTHA (furious):
> I can't stand this any longer! (She puts baby back into cradle. Camera pans with her as she hastens to door.) I'm going to talk to Randolph about this!

GRANDMOTHER (right after her):
> Yes, Randolph! First you take my son away, and now you want to alienate my grandchild!

DISSOLVE

CENTRAL PARK   1874
Nurse is pushing two-year-old Henry in a carriage.

HENRY'S VOICE:
> I was not even two, and I got involved in a triangle. At home, in the presence of the family, I was the only man in my nurse's life. I was her honeybunch, her oogi-woogie-woo. But the minute we got to the park—

Big Irish cop comes along.

COP:
> Hello, Bedelia!

NURSE:
> Well, if it isn't Patrick himself! (They sit on bench, paying no attention to baby. Baby starts crying.) Ah, shut up, you little brat! (Baby cries louder.)

CLOSE SHOT OF CRYING BABY

HENRY'S VOICE:
> No wonder I became a cynic!

DISSOLVE

CLASSROOM   FASHIONABLE BOYS' SCHOOL

HENRY'S VOICE:
> My next lesson came from Miss Chivers . . .

Miss Chivers, ruler in hand, is addressing her pupils. It is now 1880, which makes Henry and the other boys about eight years old. One seat is vacant. Henry is absent.

MISS CHIVERS:

How many times shall I tell you—heads up, chins in! (Door opens; Henry enters, stops.) Henry Van Cleve! Late again! What's your excuse now? (Henry hands her an envelope. She opens it, takes out note, starts to read.)

CLOSE-UP   HENRY

Something must be wrong, or he wouldn't look scared.

CLOSE-UP   MISS CHIVERS   READING

INSERT OF LETTER

On stationery of Henry's father, childish handwriting and misspelling:

Dere Miss Chivers:

My dere little Henry was verry sick so pleese excuse. Thank you for not beeing mean to him.

Yours truly,
Randolph Van Cleve
(Henry's father)

CLOSE SHOT   HENRY AND MISS CHIVERS

MISS CHIVERS:

Did your father write this?

HENRY (promptly takes off his coat, leans over a chair):

I knew I wouldn't get away with it. (He looks up at Miss Chivers, smiling sweetly.)

MISS CHIVERS (smiling back):

Come here, Henry. You may sit down—but never let it happen again!

HENRY (ingratiating smile as he picks up his coat):

Thank you, Miss Chivers! (As he walks to his seat, camera panning with him.)

HENRY'S VOICE:

That made me realize women love men who lean over a chair and say, "I did it."

DISSOLVE

CENTRAL PARK   1881   DAY

Henry is nine years old. Mary, a guileful little girl of nine, is pushing a doll carriage.

HENRY'S VOICE:

Then there was little Mary . . .

Henry catches up with the girl, stops her. A small box is in his hand.

HENRY:
Hello, Mary.

MARY:
Don't talk to me, Henry Van Cleve! You're a bad boy; my mother says I shouldn't talk to bad boys.

HENRY:
I bet you don't know what I have in this box.

MARY:
And I'm not interested, Henry Van Cleve.

HENRY:
Then I won't tell you it's a beetle.

MARY (showing the makings of a gold digger):
A *beetle!* (Henry opens the box. Mary looks.)

HENRY:
You like it?

MARY (a gleam in her eye):
Who doesn't like beetles!

HENRY (grandly):
It's yours.

MARY (accepting the little box):
Thank you—thank you, Henry! (As they walk along, just practicing feminine art, she pretends to reconsider.) I wonder if I should take it, Henry . . .

HENRY:
Well, if you don't want it—

MARY (quickly):
I didn't mean it that way—I was just wondering.

HENRY:
Don't worry, I have another one.

MARY (two gleams in her eye):
Another *beetle!*

HENRY:
Uh-huh. (He takes out of pocket another box, shows her the other beetle.)

Heaven Can Wait

MARY:
Oh, it's beautiful! . . . It looks rather lonely, though . . .

HENRY (beginning to suspect he is a sucker):
You mean you want *this one, too?*

MARY:
Henry Van Cleve! Do you think I'm the kind of girl who would take a boy's last beetle?

HENRY (knowing he is a sucker):
Aw, that's all right—you can have it.

MARY (grabbing the second box):
Oh, *thank* you, Henry! . . . Now if you want to, you can walk with me to the corner.

As they walk along, camera with them:

HENRY'S VOICE:
From that moment on, one thing was clear to me: if you want to win a girl, you have to have lots of beetles.

DISSOLVE

FIFTH AVENUE   NEW YORK   WEALTHY HOMES   1887
What we see on the screen illustrates the following.

HENRY'S VOICE:
I was growing rapidly, and so was New York. Yes, New York was becoming cosmopolitan, and no household was considered fashionable without a French maid. So one day a Fifth Avenue coach stopped at our house, and out of the coach and into my life came Mademoiselle.

SHOT OF COACH IN FRONT OF VAN CLEVE HOME
Mademoiselle steps out. Camera pans with her to entrance of Van Cleve home. She is attractive, twenty-five.

DISSOLVE

LIVING ROOM   VAN CLEVE HOME
Typical large living room of conservative rich family of the period. Flogdell, the butler—portly, sixty—shows Mademoiselle in.

FLOGDELL:
Mrs. Van Cleve will be here shortly.

MADEMOISELLE:
Zank you. (Mademoiselle notices the framed pictures of Mr. Van Cleve on a side table.)

FLOGDELL:
That's Mr. Van Cleve.

MADEMOISELLE (very French):
Oh—*monsieur! Charmant, charmant!*

FLOGDELL (indicating another picture):
This is Mr. Van Cleve's father. He lives here, too.

MADEMOISELLE:
Ah, Grandpa-pa! Sweet, very sweet! . . . And who is zis darling little boy?

FLOGDELL:
That's the young master—and he is not so darling.

MADEMOISELLE:
Bad boy?

FLOGDELL:
Not good.

MADEMOISELLE:
Quelle combina-zion! Sweet Grandpa-pa, charming Pa-pa—and bad boy. Looks like perfect house *pour moi.*

BERTHA ENTERS   FLOGDELL GOES OUT
Bertha is a typical Victorian matron of the period.

MADEMOISELLE:
Bonjour, madame!

BERTHA:
How do you do, mademoiselle. The agency tells me you have just arrived from France, and you are seeking employment in this country.

MADEMOISELLE:
Oui, madame. Like many French girls, I would welcome ze opportunité to intrude American home.

BERTHA:
Oh, your English is too charming! I am sure you don't know exactly what you're saying.

MADEMOISELLE:
> But, Madame be assured I know exactly what I doing.

BERTHA:
> You have references? (Mademoiselle hands references to Bertha.) Oh, they're in French!

MADEMOISELLE:
> Oui—but, madame, believe me, *toutes les références—excellentes!* Here, my last employer, the Baroness Lalotte, wishes me to be such grand success in America zat I never shall have desire to return to France.

BERTHA (trying to be international):
> The French have such a continental way of expressing their gratitude!

MADEMOISELLE:
> And here is reference from ze Duke de Polignac—which Duke write wiz own hands. He considers ze two years I spent in his house ze two most happy years of his life.

BERTHA:
> Oh, he sounds just like a duke! . . . Now, what about your wages?

MADEMOISELLE:
> Wages? Oh, *de l'argent*—money. Maybe in beginning twenty dollar ze month would give satisfac-zion.

BERTHA:
> Twenty dollars a month! For a personal maid—just to take care of my things? My husband wouldn't believe it.

MADEMOISELLE:
> If Monsieur believe twenty dollar too much for me to do sings for Madame, I can do many little sings for Monsieur, too. French maid very versatile.

BERTHA:
> No, I don't think Mr. Van Cleve would like that—he's very well taken care of. I never went higher than fourteen dollars for a personal maid. If I could only justify the difference—let's see . . . Is there anything you could do for Grandmama—no, I don't think so.

MADEMOISELLE:
> But perhaps Grandpa-pa.

Henry, fifteen, still in knee pants, appears in the door.

BERTHA:
Come in, dear. Mademoiselle, this is my little boy.

MADEMOISELLE:
Oh, *bonjour, mon petit!*

HENRY (hardboiled):
Hello.

BERTHA:
Oh, mademoiselle, you must ask him something in French—but not too difficult.

MADEMOISELLE:
Avez-vous bien travaillé aujourd'hui, mon chéri?

HENRY:
Huh?

BERTHA:
That's what I was afraid of! Now be a nice boy and go. I have an idea that I want to discuss with Mademoiselle. (Henry moves off.) A brilliant child, but a little backward in his French. And it just occurred to me—

MADEMOISELLE (getting it):
Oh, madame, it will be pleazure talk only French to little fellow. My whole vocabulaire I make present to your babee. With me in house, in one monz I assure Madame will not recognize own son— for only twenty dollar.

BERTHA (as Henry, who has gone slowly, now reaches door, having overheard):
Of course, that's six dollars more than I ever paid before, but—let's try it. (Henry goes out.)

MADEMOISELLE:
Merci, madame!

BERTHA:
If things work out, you'll find no pleasanter home than ours. I like to think of my servants as part of the family.

MADEMOISELLE:
Merci beaucoup, madame!

BERTHA:
Now suppose you start tomorrow at seven o'clock?

MADEMOISELLE:
Oui, madame. Tomorrow morning at seven o'clock I will arrive, and I will start immediately to make myself familiar. *Bonjour, madame.*

BERTHA:
Good afternoon, mademoiselle. (Mademoiselle goes.)

HALL
Mademoiselle comes from living room. Henry appears in library doorway.

HENRY:
Psst! Hey!

Mademoiselle stops, turns, sees Henry. He pantomimes to come into the library.

LIBRARY
Mademoiselle enters, very sweet.

HENRY (grimly):
You're not going to work here—I'll see to that.

MADEMOISELLE:
What's the matter? Did I make little boy angry?

HENRY:
Now, see here—that's the last time anybody's going to call me little boy.

MADEMOISELLE:
Oh, sorry if I hurt feelings. But Ma-ma—

HENRY:
Yes, Ma-ma—that's the trouble—Ma-ma and Pa-pa and Grandpa-pa and Grandma-ma. It's a conspiracy to keep me in short pants. They think they own me, body and soul.

MADEMOISELLE:
Oh, my understanding for young man is perfect. Your soul is bigger zan your pants. Zis is tragedy—great tragedy!

HENRY:
Yes, but *they* won't see it!

286

MADEMOISELLE:
You need very warm friend—with sympathy. *I* will be!

HENRY (after a moment's pause; with air of great importance):
I bet you couldn't guess in a million years what I have in my pocket.

MADEMOISELLE:
I do not know—but I am sure it is some-sing very bad. Is it?

HENRY (takes out big black cigar):
Here.

MADEMOISELLE (pretending to be overwhelmed):
Oh! You smoke big black cigar?

HENRY:
Sure! I'm going to smoke it any day now.

MADEMOISELLE:
Now we have very bad secret togezzer.

HENRY:
Oh, that's nothing! I can tell you things that would rock Fifth Avenue to its foundations.

MADEMOISELLE:
Oh?

HENRY (crosses over, closes door; comes back):
I'm going to get married!

MADEMOISELLE (genuinely astonished):
You . . . married?

HENRY (throws himself into armchair):
I have to—doggone it!

MADEMOISELLE:
Oh—zis is much worse than cigar! When did disaster take place?

HENRY:
Oh, it all happened pretty suddenly. There's a girl around the corner . . . Oh, well, *you* know . . .

MADEMOISELLE:
But I do *not* know—tell me.

HENRY:

Well, we were walking in the park, and it started raining. We climbed into a policeman's shed . . .

MADEMOISELLE:

And the policeman?

HENRY:

He wasn't there. Well, anyhow, before I knew it, I lost my head. I don't know what got into me—I took her into my arms, and then—

MADEMOISELLE:

And zen?

HENRY:

I kissed her. I may just as well face the consequences.

MADEMOISELLE (controlling her laughter):

Excuse my asking question. Zis might sound very childish to grownup young man, but did you ever consider idea of *not* marrying girl?

HENRY:

It's out of the question. It would destroy me socially. I could never go to Harvard. Why, when my father kissed my mother, she knew what he meant, and he knew she knew it.

MADEMOISELLE (sitting on arm of the chair):

I have good news for you, *mon chéri* . . . In your Pa-pa's time, Pa-pa kiss Ma-ma and then marry. But zis is 1887—time of bicycle—ze typewriter has arrive—soon everybody speak over telephone. And people have new idea of value of kiss: what was bad yesterday is lot of fun today. There is wonderful saying now in France: *"Les baisers sont comme des bonbons qu'on mange parce qu'ils sont délicieux."* Zis mean: "Kiss is like candy. You eat candy only for ze beautiful taste—and zis is enough reason to eat candy."

HENRY (getting up; intrigued):

Do you think they know that in America, too?

MADEMOISELLE (getting up):

Certainement! Today all American best home have French maids—tomorrow all American home have French ideas.

HENRY (slowly):

You mean I can kiss a girl once . . .

MADEMOISELLE:
Ten times—twenty times—and no obliga-zion!

HENRY:
Now, listen. Are you telling the truth or just trying to keep your job?

MADEMOISELLE:
I swear by ze extra six dollar I get from Madame!

HENRY:
Gosh! This is a wonderful age I'm living in!

MADEMOISELLE:
Oui! So you don't have to worry about little girl.

HENRY:
Oh, I've forgotten her already! . . . . I guess I'm pretty blasé. (Gives a little laugh.) Listen, Frenchy—

MADEMOISELLE (charmingly):
What is it, my friend?

HENRY:
If that's how things are in 1887, what do you think is going to happen in 1888?

MADEMOISELLE:
Ahhh—we make zat ze subject of ze first French lesson . . . *Au revoir, monsieur!*

Mademoiselle goes. Henry stands looking after her for a moment, then in great excitement hastens to

LIVING ROOM
Henry enters in great spirits. Bertha is busy at writing table.

HENRY:
Mother— Mother!

BERTHA (without looking up):
Yes, my baby?

HENRY:
That girl is worth the extra six dollars! (He goes quickly out as his startled mother looks after him.)

FADE OUT

FADE IN

NEW YORK STREET

A few weeks later. Around the corner comes Albert, Henry's cousin, a correct young man of fifteen. Camera precedes him as he walks toward Brentano's bookshop.

HENRY'S VOICE:

> The pride of all the Van Cleves was my cousin Albert. He was the fulfillment of a parent's dream. Always the highest in his class— never had he thrown pebbles at a window—or put a mouse in his teacher's bustle. His ears were always clean. This I think will give you a rough idea of Albert.

BRENTANO'S BOOKSHOP

Albert enters, goes to a counter.

CLERK (elderly, mild):

> Good afternoon, young man.

ALBERT (precise in diction):

> Good afternoon.

CLERK:

> What can I do for you?

ALBERT:

> I have an interesting problem. You see, tomorrow is my cousin's birthday.

CLERK:

> How old will he be?

ALBERT:

> Fifteen.

CLERK:

> Oh, we have some wonderful books for young men of that age.

ALBERT (like a schoolteacher):

> Now, you mustn't jump to conclusions. You see, while my cousin is fifteen, he has the mentality, I would say, of a boy of—well, let's be generous and say fourteen.

CLERK:

> Well, how about *The Flamingo Feather*—just published. Or *Tom the Bootblack*.

ALBERT:

> No, no—nothing trashy. It must have educational ingredients, yet it must not overtax the mind of my cousin. So, you see, we have a problem.

CLERK (annoyed):

> May I ask how old you are, young man?

ALBERT:
> That's a question which should not be answered unless the questioner states the nature of his interest. On the one hand, the questioner might have merely a superficial curiosity which confines itself to calendar years. On the other hand—

CLERK (he has had enough):
> Never mind—sorry I brought it up. I'll get you something.

> DISSOLVE

VAN CLEVE LIVING ROOM
Camera moves to a table on which birthday presents are laid out. A bicycle is leaning against the table.

HENRY'S VOICE:
> And I'll never forget the morning of my fifteenth birthday. The presents were waiting for me in the living room.

STAIRCASE
Henry's father, Randolph, a respectable specimen of the upper class, runs excitedly down the stairs.

HENRY'S VOICE:
> But suddenly Father came running down the stairs, excited and breathless.

RANDOLPH:
> Flogdell, Flogdell!

FLOGDELL (entering):
> Yes, Mr. Van Cleve.

RANDOLPH:
> Tell Robinson to go immediately and get Dr. Macintosh. Our little Henry is ill.

FLOGDELL:
> Yes, sir.

Camera pans on Randolph. As he goes upstairs, Bertha starts down and they meet.

BERTHA:
> Oh, my poor baby. The boy is acting so strangely, Randolph!

RANDOLPH (arms around her):
> Now, now, Bertha. We must keep a stiff upper lip.

BERTHA:

Oh, Randolph, he's talking all the time—as if he were in a delirium.

RANDOLPH:

What does the boy seem to be saying?

BERTHA:

If I only knew, Randolph! He's talking French—nothing but French.

RANDOLPH:

French!

BERTHA:

Oh, Randolph—our child delirious in a foreign language!

RANDOLPH (rising to the occasion):

Now, Bertha, this is an emergency. We must do everything step by step. The next move is to find out what the boy is saying. Flogdell!

LOWER HALL   LITTLE DOORWAY

Flogdell emerges, looks up. Randolph and Bertha are at head of stairs.

FLOGDELL:

Yes, sir.

RANDOLPH:

Ask Mademoiselle to come to Master Henry's room immediately.

FLOGDELL:

Very good, sir . . .

UPPER HALL

Randolph and Bertha proceed to Henry's bedroom.

BERTHA:

Oh, Randolph, I wonder if I overburdened his little mind by insisting on those French lessons.

RANDOLPH (a thinker):

That might be a possibility. You wanted to justify Mademoiselle's salary.

BERTHA:

I know it, I know it! I ruined my boy—for six dollars!

HENRY'S BEDROOM

They enter. Henry in bed asleep. Grandmother at bedside. In the background is Grandfather, a charming old man with a sense of humor. From the beginning he has been skeptical of Henry's sickness.

GRANDMOTHER:
If Grandpa would only let me rub just a *bit of garlic* on his little chest.

GRANDFATHER:
You stay away from that boy with your garlic. That boy's sick enough!

BERTHA (as Henry hiccups; in a panic):
Did you *hear that*, Randolph? Grandma—Grandpa—did you hear that?

GRANDFATHER:
I'm not deaf.

GRANDMOTHER:
The child is poisoned, that's what it is!

BERTHA:
Oh, Randolph, what shall we do—what shall we do?

RANDOLPH (sternly):
There's only one thing to do, Bertha—keep a stiff upper lip.

GRANDMOTHER:
That won't help that poor poisoned boy.

GRANDFATHER (pouring a glass of water from a pitcher):
If I had my way, I know what to do. A big glass of cold water right in that little boy's face—and I think he would start talking English.

GRANDMOTHER (stopping him):
Cold water! Hugo, you barbarian!

BERTHA:
Cold water on my little boy!

RANDOLPH:
Now, Father—please!

Mademoiselle enters. She does not seem to be feeling well herself.

MADEMOISELLE:
Did Madame send for me?

BERTHA:
Our little Henry—

MADEMOISELLE (sees Henry; frightened):
    Is sick?

BERTHA:
    Yes, mademoiselle.

MADEMOISELLE (turns; hurrying out):
    Excuse one moment—be back right away.

UPPER HALL   OUTSIDE HENRY'S BEDROOM
Mademoiselle appears, closes door quickly, lets out a solid hiccup, goes
back into the bedroom.

HENRY'S BEDROOM
Mademoiselle reenters.

MADEMOISELLE:
    Oui, madame?

BERTHA:
    The poor child is asking for something in French. You must help
    us find out what he wants.

MADEMOISELLE:
    Oui, madame.

HENRY
He opens his eyes. Everybody is in suspense. Bertha makes Mademoiselle sit at bedside. When Henry sees Mademoiselle, his face lights up.

RANDOLPH:
    Look—he's smiling!

GRANDMOTHER:
    He's far, far away . . .

BERTHA:
    He seems to be in another world . . .

GRANDMOTHER:
    He's looking at Mademoiselle . . .

BERTHA:
    Yes, yes— I wonder what he sees . . .

CLOSE SHOT   HENRY AND MADEMOISELLE

HENRY (with a faraway smile):
Oh . . . *je suis si malade . . . mon estomac me fait si mal . . .*

WHOLE GROUP

BERTHA:
Is it clear?

RANDOLPH:
Does it make any sense?

MADEMOISELLE (getting up):
His French is absolutely perfect. What beautiful grammar!

RANDOLPH (severely):
Mademoiselle, at the moment we are not concerned with the young man's linguistic accomplishments.

BERTHA:
Randolph, don't be harsh!

RANDOLPH (to Mademoiselle):
I'm sorry if I seem to have lost my temper, but the occasion is a trying one. If you could only tell us what the child is saying, it might help us to meet the situation.

GRANDFATHER (still holding the glass of water):
I say a big glass of cold water right on the child's head.

GRANDMOTHER:
Hugo! Shh!

BERTHA:
Father Van Cleve!

Henry hiccups again; everybody again in suspense. Then Mademoiselle suddenly hiccups; everybody stares at Mademoiselle.

MADEMOISELLE (embarrassed):
Must be contagious disease.

GRANDFATHER (still holding glass of water; to Randolph):
Son, step out with me for a moment.

As Grandfather and Randolph go, Albert enters.

CLOSE SHOT   ALBERT

ALBERT (as he passes the two men):
Good morning, Uncle Randolph—good morning, Grandfather—
(Seeing Henry in bed.) Oh . . . what's going on?

GRANDMOTHER:
Shh!

UPPER HALL   NEAR HENRY'S BEDROOM DOOR
Grandfather and Randolph have come out. During following scene
Grandfather puts glass of water on a table.

GRANDFATHER (losing patience):
Now, Son—you still don't know what's the matter with that boy?

RANDOLPH:
Father, I wouldn't presume to make a diagnosis. After all, I'm not
a man of medicine.

GRANDFATHER:
Randolph, how old are you?

RANDOLPH:
What an odd question, Father. I'm forty-three.

GRANDFATHER:
Well, I think you're old enough to be told the facts of life.

RANDOLPH:
Father, what are you driving at?

GRANDFATHER:
Now, Son, don't look at me with those big wondering eyes. It
breaks my heart, but I have to shatter your illusions. Randolph,
my boy, there is no Santa Claus. And that child of yours—
(Pauses.) Listen, don't you really know what's the matter with
him?

Door opens. Bertha, Grandmother, and Mademoiselle come seething
out.

GRANDMOTHER (to Mademoiselle):
Get out of here!

BERTHA:
You disgraceful creature!

RANDOLPH:
What is it, Bertha?

BERTHA:
Randolph, call the police at once.

GRANDMOTHER:
Yes, let's put her where she belongs!

GRANDFATHER:
Now, quiet, quiet! We don't need the police.

RANDOLPH:
Bertha—Mother—I'd appreciate it if someone would take the trouble to tell me what this is all about.

MADEMOISELLE:
Believe me, monsieur—ze excitement is greatly exaggerate—

BERTHA:
How dare you speak!

GRANDMOTHER:
Have you no shame?

MADEMOISELLE:
Please, Grandpa-pa—

GRANDMOTHER:
Don't you call him Grandpa-pa!

BERTHA:
Don't you dare—you outrageous person!

GRANDFATHER:
Girls, girls—shut up! (To Mademoiselle.) Go ahead—call me Grandpa-pa.

MADEMOISELLE:
Merci, monsieur—merci beaucoup. You are so kind!

GRANDFATHER:
Yes, I am very kind. But you'd better go now and pack your things. And if you're not out of the house in a very short time—I'll come down to your room and *help* you pack.

MADEMOISELLE:
I wish you would, Grandpa-pa!

BERTHA:
Shameless! Shameless!

GRANDMOTHER:
Leave this house—go!

MADEMOISELLE (pausing; giving herself an exit):
Zere is old French saying: If you are thrown out of house, you better resign. Au revoir! (Mademoiselle hiccups and goes downstairs.)

SHOT ON REMAINING GROUP

RANDOLPH:
I *still* would appreciate it if *someone* would tell me what all this has to do with our little Henry!

ALBERT (coming out of the bedroom, turns to Randolph; importantly):
Fortunately, Uncle Randolph, French always being one of my favorite subjects, I was able to understand the incredible conversation between Henry and Mademoiselle. (He gets everyone's instant attention.) I don't know how to begin . . .

GRANDFATHER (fed up):
All right. Henry had a glass of wine. We all know that.

RANDOLPH:
Henry—intoxicated!

ALBERT:
From what I overheard, at or about ten o'clock last night Henry and this foreign young woman slipped out of the house. Before doing this, however, Henry wrongfully took possession of his father's dress clothes, including twenty dollars which Uncle Randolph was negligent enough to leave in his pocket.

BERTHA:
Imagine—they went to Delmonico's!

GRANDFATHER:
Did they have a good time?

GRANDMOTHER:
They drank champagne!

BERTHA:
Our little baby drank champagne!

GRANDFATHER (wanting no more of Albert):
Thank you, Albert, thank you.

ALBERT (unstoppable):
That's not all, Grandfather. It seems, from what I could gather, that Mrs. Asterbrook, of the Asterbrooks, who was sitting at an adjoining table, resented the idea of Henry dropping a nickel into her décolletage and then complaining to the management because no chocolate bar dropped out of Mrs. Asterbrook.

BERTHA (horrified):
Mrs. Asterbrook! How shall I ever face her!

GRANDMOTHER:
What a disgrace!

RANDOLPH:
I'm going to teach that boy a lesson!

GRANDFATHER:
Yes, that's what he deserves . . . throwing nickels around like that! Knowing the Asterbrooks, I can tell you right now we'll never see that nickel again.

RANDOLPH (actually stern):
I've reached my decision—that boy's going to be spanked, and severely!

Randolph strides back into the bedroom. Bertha and Grandmother follow.

BERTHA:
Please, Randolph, don't hurt him—don't hurt him!

GRANDMOTHER:
Yes—he's such a baby!

Henry hiccups from inside as Grandmother closes door.

CLOSE SHOT   ALBERT AND GRANDFATHER IN HALL
Grandfather is disliking Albert more and more.

ALBERT:
Well, I assume there will be no further birthday celebration.

GRANDFATHER:
I'm afraid not.

ALBERT:
   I believe I can utilize this time beneficially, so I'll say goodbye.

GRANDFATHER:
   Goodbye, Albert. You're a real credit to the family.

ALBERT:
   Thank you, Grandfather.

CAMERA PANS WITH ALBERT
as he goes down stairs. When he reaches lower hall, he looks for his hat and schoolbooks. They are on a chair below the railing where Grandfather stands. As Albert is about to pick them up—

UPPER RAILING
Grandfather is leaning over, looking down grimly. Now he hastens to the table, and, like a mischievous boy, takes glass and pours water down over Albert's head.

LOWER HALL   CLOSE-UP OF ALBERT
as water strikes him.

UPPER HALL   CLOSE-UP   GRANDFATHER
He hides behind a chair.

                                                    FADE OUT

FADE IN
LIVING ROOM   ELEVEN YEARS LATER
Furnishings are only slightly altered. Birthday presents again laid out on the table. Randolph, in cutaway, and Bertha, in formal day dress, are pacing nervously up and down. Grandfather sits in chair, background.

HENRY'S VOICE:
   It was a Sunday morning, the day of my twenty-sixth birthday . . .

BERTHA (dolorously):
   Oh, that boy! At least poor grandmother, may her soul rest in peace, has been spared seeing a day like this. Oh, Randolph, where can he be? Where can he be?

RANDOLPH:
   Now, Bertha, I would like to give you some consolation, but all I can say is—chins up!

BERTHA:
Randolph, Randolph, where does the boy get it from?

RANDOLPH:
I give up, Bertha. *I* never gambled in my life. *I* never got entangled with any girl, until I met you.

BERTHA:
Randolph! You call it *entangled?*

RANDOLPH (earnestly):
I mean, you entangled my *heart.*

BERTHA:
Of course, Randolph—we entangled *each other's* hearts.

RANDOLPH:
Believe me, Bertha, I never knew what a musical comedy girl looked like.

BERTHA:
What can he *possibly* derive from their company?

RANDOLPH:
To me they were creatures from another planet.

BERTHA:
Where does the boy *get* it from? Nobody in our family was musical!

RANDOLPH:
To this day I wouldn't know how to find the stage entrance to a theater.

GRANDFATHER (who has had all he can take):
It's always around the back. Up an alleyway. It has a sign over the door—Stage Entrance—you can't miss it!

RANDOLPH:
But I'm not interested, Father—I never was.

BERTHA (with rising emphasis):
Where does he get it from—where does the boy *get* it from?

RANDOLPH (answering):
Father built up the Van Cleve Importing Company from nothing. When Father stopped, I carried on. Dad, you must admit that from the day I left Harvard I earned every dollar I ever spent.

GRANDFATHER:

Then why do you give him money without making him work for it?

RANDOLPH:

I had to save the family name. But what about you? Handing him hundreds of dollars. If I had ever come to you for money, would you have given it to me?

GRANDFATHER:

No.

RANDOLPH (hurt):

But you give it to him. Why, why, why?

GRANDFATHER:

Because I like him.

RANDOLPH (incredulous):

Father, does that mean, by chance, that you didn't like me?

GRANDFATHER:

Son, I love you. Now shut up and leave me alone.

ALBERT

enters briskly. He is now twenty-six and has developed into everything he threatened to become.

ALBERT:

Good morning, Grandfather.

GRANDFATHER:

Good morning, Albert.

ALBERT (bringing in a little present):

Good morning, Uncle Randolph! Good morning, Aunt Bertha!

RANDOLPH AND BERTHA:

Good morning, Albert.

ALBERT:

Just came in to bring a little birthday remembrance for Henry . . . Anything wrong? Isn't he home? . . . (Looks around.) Well, it's eleven o'clock Sunday morning, and if I know my cousin Henry, he's probably still in church. (Laughs.) I mean that humorously.

GRANDFATHER:

Albert, I'm struggling successfully against the gout. I'm waging a terrific battle with my liver. And I'm holding my own against the asthma. But I doubt if I have the strength to survive your jokes! You're a successful lawyer—let it go at that. I love you, Albert.

GROUP SHOT

BERTHA (tactfully to Albert, who has received Grandfather's snub with hurt dignity):
    It was sweet of you to drop in so early, Albert. I hope Henry will be here tonight to thank you.

ALBERT:
    I hope so, too. Otherwise, I'd be in the most embarrassing position so far as my future in-laws are concerned.

BERTHA:
    Oh, we are so eager to meet your fiancée. How does she like New York?

RANDOLPH:
    Yes, is she enjoying herself?

ALBERT:
    Well, she's only been here for two days, and naturally the impression is overwhelming. I took her to the aquarium; then we rode up and down the elevator in the Flatiron Building—and naturally we ended up in Grant's Tomb.

GRANDFATHER:
    Naturally.

BERTHA (again tactfully bridging Grandfather's insult):
    And her parents—?

GRANDFATHER:
    Oh, yes—how does the big Kansas City butcher like New York?

RANDOLPH:
    Father—please!

ALBERT (with dignity unshakable):
    I assume that you are referring to my future father-in-law, who happens to be one of the great meat-packers of our time.

BERTHA:
    Yes, Father Van Cleve. Don't you realize that every piece of beef we eat comes from one of Mr. Strabel's many, many plants?

GRANDFATHER:
Does that include the steak I fought ten rounds with last night?

ALBERT:
Grandfather, you don't seem to have any idea of the importance of Mr. Strabel. He created the most famous character in American advertising—Mabel, the cow.

RANDOLPH:
You've seen her on billboards, Father.

BERTHA:
That big, happy cow smiling at you over the fence—and saying in big letters—how does it go—?

ALBERT (proudly):
To the world my name is Mabel,
Which you'll find on every label.
I am packed by E. F. Strabel,
For the pleasure of your table.

GRANDFATHER:
No cow in its right mind could have said anything like that. Sounds more like Mr. Strabel.

ALBERT (really getting nervous):
Grandfather—please—I beg of you. The family understands your humor, but it's a typical kind of New York humor—

GRANDFATHER:
In other words—it's not for yokels.

Albert is petrified. Flogdell enters.

FLOGDELL:
I beg your pardon—Mr. Henry has just come home. He went directly upstairs.

Flogdell goes. There is a moment's suspense. Then Randolph seems to have reached a decision. He walks out of the room like a warrior going to battle.

LOWER HALLWAY
at door to living room. Camera pans with Randolph as he comes out, goes upstairs into Henry's bedroom, and slams door.

LOWER HALL   CLOSE SHOT

at door to living room. Bertha comes out, agitated about what might be going on upstairs. Albert also comes out.

ALBERT (picking up his hat):
Aunt Bertha, when you see Henry, will you tell him that as a Van Cleve I have a right to demand that he keep the shadow of scandal off our name. You see, my future in-laws are, so to speak, pioneer people—

GRANDFATHER'S VOICE (from living room; clears throat, then):
Packed by E. F. Strabel—for the pleasure of our table. Holy smoke!

ALBERT (instantly stopped):
Goodbye, Aunt Bertha!

Albert rushes out. Camera pans with Bertha as she starts up stairs, then pauses, flurried and polite:

BERTHA:
Goodbye, Albert.

UPPER LANDING   AT HENRY'S BEDROOM DOOR

Randolph comes out. Camera pans as he starts down. He meets Bertha on staircase.

RANDOLPH:
This time I was firm.

BERTHA:
Good, Randolph. What happened?

RANDOLPH:
He asked for a hundred dollars—but I told him I'd let him have only fifty—

BERTHA:
Randolph!

RANDOLPH:
And not right away!

BERTHA (severely):
For the first time in twenty-seven years of marriage, I feel like criticizing you.

RANDOLPH:
Well, what do you want me to do—spank a twenty-six-year-old boy?

BERTHA (resolutely):
No, but at least I expected a verbal lashing.

Still determined, she goes up stairs. Camera pans with her as she enters Henry's room.

HENRY'S BEDROOM
Henry has become a playboy. He is in tails, just taking off his evening cape as Bertha enters. She sternly looks at him. He seems embarrassed. Then he gives her a repentant look, and her severity vanishes.

BERTHA:
Are you all right, my boy?

HENRY:
Yes, Mother.

BERTHA (kissing him):
Many happy returns of this day!

HENRY:
I'm sorry, Mother, if I made you unhappy.

BERTHA (trying to be severe):
Father and Grandfather and I—we're worrying ourselves to death. But you don't give your family a single thought. All that matters to you is having what you call a good time.

HENRY (in a romantic, melancholy mood):
Mother, I went out last night to raise Cain—

BERTHA:
Son, you mustn't talk like that!

HENRY:
Don't worry, Mother, I didn't. I couldn't. I couldn't get her out of my mind.

BERTHA:
Son, you worry me. Are you well?

HENRY:
Mother, when you saw Father the first time, did you feel that unmistakable something . . . an electric spark from your head to your toes that swept over you like a hurricane and lifted you off the ground, but you bounced up again and floated right over treetops?

BERTHA:

Spark! Hurricane! Heaven forbid, I never had such a feeling. Oh, Henry, where do you get it from? Not from me! And your father certainly never had any *spark!*

HENRY:

Mother, all I'm trying to say is—I met a girl yesterday—

BERTHA (relieved; no hurricane):

Oh! . . . Well, I hope she's from a good family.

HENRY:

I don't know—and, frankly, I don't care. (Romantic again.) Mother, if one sees a lovely rose—

BERTHA:

One can be certain she comes from a fine rosebush.

HENRY (gently):

Mother, even if this girl came from a family of buttercups, I wouldn't care.

BERTHA:

Well, what's her name—where does she live?

HENRY:

I wish I knew.

BERTHA (suspiciously):

She isn't one of those musical comedy girls?

HENRY:

No. This time it's entirely different music. It's not hootchy-koot-chy; its not the cancan . . . It's like a waltz by Strauss, like a minuet by Mozart.

BERTHA (helplessly):

Henry, where do you get it from?

HENRY:

From you, Mother. Now, be just. When I was a little boy, you wanted me to believe in fairy tales. And now, when one really happens . . . (He is sitting and draws his mother to his knee.) You remember that story about the young man—I think he was a shepherd—who was walking in the woods—

BERTHA:

Oh, you've been in the country?

HENRY (impassioned):

No, it happened right on Broadway. Suddenly the young man saw a big castle, and out of the window leaned the most beautiful princess. Nothing could stop him! He climbed up the parapet of the castle—

BERTHA:

Henry! You haven't broken into the Waldorf again?

HENRY (giving up):

Mother, darling—let's forget the fairy tale! (Both have risen.)

BERTHA (back to her duty):

Well, it's time you grew up! I came here to scold you, and I'm going to. Look at your cousin Albert—not much older than you and already a corporation lawyer, engaged to a lovely girl of a well-known family. Henry, this may sound severe, but you *must* pull yourself together and settle down.

HENRY (with feeling):

I don't think I'll ever find that girl, Mother, but if I did, *all your troubles would be over*. If she didn't want me to gamble, I wouldn't look at another card. I would stay home every night. Mother, I might even go to work.

BERTHA (finally impressed):

Henry, that's wonderful! I don't know about the girl, but the fact that you have the desire to settle down makes me so happy. For the first time you're beginning to sound like your father.

HENRY:

Well, anyway, Mother, I don't know where she is, so don't expect too much.

BERTHA (putting her arm around him):

Now listen to your mother. Don't worry about that girl. Another girl will come along. I'll look for one myself—how's that?

HENRY:

Fine, fine, Mother.

BERTHA (going strong):

And when *I* find a girl for you, she'll be Miss Right. And do you know *where* we'll find her? In the home of *Mr.* and *Mrs.* Right. Oh, Henry, you're making me so happy! (She kisses him.)

HENRY (starting a new move; sheepishly):
> Mother . . . I've been riding for hours and hours trying to forget this girl . . .

BERTHA:
> Now, child—stop worrying.

HENRY:
> But it was pretty expensive. The cab is still waiting out in front. And the cab driver was so nice to me I promised him—

BERTHA:
> I know—your heart is always bigger than your father's pocketbook. Well—look under your pillow. I put something there last night. (Henry goes to the bed, looks under the pillow, finds several bank notes, takes them, is really touched.)

HENRY (embracing Bertha):
> Mother, sometimes I wonder if you're not spoiling me. (He kisses her.)
>> FADE OUT

FADE IN
LIVING ROOM   VAN CLEVE HOME
Evening of the same day. The Van Cleve tribe is assembled to celebrate a double occasion—Henry's birthday and the introduction of Albert's fiancée. Henry is still upstairs. The guests of honor have not yet arrived. Relatives move in and out from the hall. Randolph and Bertha stand talking to Albert's parents, who look worthy of Albert.

RANDOLPH:
> Well, this is a great day. You must be proud of your Albert.

ALBERT'S FATHER:
> Yes, I think we have a pretty good son.

BERTHA:
> And I hear the Strabel family—

ALBERT'S MOTHER:
> We couldn't ask for anything better for our Albert.

FLOGDELL (at the entrance door, announces):
> Mr. and Mrs. Frabel and Miss Frabel!

Conversation stops. Everybody looks toward the door. Albert enters, then Mr. and Mrs. Strabel, then Martha, who is not clearly visible behind the portly figures of her parents. Mr. and Mrs. Strabel are two representatives of the *nouveau riche* from the cow country.

ALBERT:

Good evening, Grandfather. (Proud and businesslike.) Uncle Randolph—Aunt Bertha. Dear, dear family, it is my privilege and honor to present Mr. and Mrs. E. F. Strabel. And last, but not least—well, here she is! (He takes Martha's hand and brings her forth. Martha, beautiful, creates a most favorable impression.)

GRANDFATHER (as the head of the family; to Mrs. Strabel):

How do you do, madame?

MRS. STRABEL:

How do you do?

GRANDFATHER:

I can't tell you how much I've been looking forward to meeting you. All my life I've wanted to see the wide open spaces. Well, if Mahomet can't go to the mountain, the mountain must—here it is! Welcome, Mrs. Strabel!

MRS. STRABEL (sturdy western stock and somewhat mountainous):

Yes—we're pretty proud of Kansas.

GRANDFATHER:

Naturally. And you, Mr. Strabel—welcome to our family.

STRABEL (even more hefty than his wife):

Mr. Van Cleve, we people from the West don't talk much, but when we say something we mean it: Thank you!

GRANDFATHER:

Thank *you*—for giving me the chance to meet the man who feeds the nation. I hope this is the beginning of a lifelong friendship. (Albert smiles happily.) May you lie as solidly anchored in our hearts as you do in our stomachs.

ALBERT (quickly):

And, Grandfather—this is Martha.

GRANDFATHER (falling for her at sight):

So this is Martha? (Steps close, takes glasses from pocket, looks her over, likes her; complete change of tone.) Well, Martha!

MARTHA (a lovely girl about twenty; shyly):
Yes, Mr. Van Cleve.

GRANDFATHER (correcting her):
Grandpa.

MARTHA:
Yes, Grandpa.

GRANDFATHER (warming up):
If I were fifty years younger, I would take you right away from
that . . . (Albert looks frightened) s-s-splendid young man you're
going to marry—and who is going to make you a wonderful husband. (Embraces her; Albert beams again.) Kiss your grandpa!
(They kiss; whole family almost applauds, and all crowd around
Strabels and Martha. Martha has conquered their hearts.)

HALLWAY   HENRY AND FLOGDELL
Henry comes down, pauses on stairway where he can see the living
room but not be seen. Flogdell is in rear of hall.

HENRY:
Well, I see the mob has assembled.

FLOGDELL:
Yes, sir.

Henry glances into the living room. His expression becomes increasingly sardonic.

HENRY:
Flogdell, is that—is that—?

FLOGDELL (with dignity):
That's Mr. Strabel.

HENRY:
And that spreading chestnut tree under which my grandfather is
standing?

FLOGDELL:
That's Mrs. Strabel.

HENRY:
And where's the lucky girl?

FLOGDELL:

> The young lady standing by your aunt Minetta, with her back to us— She's just turning around . . . (Suddenly Henry's expression changes. He does not believe what he sees. He is speechless.) Charming young lady, if I may say so.

HENRY (very nervous):

> Flogdell, I don't think I can stand this party. Get my hat and coat.

FLOGDELL:

> But, sir—

HENRY:

> My hat and coat! (Flogdell exits toward wardrobe. In same moment, Albert enters from living room.)

ALBERT:

> Oh, there you are! Many happy returns.

HENRY:

> Thank you.

ALBERT:

> Now it's about time for you to come and meet the Strabels. (Flogdell brings Henry's hat and coat, which puzzles Albert.) Where are you going?

HENRY (behaving strangely):

> Out.

ALBERT (sternly):

> I beg you to stay and behave like a Van Cleve just once! The Strabels know it's your birthday, and they want to congratulate you. (Camera pans with him as he hastens to the living room doorway.) Martha! Martha! (Martha appears.)

MARTHA:

> Yes, Albert.

ALBERT (takes her over):

> Dearest, I want you to meet Henry Van Cleve. The cousin whose birthday we're celebrating today.

MARTHA (sees Henry and is just as stunned as Henry was when he saw her; controlling herself):

> Many happy returns, Mr. Van Cleve.

ALBERT (a family man):
"Cousin Henry."

MARTHA (with a forced smile):
Cousin Henry.

HENRY (no smile):
Thank you, Cousin Martha. (There is no doubt that these two have seen each other before.)

ALBERT (proudly):
Well, Henry—here she is! Now I've done my duty, bringing some new blood into the family. It'll be your turn next.

HENRY (grimly):
That's most unlikely.

ALBERT:
Oh, nonsense! All you need is to find the right girl.

HENRY:
That's difficult, Albert. I'm afraid I'll never have your luck.

ALBERT:
Yes—no question about it, I'm lucky. Well, shall we go in? (Calling.) Father Strabel—Father Strabel!

LIVING ROOM
All go to the living room, Albert first.

HENRY (to Martha, lagging behind a little; voice lowered):
Don't be afraid.

MARTHA (voice low; distressed):
I should have told him! It would have been the thing to do.

HENRY:
It shall remain our secret—I promise.

MARTHA:
Thank you!

                                                          DISSOLVE

WANAMAKER'S DEPARTMENT STORE

HENRY'S VOICE:
Yes, we shared a secret—the most innocent secret I ever had. It

313

happened on Saturday morning in Wanamaker's department store . . .

Henry goes toward a telephone booth.

TELEPHONE BOOTHS
Henry goes into one. Its door is open; so is door of adjoining booth, where stands Martha. Henry is about to make his call when he hears Martha's voice.

MARTHA (into telephone):
Mother, I'm at the hairdresser's—they're still doing my hair . . . Just a moment, and I'll ask how long it will be . . . (She covers mouthpiece, faking time out.)

HENRY'S VOICE:
Here was a girl lying to her mother. Naturally, that girl interested me at once.

MARTHA (into telephone):
They say it'll take about fifteen minutes. I'll be home, at the most, in a half hour . . . Don't worry, Mother—goodbye!

She comes out of booth and leaves. Henry follows her. So far he has not been able to see her face.

INT. DEPARTMENT STORE
Martha stops at a counter and appears interested in a handbag. Henry stops at a slight distance. She turns to look at another handbag, and Henry sees her face. He is smitten. Martha goes out of the store. Henry follows.

STREET
Henry follows Martha. She stops in front of Brentano's bookshop, looks around to be sure that she has not been seen, goes in. During this:

HENRY'S VOICE:
Why was this angel lying to her mother? I had to find out. So I followed her. But even if she hadn't lied to her mother, I would have followed her anyway.

BRENTANO'S BOOKSHOP
Martha enters. It is crowded—many customers and clerks. Martha

314

goes to one of the counters in center. Henry enters, quickly puts hat and cane on a chair, and appears on other side of counter, posing as a clerk.

HENRY:
  May I help you, miss?

MARTHA (embarrassed):
  Thank you. I'd like to see . . . (Pause.) Are there no women clerks?

HENRY:
  Unfortunately not. But you might feel a little easier if I mention that I am the one who is usually chosen by the management to handle the more delicate situations. As a matter of fact, they call me the bookworm's Little Mother.

MARTHA (still embarrassed):
  Well, it's—maybe I'd better come some other time.

HENRY:
  Please, miss—the manager is watching, and if he sees me losing a customer, it might cost me my job.

MARTHA:
  Oh, I'm sorry! Naturally, I wouldn't like to deprive you of your livelihood.

HENRY:
  Thank you, thank you! Thank you again and again! I could tell the moment I looked at you that you had a very kind heart.

MARTHA (confused):
  Perhaps I can buy some other book.

HENRY:
  Why *another* book? You must have confidence in your book salesman. Your book salesman is your literary confessor. So please speak freely.

MARTHA:
  Well, the title of the book is—

HENRY (encouragingly):
  Yes?

MARTHA:
  I saw it in the corner of the window between *To Have and to Hold*

and *When Knighthood Was in Flower*. (Henry goes to show window and takes book out.)

INSERT

HOW TO MAKE YOUR HUSBAND HAPPY
by Dr. Blossom Franklin

BOOKSHOP
As Henry brings book over to her. Camera moves up to

CLOSE SHOT ON THE TWO

HENRY (as he gives Martha the book):
I probably should apologize. I imagine I should have called you Madame.

MARTHA:
No—it's still Miss.

HENRY:
But not for long, I presume?

MARTHA:
That's quite right. How much is the book?

HENRY (fishing):
Oh—we'd be only too glad to charge it, if you'll be kind enough to give me your name and address.

MARTHA:
Thank you, but I'd rather pay. How much?

HENRY (stalling):
It's—it's very expensive.

MARTHA:
Oh, that's all right.

HENRY (moving closer, in a low tone):
Now—this is against the interests of Mr. Brentano—but since I am, so to speak, your literary confessor, I must be honest with you. Don't buy this book! You don't need it. I'll tell you something much more appropriate for you—*Leave Your Nest and Fly Away with Me*.

MARTHA (blushing, bewildered):
I might buy that book, too.

HENRY:

Well, it's not in stock right now. But I'd love to discuss the *idea* with you—and if you like it—

MARTHA (pleadingly):

I'm afraid I haven't much time. So, please—will you tell me how much is *How to Make Your Husband Happy*?

HENRY (points to picture on the book jacket):

Look at her!

INSERT

Picture of Dr. Blossom Franklin—a forbidding-looking woman with glasses.

HENRY AND MARTHA

HENRY:

Dr. Blossom Franklin! Now where could a woman like that have learned how to make a husband happy? You certainly don't want any lessons from *her*. You're so charming—so young—so beautiful!

MARTHA (completely upset):

I beg your pardon—you shouldn't say such things!

HENRY (fast on his feet; smooth and soothing):

You see, miss—when selling literature, one gets poetic—and you must forgive me if I take poetic license once in a while.

MARTHA (angrily):

I'd rather not discuss it! And if you don't mind, I'd like to buy *this* book.

HENRY (fervently):

I *do* mind . . . Imagine that I'm the man you're going to marry.

MARTHA:

I couldn't imagine any such thing!

HENRY:

What's the matter with me? You think I'm that terrible?

MARTHA (helplessly):

Please—I just came in here to *buy a book*—that's all!

HENRY:

I understand. But for the sake of discussion, let's say we're getting married. Believe me, I don't want *anybody* to tell you how to make me happy. The greatest gift you could bring me is to be *just as you are—adorable* . . .

MARTHA (helplessly):
All I want is a book—*just one book!*

HENRY (shifting again):
Stubborn, eh?

MARTHA:
What?

HENRY:
Pardon my poetic license.

MARTHA (furious):
If you don't change your attitude, I shall have to complain to your employer!

HENRY (helplessly in love):
I'm not employed here—I'm not a book salesman. I took one look at you, and I followed you into this store. If you had gone into a restaurant, I would have become a waiter. If you had walked into a burning building, I would have become a fireman. If you had stepped into an elevator, I would have stopped it between two floors and we'd have stayed there for the rest of our lives!

Desperate, she runs out of the store. Henry grabs hat and cane and follows her.

STREET   FRONT OF BRENTANO'S
Martha hastens toward the corner. Henry follows, comes up behind her.

HENRY:
Please forgive me—but you can't walk out of my life like that.

MARTHA:
I think your behavior is outrageous—it's mad—and I must insist that you leave me at once!

HENRY:
Never! Never! (They have reached the corner. A policeman comes up.)

POLICEMAN:

Is this man annoying you? Just say the word and I'll take care of him.

HENRY (facing Martha):

Am I annoying you? Tell the officer!

MARTHA (after a slight pause):

No—the gentleman was just saying goodbye . . . Well, goodbye!

HENRY:

Goodbye!

Policeman stands by suspiciously as Martha gets into a cab; cab drives away, Henry looking after.

CLOSE SHOT   CAB

Camera following cab. Martha's head emerges from back, giving Henry a last look. She was not uninterested.

DISSOLVE

HALL   VAN CLEVE HOME

Later the present evening. Through the wide open doorway of the living room we see the whole tribe in rows of chairs, as at a concert, listening to the vocal solo of Mrs. Cooper-Cooper, a not-too-gifted amateur. Martha suddenly emerges, followed by a very nervous Albert. The singing continues on the sound track during this scene. They speak in lowered voices.

MARTHA:

I'm terribly sorry, Albert!

ALBERT:

Dearest, you don't seem to realize who is singing.

MARTHA:

I know—Mrs. Cooper-Cooper.

ALBERT:

If it were just a relative, it wouldn't be half so embarrassing.

MARTHA:

Mr. Cooper-Cooper is one of your most important clients—I haven't forgotten. But what could I do? I had to sneeze.

ALBERT:

You did it right in the middle of her aria—and five times.

MARTHA:

Because I had to *sneeze* five times. Albert, tell me—suppose some-day in the future I have to sneeze . . .

ALBERT (generously):

Then you sneeze! Naturally! Don't you worry! After all, I'm taking you for better or for worse . . . (With anxiety.) Do you think you may have to sneeze again?

MARTHA:

I don't know—I can't guarantee it.

ALBERT (steers her to library; hastily):

Well, then let's not take any chances. Why don't you go into the library and rest awhile and see how things develop? Make yourself comfortable. Read a book. I think I had better go back for the en-core.

MARTHA:

Yes, dear.

He blows her a kiss as she goes into library. He hurries back to living room.

LIBRARY

Martha has entered. She suddenly sees Henry sitting in corner, appar-ently very bored.

HALL   CLOSE SHOT   NEAR LIVING ROOM DOOR

Albert is just about to enter as Mrs. Cooper-Cooper reaches new heights. But he turns and tiptoes back to library door. We think he is going to find Martha and Henry. Instead he reaches for door, which is slightly open, and very carefully closes it.

LIBRARY

Martha stands uncertainly. Henry sits, says nothing. Martha takes a book from a shelf in instinctive self-defense. Henry gets up, goes to her, pulls book away, takes her in his arms, and kisses her. Martha comes out of the kiss, gives Henry a terrified look, and dashes out of the room.

HALLWAY

Camera pans with Martha as she almost runs from library toward living room, where the singing goes on. Before she reaches the living room she suddenly stops, fights a sneeze, then sneezes. The next moment Albert appears in living room doorway, horrified, and motions her to get back to the library. Martha stands an instant, then goes back.

LIBRARY
Henry is pacing up and down. Martha enters.

MARTHA (with determination):
  Cousin Henry—

HENRY:
  Yes, Cousin Martha?

MARTHA:
  You must never do anything like that again!

HENRY (close to her):
  Is that what you came back here to tell me?

MARTHA:
  I think it's outrageous! I hardly know you! Even Albert, my own fiancé, never dared to—

HENRY:
  To kiss you?

MARTHA:
  Of course, he kissed me—why not? After all, we're engaged. But he never kissed me like that.

HENRY (coming closer):
  Like what?

MARTHA:
  Oh, I hate you! I hate you! I don't know why I stay in the same room with you.

HENRY (earnestly, taking a different tack):
  Please forgive me. But can't we be friends—just friends?

MARTHA:
  Never!

HENRY (taking her hand; sensibly):
  Now, look—we're going to be related, aren't we? We're going to see each other—how can we help it?

MARTHA:
> I suppose we can't.

HENRY:
> And when we meet in the future, we don't have to talk about personal things—about you and me. We can talk about something neutral. For instance, Albert.

MARTHA:
> Why not?

HENRY:
> By the way, do you love Albert?

MARTHA (indignantly):
> I'm marrying him, am I not?

HENRY:
> *Are* you?

MARTHA:
> Yes, I *am*.

HENRY:
> No, you're not. You *can't*. You haven't got that book.

MARTHA:
> What book?

HENRY:
> *How to Make Your Husband Happy.*

MARTHA:
> Well, it might interest you to know I went back and bought it.

HENRY:
> Does it tell you how to make a man happy that you don't love?

MARTHA:
> Albert's a fine man! He's good! He has integrity! He's full of high ideals!

HENRY:
> *Do you love him?*

MARTHA (desperately):
> Well, I'm going to make him a fine wife—at least I'll try my best. There'll never be a day in his life that he'll regret having married

me! And if you ask me *one more question* . . . I'm going to leave this room and I'll never come back again—never! (Suddenly she bursts into tears, hurries to the window as if to hide some secret feeling. Henry comes over and puts his arms gently around her.)

HENRY:

I still can't understand—an angel like you—and Albert. It doesn't make sense. Why do you want to marry him?

MARTHA (sobbing):

I've always wanted to live in New York. I don't want to say anything against Kansas, but life on my father's estate—don't misunderstand me, we have all the modern conveniences and luxuries—but you don't know Father and Mother.

HENRY:

Well, I've only just met them—

MARTHA (between sobs):

Don't you think they're sweet?

HENRY:

Oh, very sweet.

MARTHA (still sobbing):

Yes, they are, but it's not very easy to live with them. You see, most of the time they don't talk to each other. And whenever a young man—and there were some very nice ones—

HENRY (holding her closer):

I'm sure of it.

MARTHA (rising to a crescendo of sobs):

If one asked for my hand and my mother said yes, my father said no. And when my father said yes, my mother said no. But Albert came in one of the rare moments when they were both on speaking terms. And if *I* hadn't said yes, who knows when my parents would have been talking to each other again? *I might have spent the rest of my life in Kansas!* Don't misunderstand me—I love Kansas—I just don't feel like *living* there! And besides, I didn't want to be an old maid—not in Kansas!

HENRY (with finality):

Well, you're going to live right here in New York—and you don't have to marry Albert.

MARTHA (staring up at him):
   I don't know what you're talking about.

HENRY:
   Yes, you do! You're going to be married—but not to Albert. And
   yet you won't even have to change the initials on your linens. (By
   now he is kissing her again, and quite thoroughly.)

MARTHA (as they come out of the kiss; repeating dimly):
   I *don't* know what you're talking about.

HENRY:
   You're going to marry *me*.

MARTHA (incoherently):
   We *can't!* How can I marry you? I'm not even *engaged* to you!

HENRY:
   Martha—*do you love me?*

MARTHA:
   I—I—I hardly *know* you!

HENRY (holding her close; ardently):
   You don't need to know anything when you *love*. Love doesn't
   need introductions. You love or you don't love.

MARTHA (coming to herself):
   You're mad! You don't know what you're saying! You must be out
   of your mind!

HENRY:
   Do you love me or don't you?

MARTHA:
   Trying to take away the fiancée of your own cousin! Causing a
   family scandal!

HENRY:
   Do you love me?

MARTHA (to her own surprise):
   Yes! (Tragically.) *Oh, why did you ever come into my life?*

HENRY:
   To make you happy—to hold you in my arms forever.

MARTHA:
I'll never be able to look my father in the face. I'll never be able to go back to Kansas again!

HENRY:
Isn't that *wonderful?* (He kisses her again. She loves it. As they come out of it:)

MARTHA (happily):
I wish I were dead!

HENRY (dynamic):
Look—let's get out! Let's get married immediately—tonight—right away!

MARTHA:
You mean *elope?*

HENRY:
That's what I mean.

MARTHA:
Where would we *go?* I never *did* such a thing before! I feel so helpless—I haven't anything *with* me! Oh, I wish I were dead!

HENRY (surging into reckless and contradictory imagery):
When Romeo and Juliet ran away from home, they didn't stop to say goodbye. When Leander swam the Hellespont to his beloved, he didn't bother with a suitcase. When Tristan falls in love with Isolde, they have to sing for three and a half hours. All I ask *you* to do is hop into a cab with me and drive to the first justice of the peace. *What are we waiting for?* (He gathers her into his arms and carries her out of the room.)

HALLWAY   AN ENCORE IS BEING SUNG
As Henry carries Martha past the open living room doorway, suddenly they are seen by the tribe. Everybody rushes toward the hall. Martha slips out of Henry's arms. Albert comes out. The Strabels come out. Before anyone can speak, Henry picks Martha up again and, a wild man, carries her out through the front door. Flogdell, standing by door, rushes out after them. Family is paralyzed. Finally the dazed Albert stumbles to the door as Flogdell comes back.

ALBERT:
What happened?

FLOGDELL:
They left in a cab. They—they're going to be married.

RELATIVES:
What? *Married!* Not Martha! Not *Henry!* It seems incredible! It's hard to believe! How could they do *such* a *thing!* That *such* a *thing* could happen in *our family!* Why, he just *met* her today!

BERTHA (nearly fainting):
Where does he get it from?

RANDOLPH (trying to save the family honor; to Strabel):
Sir, I'm still too dazed to express myself clearly—but I assure you that the sentiments of our family are with you.

MRS. STRABEL:
If this happened at home, my husband would get on a horse and lasso them back.

STRABEL:
Don't you tell me what I would do! But one thing I *am* going to do—disinherit her! She'll never get another quarter, a dime, a penny!

MRS. STRABEL (mournfully):
We came here from Kansas, a happy family—

STRABEL:
Well, anyway, a family.

MRS. STRABEL:
We loved our Martha.

STRABEL:
Don't mention her name again! If she comes crawling back on her knees, she'll find the door closed. And don't *you* open it!

ALBERT (rising to the occasion):
Please! . . . Dear family—thank you for the efforts you have made to comfort me in my bereavement, but I feel there are others who need even more consolation than I do. Uncle Randolph and Aunt Bertha—you must learn to forget, as the years pass by, that you are the parents of the guilty party. And you, Mr. and Mrs. Strabel, there's very little I can say to sustain you. As for you, Mrs. Cooper-Cooper— (Turns to an unattractive woman.) I offer our deepest apology for the unfortunate interruption of your beautiful *aria*

. . . I would like to say more, but the strain is too much. (Acting the part of a broken man, he returns to the living room, followed by the others, leaving Grandfather and Flogdell.)

GRANDFATHER (intimately):
Flogdell, do you know where they were going?

FLOGDELL:
No, sir.

GRANDFATHER:
Flogdell, we've been together for thirty years, and you've never lied to me. *Do you know where they were going?*

FLOGDELL:
Yes, sir!

GRANDFATHER (getting into action):
Get your hat and coat. Get a cab—tell the driver to go like lightning.

FLOGDELL (starting):
Very well, sir.

GRANDFATHER (a wad of bills in hand):
I think they should have a honeymoon, don't you?

FLOGDELL:
I think so, sir!

GRANDFATHER (giving him the money):
Hurry, hurry! (Flogdell hurries out happily. As Grandfather starts back to the living room he makes up a little poem:)

> She was packed by E. F. Strabel,
> To be served at Albert's table—
> But that Henry changed the label.
> That's poetry!

FADE OUT

FADE IN
On the screen we see a brief documentary sequence going with:

HENRY'S VOICE:
In the next ten years old houses were torn down. New houses rose taller and taller. New York was changing all over. But our marriage lasted just like our four-story brownstone home.

The camera is now in front of the Van Cleve house. It moves to entrance door.

DISSOLVE

HALL   VAN CLEVE'S HOUSE

Ten years later, early morning. Thomas, the new butler, busy in the hall. Grandfather comes downstairs. He has aged considerably but is still spry.

GRANDFATHER (clearing his throat the way old men do):
  Good morning, Flogdell.

THOMAS:
  Good morning, sir.

GRANDFATHER (taking another look):
  Oh, you're a new man, aren't you?

THOMAS:
  Yes, sir. The name is Thomas, sir.

GRANDFATHER:
  How long have you been here?

THOMAS:
  I would say about a year.

GRANDFATHER:
  Oh, yes, yes, yes. (He goes into the dining room, again clearing his throat vigorously.)

UPPER HALLWAY

Jackie appears. He is Henry and Martha's eight-year-old boy, resembling Henry. Schoolbooks under one arm, he loafs in the hall, idly bouncing a ball and whistling. Henry, dressed, comes out of bedroom, motions to Jackie.

HENRY:
  Shh! Jackie!

JACKIE:
  Good morning, Daddy.

HENRY:
  Good morning, Jackie. (As both go downstairs.) You know very well you're not supposed to bounce that ball until your mother is up.

JACKIE (insincerely):
　I'm sorry, Daddy.

HENRY:
　Now, I've told this to you many times—

JACKIE:
　And I'm always sorry, Daddy. Daddy, I bet you'd like to know what I'm going to give you for your birthday.

HENRY:
　I'm dying to know.

JACKIE (holding off):
　It's something to wear.

HENRY:
　Now let me see . . . Is it a tie?

JACKIE:
　I'll give you a hint. It has twenty-two colors in it.

HENRY:
　No tie has that many colors, so it can't be a tie.

JACKIE:
　It can't be, huh? (Laughs.) Now, I'm not saying it *is* a tie. But if it *were* a tie, there wouldn't be any other one like it in the world.

HENRY:
　Oh, I believe that, Jackie. I can hardly wait to find out what it is. (They are now downstairs.)

JACKIE:
　Daddy, how old are you going to be?

HENRY:
　Thirty-six.

JACKIE:
　That's pretty old, isn't it?

HENRY:
　I never thought about it, but I guess it is.

JACKIE:
　Daddy, when you were as old as me, what kind of kid were you?

HENRY:

Well, when my parents said go to bed, I *never* argued about it. I did *all* my schoolwork. I brushed my teeth *every morning* . . .

JACKIE:

Gee, Daddy, I guess you were a wonderful boy.

HENRY:

Well, I suppose I was.

JACKIE (at the door):

Then old Grandpa must be a terrible liar. Goodbye, Daddy!

HENRY (cheerfully):

Goodbye, Jackie! (After Jackie has shut the door.) Where does he get it from? (Goes into dining room.)

DINING ROOM

Grandfather and Bertha at breakfast. Henry enters.

HENRY:

Good morning, Mother.

BERTHA:

Good morning, Henry.

HENRY:

Good morning, Grandfather—how are you feeling? (Grandfather coughs, grunts, clears throat, creating a barbaric noise.) That's fine! (Sits down to breakfast.) Mother, I want you to see this. (Takes bracelet out of pocket.) Do you think Martha will like it?

BERTHA:

Oh, it's beautiful!

HENRY:

After ten years with me, I think she's entitled to it.

BERTHA:

Yes, it'll be ten years on Monday, and you'll be thirty-six. Oh, if your dear father could be here to share this happiness with us! But I always thank Heaven that he lived long enough to see you settle down and become a fine husband, a good father—and a wonderful son.

HENRY:

Well, it's Martha, and only Martha. Mother, I'm the luckiest man in the world.

BERTHA (judiciously):

Yes, she's a fine wife. And she has a good influence on you. But she's pretty lucky herself.

HENRY:

Now, come on—don't be a mother-in-law.

BERTHA (being a mother-in-law):

By the way, isn't she coming down for breakfast?

HENRY:

I didn't go into her room. You know, the opera lasted until after midnight, and she's probably tired. (Thomas enters with telegram, hands it to Henry. Henry reads it, is stunned.)

BERTHA:

Anything serious?

HENRY:

No, nothing. (Grandfather looks at him. He senses something about that telegram. Henry gets up.) Excuse me. I'll be right back. (He leaves quickly.)

HALL

Henry runs upstairs.

MARTHA'S BEDROOM

Henry enters. Room is empty. He looks into dressing room, which is in disorder. Martha must have done some quick packing. He steps back into bedroom and stands completely dazed. Grandfather enters.

GRANDFATHER (sternly):

Where is she? (Henry doesn't answer.) Show me that telegram.

HENRY:

It's just something personal—it has nothing to do with—

GRANDFATHER:

So, you don't trust me anymore? I'm getting too old? (Henry hesitates, then hands over the telegram. Grandfather reads it.)

331

INSERT TELEGRAM

> HENRY VAN CLEVE 921 FIFTH AVE. N.Y.C.
> PLEASE DON'T TRY TO FOLLOW ME. AS SOON AS I HAVE SETTLED
> DOWN I WILL MAKE PLANS ABOUT JACKIE. DON'T LET HIM KNOW
> ANYTHING. WITH YOUR INGENUITY IT WILL BE EASY TO MAKE
> UP A STORY. MARTHA

CLOSE SHOT   GRANDFATHER AND HENRY

GRANDFATHER (deeply moved):
   Henry—you mean we've lost Martha?

HENRY (miserable):
   It's impossible! It's incredible—just doesn't make sense—Martha
   leaving me!

GRANDFATHER:
   What did you do? What happened, Henry?

HENRY:
   I just can't go on living without her. Grandpa, I love Martha. I love
   her more than anything in the world.

GRANDFATHER:
   I didn't ask you that. I asked you what happened.

HENRY:
   I don't know . . . I always thought she was very happy. I don't
   know *what* she's heard. No man is perfect. But running away like
   this! Believe me, I can't see *any* reason for it.

GRANDFATHER:
   If a woman like Martha runs away from her husband, there *must*
   be a reason. (Henry sinks into a chair.) Now, look here, Henry. You
   were the only Van Cleve I really cared about. I loved you; you were
   like me—that's what I thought. You were all the things I wanted to
   be. You did everything I wanted to do, and didn't do . . . And now
   you've let me down.

HENRY (in despair):
   Grandpa, I can't live without her. What am I going to do?

GRANDFATHER:
   That's up to you. But let me tell you one thing: I'm an old man,
   and I might have to go any day; and if you can't make her forgive

332

you, I'll be standing up there— (pointing above) right in the entrance—and if you ever try to climb that ladder, I'll hit you on the head with a baseball bat.

DISSOLVE

TRAIN   SPEEDING ALONG
Shot of landscape indicating a trip from New York to the Middle West.

DISSOLVE

ENTRANCE   STRABEL ESTATE IN KANSAS   A DRIZZLY SUNDAY MORNING
Camera moves down the driveway. In front of Strabel mansion, part of the lawn decoration is a big statue of a cow, and on the bronze pedestal we see, in large engraved letters, MABEL.

DISSOLVE

DINING ROOM OF THE STRABELS
Breakfast time. A long dining table. At one end Strabel, at the other end Mrs. Strabel. Mrs. Strabel is reading the funny papers. They are not on speaking terms.

STRABEL (grouchily):
Jasper! (An aged, courtly Negro servant enters.)

JASPER:
Yessuh.

STRABEL:
Where are the funny papers?

JASPER (stalling, diplomatic):
Why, you see—it's like this, suh—

STRABEL:
Get 'em! And get 'em right now! I want to know what happened to the Katzenjammer Kids!

JASPER:
Yessuh. (Calmly makes what is apparently a familiar trek along the length of the table to Mrs. Strabel.) Good mawnin', Mrs. Strabel.

MRS. STRABEL:
Good morning, Jasper.

JASPER (suave and urbane):
We're havin' bad weathuh today. When I see it pourin' like that, I wonder *where* does it all *come* from—

333

MRS. STRABEL:

You tell Mr. Strabel that he'll get the funny papers when *I'm through*—and not one second sooner.

JASPER (cheerfully):

Yes, *ma'am*, I certainly *will*. 'Scuse me, ma'am. (Trudges back to Strabel.) I just had a *fine* conversation with the missus. She asks you to be kind enough to give the matter a little patience. As soon as she finishes with the Katzenjammer Kids, I think—

STRABEL (exploding):

I came down early this morning to find out if Der Captain got out of that barrel! It's the same every Sunday! Well, I'm not going to stand for it anymore!

MRS. STRABEL (sharply):

Jasper!

JASPER:

'Scuse me, Mr. Strabel. (Journeys back to Mrs. Strabel.) Yes, ma'am?

MRS. STRABEL:

You can tell Mr. Strabel that Der Captain got out of the barrel.

JASPER (rushes back to Strabel):

Boss, I got good news for you. Der Captain's out—ain't that fine? Now I think you can have a few more wheat cakes.

STRABEL (broodingly):

All right. A couple more . . . (As Jasper piles the plate high with wheat cakes.) I don't see how he ever got out of that barrel. Why, that barrel had wooden slats nailed down on the top and the bottom, and there were steel bands all around it, and they put it way out in the middle of the desert. *How could he get out?*

JASPER (soothingly):

Now, you eat them wheat cakes while they're hot. I'll see what I can find out. (Wends his way back to Mrs. Strabel.) Another lamb chop, Mrs. Strabel?

MRS. STRABEL:

I don't mind. (As Jasper serves.) About that barrel. The way he got out of it was: A friendly snake came crawling up—

334

STRABEL (yelling):
> *Don't tell me!* You know it's no good unless I read it by myself! What are you trying to do—ruin my Sunday?

MRS. STRABEL (devastatingly calm):
> Will you tell Mr. Strabel that I was talking to *you?* (Continuing relentlessly.) Now, Jasper, as I was saying, the snake came *crawling along* in the desert. It *wound* itself *around* the barrel, and then— cr-r-runch—

STRABEL (jumps up):
> I can't live in this house any longer! (Before Strabel reaches the door, the Negro maid enters.)

MAID:
> Mr. Strabel—

STRABEL:
> What is it, Daisy?

DAISY:
> There's a gentleman calling. He says he's from New York—a Mr. Van Cleve. (Strabel stops cold, and his wife stiffens in her chair, dropping the newpaper.)

STRABEL:
> Van Cleve?

DAISY:
> That's the gentleman's name—yessuh.

MRS. STRABEL:
> The nerve of him—trying to walk into this house! You tell him to go back where he came from.

DAISY:
> Yes, ma'am.

STRABEL:
> Just a minute, Daisy.

DAISY:
> Yessuh.

STRABEL:
> Maybe *I* want to see Mr. Van Cleve. And if I want to see him, he'll come in. And if I want him to *stay* here—he'll stay *right here . . .*

(Momentous pause. Then:) You tell that man if he's not off these premises in ten seconds, I'll break his neck!

DAISY:

Yessuh—I'll tell him. (Daisy goes. Strabel sits down again.)

STRABEL:

Jasper, dish me some fresh hot cakes.

JASPER:

Yessuh. (As he serves.) 'Scuse me—but I was just wonderin', maybe somethin' done happen to Miss Martha.

STRABEL:

You talk too much, Jasper.

JASPER:

Yessuh.

MRS. STRABEL (taking her turn):

Jasper.

JASPER:

Yes, ma'am?

MRS. STRABEL:

Tell that man to come in.

JASPER:

Yes, *ma'am*. (He is about to go, pauses, looks at Strabel, expecting contrary order.)

STRABEL (apparently won over):

Hurry up!

Jasper leaves. In a few seconds Albert enters. His dignity has increased with the years.

ALBERT:

How do you do!

STRABEL:

Oh, it's the other one!

MRS. STRABEL (crustily):

It's Albert! Hello, Albert.

ALBERT:

How do you do, Mrs. Strabel.

STRABEL (almost hospitable):
Why, we haven't seen each other . . .

ALBERT:
Not since that ill-fated occasion—ten years ago tomorrow.

STRABEL:
Did you have breakfast?

ALBERT:
Yes, thank you.

STRABEL:
Sit down anyway. (As Albert sits.) Got some business in Kansas?

ALBERT:
No, I was on my way to California, but I said to myself, why shouldn't I stop and pay my respects to those charming Strabels?

STRABEL (uncharmingly):
Well, what do you want?

ALBERT:
Oh, nothing—nothing in particular.

STRABEL:
Good.

ALBERT:
Uh, yes—there *is* one bit of news . . . I bet you can't guess whom I met accidentally on the train.

STRABEL (not guessing):
Probably not. How is business in New York?

ALBERT:
Very good . . . Well, I don't want to keep you in suspense any longer. I met your own daughter Martha.

STRABEL:
Don't mention her name in this house!

MRS. STRABEL (right with him):
We don't want to hear anything about her!

ALBERT (up to his neck in dignity; a lawyer building a case):
My dear friends. Speaking as a jurist, may I say that even in our penal code we have wisely provided a system of parole. And I

337

have excellent reason to believe that the party—whose name I naturally will not mention in this house—has amply paid for her mistakes—

STRABEL:
Good!

ALBERT:
And I am sure she would like nothing better than to come back to the paternal nest.

MRS. STRABEL:
So she wants to leave him. And *now* she remembers us!

STRABEL:
No chance, Albert—that's final.

ALBERT (getting up; masterful):
Well, she's waiting in a carriage in front of this very house.

MRS. STRABEL (she and Strabel are on their feet):
Martha?

STRABEL:
Martha—*here?*

ALBERT (triumphantly):
Yes, Mr. and Mrs. Strabel! (A stunned pause.) Shall I bring her in?

STRABEL:
I don't know what Mrs. Strabel thinks—

MRS. STRABEL:
Well, I—

STRABEL:
—and I don't *care*—

MRS. STRABEL:
And *I* don't care what *you* think. She might just as well come in and stay until the rain is over.

STRABEL (sourly):
All right! (Albert goes, the Strabels following him.)

HALLWAY
Albert hastens out through the entrance doorway. The Strabels, with

338

grim slowness, approach. Then Albert opens door and escorts Martha in. The atmosphere is strained.

MARTHA (shyly):
Hello, Father.

STRABEL:
Hello.

MARTHA:
Hello, Mother.

MRS. STRABEL:
Hello, Martha. (Jasper comes in with Martha's suitcase and puts it down.)

JASPER (happily):
Welcome home, Miss Martha!

MARTHA:
Thank you, Jasper.

JASPER:
We all missed you, Miss Martha.

STRABEL:
Get out of here—you talk too much! (Jasper goes.)

ALBERT (displaying tact):
Well, I assume there are things between daughter and parents which are better left to the daughter—and the parents. If you'll excuse me . . . (Goes toward dining room.)

MARTHA AND THE STRABELS   ALL STANDING

MRS. STRABEL:
I guess it was a pretty muddy ride from the station in all that rain.

MARTHA:
Yes, I suppose it was.

MRS. STRABEL:
Do you want some breakfast?

STRABEL:
It's Sunday morning—we have wheat cakes.

MARTHA:
Thank you, Father, but I'm not hungry.

STRABEL (after pause):
Well, the place hasn't changed much, has it?

MARTHA:
No, it looks exactly the same.

STRABEL:
Maybe now you'll appreciate your home.

MRS. STRABEL:
It took you ten years to find out we were right. If you had listened to your mother—

STRABEL:
And your father—things would have been different.

MARTHA (with dignity):
I think I'd better be going.

STRABEL:
Getting touchy, huh? If anybody has a right to be angry, it's me.

MRS. STRABEL:
And me. But we're willing to let bygones be bygones—

STRABEL:
After all, we're not made of stone. And when a daughter comes home and is sorry—

MARTHA:
I'm *not* sorry—and I don't want your forgiveness.

STRABEL:
Then what did you come home for?

MARTHA:
I came because I felt I wanted to see you, but if you expect me to get down on my knees . . .

STRABEL (beginning to soften):
Forget it. You were young—and it was probably all the fault of that—

MARTHA:
Please, Father—I don't want to hear a single unpleasant word about the last ten years—or I'll have to go. (Slight pause.)

MRS. STRABEL (breaking down, takes Martha into her arms):
> Martha! You look so tired.

STRABEL:
> No wonder, after what she—

MRS. STRABEL:
> Can't you keep still? It's all dead and buried, and let's forget it! (To Martha.) Come upstairs, child. You're going to have a nice hot bath, and then you're going to lie down and rest . . . (Her arm is around Martha as they go up. Strabel looks after them; then, blowing his nose and wiping his eyes, he takes Martha's suitcase and follows them up.)

"Home on the Range" is playing on the sound track as we

FADE OUT

FADE IN
LIVING ROOM   STRABEL HOME   EVENING
Same day, after dinner. Mrs. Strabel knitting, Martha trying to read a book, Strabel with the funny papers at last. Albert, with briefcase, is going over legal notes. Fire in fireplace. A family picture. After a few moments of silence:

STRABEL (marveling to himself):
> So he really got out of that barrel. What do you think of that!

Again silence. From behind the rainy window on the outside, suddenly a face appears.

CLOSE SHOT   WINDOW
It is Grandfather Van Cleve, wearing a winter cap, overcoat collar turned up, neck wrapped in heavy scarf. He motions to someone. Henry's face appears. Both look in, unseen by the people in the room. They look first at Martha.

CLOSE-UP   MARTHA   FROM HENRY'S VIEW

CLOSE-UP   HENRY AND GRANDFATHER
Henry is looking longingly at Martha. Grandfather scolds him.

LIVING ROOM   GROUP FROM HENRY'S VIEW
Albert, seated so that he cannot be seen by Henry or Grandfather, now gets up and goes to desk with his papers.

CLOSE-UP   HENRY AND GRANDFATHER
Furious at sight of Albert. They talk to each other excitedly. Suddenly a dog barks, and they scurry out of picture.

LIVING ROOM   MARTHA AND ALBERT AND THE STRABELS
Dog continues barking. Jasper enters.

STRABEL:
> What's all that noise about?

JASPER:
> Yes*suh*. I just talked to Mr. Chuck. He say somebody saw a couple prowlers somewhere on the grounds. May be some of them horse thieves.

STRABEL:
> Tell Chuck to keep after 'em.

JASPER:
> Yes*suh*.

STRABEL:
> And if necessary shoot 'em.

JASPER:
> Yes*suh*. (He goes.)

MARTHA (bored; rising):
> Excuse me—but if you don't mind, I think I'll go upstairs. I'm pretty tired. Good night.

STRABEL:
> Good night, Martha.

MRS. STRABEL:
> Good night, Martha. Breakfast at seven thirty.

MARTHA:
> Yes, Mother . . . Good night, Albert.

HALL
Camera pans with Martha as, without pausing for Albert's response, she goes from living room to foot of staircase.

ALBERT'S VOICE:
> Martha!

ALBERT (quickly joining her; in paternal tones):
Now, Martha. I want you to have a restful night—and why not?
Your troubles are actually over.

MARTHA (sadly):
I suppose you're right.

ALBERT:
I know I am. You paid for your mistakes—and paid dearly.

MARTHA (on edge):
Now, Albert, I don't want anybody to get the impression that I'm
a victim of ten years of misery. Nothing of the kind! On the contrary, I can say there were moments in my marriage which very
few women have been lucky enough to experience.

ALBERT (a lawyer to the hilt):
There were times when you were lifted way up to the sky?

MARTHA:
Yes—way up!

ALBERT:
Only to be dropped way *down* afterward! That's not the purpose of
marriage. Marriage is not a series of thrills. Marriage is a peaceful,
well-balanced adjustment of two right-thinking people.

MARTHA (cowed):
I'm afraid that's only too true! Good night, Albert.

ALBERT (moving in):
And, Martha—there's one other thought I want you to sleep with:
My feelings for you have remained unchanged.

MARTHA (gently):
That's very kind of you, and I'm touched.

ALBERT:
Naturally, I'm not the flashy type like some people. I'd say I'm
rather on the conservative side. If I were, for instance, a suit of
clothes, you would not call me a stylish cut. And I *prefer* it that
way. But I can safely say that I am made of solid material. I am
sewed together carefully, and my lining is good, Martha. Frankly,
I believe I wear well. I'm not too hot in summer; I give protection
in winter . . . Need I say more?

MARTHA:

No, Albert. You've given a complete and accurate description of yourself.

ALBERT (complimented):

Thank you, Martha!

She says good night and goes upstairs, camera with her. As Martha reaches upper landing Jasper approaches.

JASPER (in a low voice):

Miss Martha—'scuse me but that horse thief we was lookin' for—

MARTHA:

Did you catch him?

JASPER:

He's right in your room—waiting for you.

MARTHA:

In my room? You mean . . . (She suddenly gets it.)

JASPER:

Yes, ma'am—that's him! (Martha rushes to her room.)

MARTHA'S ROOM

Henry is pacing up and down. Martha enters. They look at each other for a moment.

HENRY:

Martha—darling—sweetheart! How could you do this to me? Don't you realize what I went through? Running away like that without a word. Can't you imagine what I suffered? (Sinks into a chair; dramatically.) Oh, Martha, Martha!

MARTHA (very cool):

Henry, it won't work anymore.

HENRY (gets up; the jealous husband):

What's Albert doing here?

MARTHA:

I met him by accident—on the train. And he was very nice and—

HENRY:

Accident! You expect me to believe that? Here I am—looking all over the world for my wife—going insane with despair—and where do I find her? Two thousand miles away in a lonely country place with another man!

MARTHA (unmoved):
Henry, it won't work.

HENRY (another shift):
Very well! If it comes to the point where a woman doubts her husband's sincerity, there's nothing more to do. Everything is over. Goodbye, Martha!

MARTHA (serenely):
Goodbye, Henry.

HENRY (goes to door; at door he turns):
Martha, I really mean this—I'm going!

MARTHA:
I know you mean it.

HENRY (tries another approach; goes to chair and sits):
Just give me five minutes to pull myself together, and you'll never see me again—never, never.

MARTHA:
Henry, I know your every move. I know your outraged indignation. I know the poor, weeping little boy. I know the misunderstood, strong, silent man—the worn-out lion who is too proud to explain what happened in the jungle last night.

HENRY (putting it on thick):
So I'm a fake. I'm false. I'm cheap.

MARTHA:
Henry—please!

HENRY:
I brought you nothing but unhappiness . . .

MARTHA:
You know that's not true.

HENRY (shifting again):
So we did have some good times together?

MARTHA:
Some wonderful times.

HENRY:

> Then what do you *want?* What did I *do?* Even a murderer has a
> right to defend himself. You can't— (She is so familiar with this
> routine that she joins him.)

MARTHA AND HENRY TOGETHER:

> Hang a man without evidence!

MARTHA:

> I know!

HENRY (switching again):

> If I only *knew.* What *particular thing* is in your mind? Have you seen
> Aunt Minetta recently?

MARTHA:

> Of course I have.

HENRY:

> Well, now everything is clear! Now, let me tell you—this is some-
> thing I didn't even want to mention; it's so unimportant. When
> she saw me—yes, I was having tea at the Plaza and at the table
> with me was a handsome young woman. But believe me, there
> was *nothing to it.* I would have come to you and told you myself,
> but—

MARTHA:

> But you didn't want to make me uncomfortable—even for one
> second.

HENRY:

> That's right, darling—that's *exactly right.*

MARTHA:

> It won't work, Henry. And besides, Aunt Minetta hasn't said one
> word about you. And as for the beautiful young lady in the
> Plaza—

HENRY:

> Darling, I can easily explain.

MARTHA:

> I *know* you can—you're a master at that.

HENRY (still another squirm; dejectedly):

> All right—I'm fighting a losing battle, I see . . . I *don't* love you. I
> *never* loved you. I love everybody in New York more than you.

MARTHA:

There you go again! (The scene is interrupted by a distant church bell striking twelve. She pauses to listen; it changes her mood.) It's the twenty-fifth of October . . . Many happy returns!

HENRY (going to her; with real feeling):

Thank you, Martha. But it's something much more important than my birthday. It's our anniversary. Ten years ago today I was almost as much in love with you as I am right now.

MARTHA (softly):

It's very difficult for a woman to send her husband away on their tenth anniversary—especially when he speaks as beautifully as you do . . . (Resolutely.) *But I must do it.*

HENRY (apparently surrendering):

All right, darling. I know it's all over. I'm sure you'll find someone else who will really be worthy of you. But can't we pretend—for just one minute? (Takes out of pocket an overwhelmingly expensive bracelet and hands it to Martha.) Happy anniversary! (As she calmly examines the bracelet.) Do you like it?

MARTHA:

I would say it cost at least ten thousand dollars. For that money, it's a very good purchase.

HENRY (this is a ten-thousand-dollar blow):

Martha, how can you talk like that?

MARTHA:

If you had merely forgotten to give me this bracelet, I probably would have been foolish enough to be in your arms right now. But you've no idea of the real mistake you made. The magician played one trick too many. (Goes to night table, opens purse, takes out a bill.) The other day I was having a new photograph made of Jackie and me, and I wanted to have it the right size to fit into your wallet. So I slipped into your room . . . This is what fell out of your wallet. (Hands him bill.)

INSERT OF CARTIER BILL OF THE PERIOD

May 2	1 bracelet delivered	$	500.00
May 21	1 bracelet delivered		10,000.00

MARTHA AND HENRY

MARTHA:

And *I* don't remember having received any bracelet from you on or about May *second*.

HENRY (with a false air of great relief):

Oh—so that's what it's all about! (False laughter.) To think you had to go through all this only because the jeweler made a mistake! That's what the whole thing is—a mistake. I *never bought* this five-hundred-dollar bracelet.

MARTHA:

Has Cartier ever made a mistake on any of our bills before?

HENRY:

Darling, I love you. Do you really believe there is any woman good enough to win me away from you? And if there were such a woman—do you think she'd be only worth a five-hundred-dollar bracelet? (Reaching for telephone.) Martha, I'll make you a bet. If Cartier doesn't admit that the whole thing is a terrible mistake . . .

MARTHA:

Then we won't buy there anymore!

GRANDFATHER (suddenly stepping out from behind a screen):
Henry, it won't work!

MARTHA (hardly believing her eyes):
Grandpa! (She rushes to him; they embrace and kiss.)

GRANDFATHER (tenderly):
Martha—my darling! (Brisk and businesslike.) Now, come on—let's get started! Let's pack!

MARTHA (dazed):
What do you mean?

GRANDFATHER:

Well, naturally, you're going back with us to New York. (To Henry.) What are you standing there for? You're doing a pretty bad job. Come on, sweep her off her feet! Otherwise we'll miss the next train.

HENRY (playing obstinate):
If I can't make her happy, then I don't want her to come back.

GRANDFATHER (recognizing a new approach):
 That's better!

HENRY:
 No, I mean it.

GRANDFATHER:
 That's why it's good.

HENRY:
 Now, Martha, let's face it. You want a divorce?

MARTHA:
 I see no other way. (Grandfather, now having confidence in Henry, begins packing Martha's things.)

HENRY:
 What about Jackie?

MARTHA:
 Naturally, I want him.

HENRY:
 I think you're right. The boy should get away from me.

MARTHA:
 Oh, I didn't mean it that way.

HENRY:
 But I did. I adore that boy; therefore I think he shouldn't be with me.

MARTHA:
 I don't think a child should be deprived of his father.

HENRY:
 Do you want him to turn into another Henry Van Cleve—and on his thirty-sixth birthday make his wife as unhappy as I've made you?

GRANDFATHER (loving what he hears and moving everywhere):
 Now, where are the rest of your things, Martha?

MARTHA (without realizing that she has already made up her mind):
 In the closet, Grandpa.

HENRY (on the right track at last):
 For instance, do you know what little Jackie did the other day?

MARTHA:
What?

HENRY:
He bought ice cream for a little girl.

MARTHA:
What's wrong about that? I think it's charming.

HENRY:
But the girl he bought the ice cream for was not the girl he should have bought it for.

MARTHA (amused and proud of the little rascal):
It wasn't?

HENRY:
No.

MARTHA (beaming):
The little devil!

HENRY:
And when the one little girl found out that the other little girl . . .
Well, that boy got himself into such a mess—!

MARTHA:
Oh, if I could only have been there . . .

HENRY:
Well, you should have seen our little Jackie trying to get out of it.

MARTHA:
Did he?

HENRY:
The little girl likes him better than ever.

MARTHA:
What a child!

HENRY:
But let me tell you, he's a problem.

MARTHA:
I suppose so . . . But when he comes and makes up his little sto-ries, and you *know* they're just little stories, but he wants you to believe them so *badly* that you *wish* you could, and finally . . . Well,

what can you *do?* (Suddenly she realizes she has been giving forgiveness and blessings to Henry. They look at each other. Grandfather comes over, takes Martha's hand.)

GRANDFATHER:
Happy anniversary!

MARTHA:
I'm still too confused . . . I have to collect myself.

HENRY:
Give her a little time to think it over, Grandpa.

GRANDFATHER:
She can do it on the train.

MARTHA:
What am I going to say to my parents?

GRANDFATHER:
Send them a telegram.

MARTHA:
You mean . . . sneak out of the house . . . in the middle of the night . . .

HENRY:
Exactly!

MARTHA:
Like burglars?

HENRY (romantically):
Yes—like thieves!

MARTHA (remembering):
We did it once before . . .

HENRY:
Why shouldn't we do it again? How many people are lucky enough to have the thrill of eloping twice in one marriage?

GRANDFATHER (like a cheerleader):
That's it—that's it!

HENRY (going good again):
How many women love their husbands enough so they're willing to forgive them, and take them back, and start all over again?

GRANDFATHER:
> Good, good!

HENRY:
> And how many husbands love their wives enough so they're will-
> ing to lie and say they're guilty, when they really have done noth-
> ing wrong?

GRANDFATHER:
> Careful, Henry!

HENRY (still fast on his toes):
> At least nothing that amounts to very much.

GRANDFATHER:
> Don't go into it! We'd better get started—I'll see if the coast is clear.
> (Goes quickly.)

UPPER HALLWAY
Grandfather sneaks out of Martha's bedroom, looks around.

GRANDFATHER (whispering):
> Jasper! Jasper! Everything ready?

JASPER (appearing):
> Yessuh—right out in front.

GRANDFATHER (peeling money off his roll):
> Jasper, all my life I wanted to run away with a woman—and Jasper,
> it's happening! Here— (Hands him money.)

JASPER:
> Thank you, Mistuh Van Cleve! (Jasper goes. Grandfather opens
> bedroom door.)

GRANDFATHER:
> All right—come on!

Martha and Henry come out, Henry carrying her suitcase. Camera
pans with them as they tiptoe downstairs. As they reach lower hall we
hear and see Strabel through living room doorway, snoring. Albert is
occupied at desk.

LOWER HALL   IN FRONT OF LIVING ROOM DOORWAY
Strabel opens one eye, sees Martha leaving as if in a dream. Henry
grabs her, lifts her off the floor, and, with the help of Grandfather,

carries her out the front door. It takes Strabel a moment to recover. He jumps up and calls, "Albert!" Albert, at the desk, gets up, startled.

STRABEL MANSION   FROM OUTSIDE   A HORSE-DRAWN PHAETON   RAIN
Albert and Strabel hasten out, dash a few steps toward the road, stopping by the Mabel monument.

THE PHAETON   FROM STRABEL AND ALBERT VIEW
It is moving fast toward the highway, Henry driving, Martha next to him and, in the back seat, Grandfather. Just before they reach the gate, Grandfather turns toward Albert and Strabel.

GRANDFATHER (gaily):
    And so farewell, dear E. F. Strabel.
    We take Martha—you keep Mabel.
    Whoopee!

CLOSE-UP   ALBERT AND STRABEL
Never in their lives have they looked more foolish than now as they stand beside Mabel.

                                                            FADE OUT

FADE IN

HENRY'S VOICE:
    Then one birthday began following another—faster and faster. Each year there were more and more candles and less and less *phhht*.

Against Henry's voice, we see, in rapid succession:

BIRTHDAY CAKE
with many candles, which are being blown out by someone out of the picture.

                                                        QUICK DISSOLVE

MORE BIRTHDAY CAKES
each of them having more candles, always being blown out by someone out of the picture.

                                                            DISSOLVE

A BIG BIRTHDAY CAKE
with more candles than ever before. Again the unseen Henry tries to blow out the candles, but succeeds only in blowing out some of them.

                                                            DISSOLVE

HENRY'S HAND
opening a telegram. We read:

> CONGRATULATIONS. YOU ARE FORTY-FIVE TODAY AND THIS NEED
> NOT DEPRESS YOU IF YOU VISIT DR. EMANUEL SCHRAMPS HEALTH
> EMPORIUM STOP BE GENTLE TO YOUR ARTERIES AND THEY WON'T
> HARDEN UP ON YOU. DR. EMANUEL SCHRAMPS, PRES.

Henry's hand tears up the telegram.

WASTEBASKET
We see this and other telegrams being thrown in. We hear:

HENRY'S VOICE
>   Yes, I became forty-five. Then came forty-six, forty-seven—and I
>   stopped counting. On one of these birthdays . . .

DISSOLVE

GLITTERING BROADWAY NIGHT SCENE OF THE PERIOD WITH BIG "ZIEGFELD
FOLLIES" ELECTRIC SIGN IN FOREGROUND

DISSOLVE

INT. THEATRE   SHOT   FROM AUDIENCE VIEW   ON STAGE

HENRY'S VOICE (continuing):
>   . . . Martha and I—just the two of us—went to the Follies . . .

On stage we see a typical gorgeous show girl number with a typical
magnificent staircase. Peggy Nash, a super show girl, comes slowly
down in a ravishing and revealing costume.

HENRY'S VOICE:
>   To me, she was just another attractive girl, but I must admit—at-
>   tractive. Anyway, a few weeks later, I happened to learn her name
>   was Peggy Nash, and I happened to hear things about her which
>   made me eager to meet Miss Nash.

DISSOLVE

A LUXURIOUS PARK AVENUE APARTMENT
in good show girl taste. A maid opens the door.

MAID:
>   Will you come in, Mr. Jones? Miss Nash will be with you in a
>   minute.

Mr. Jones enters. He is none other than our Henry. The maid leaves.
Henry has aged considerably, gained in weight. He has a little bulge.

He is, as always, elegantly dressed, but now with a touch of the conservative. He looks around with curiosity—a man no longer familiar with such places. Miss Nash comes in from another room. She is dressed to kill.

PEGGY (ritzy, but inviting):
How do you do, Mr. Jones?

HENRY:
How do you do, Miss Nash?

PEGGY:
Thank you *so* much for those beautiful, beautiful roses.

HENRY:
When I saw you the other night, coming down that stairway, I said to myself—

PEGGY:
"That's the girl of my dreams!"

HENRY:
That's right! You see, Miss Nash—

PEGGY (sitting):
Call me Peggy.

HENRY:
This is delightful . . . (Sitting.) Hello, Peggy!

PEGGY:
Hello, Jonesy! (Henry is a bit thrown by the speed of this new generation.) Well, Jonesy, let me tell you, that note that came with your flowers—

HENRY (flattered):
You liked it?

PEGGY:
Who wouldn't? That note was so full of charm. It was so sweet—it had all the quaintness of bygone days.

HENRY (unflattered):
Really!

PEGGY:
Oh, yes! You know, men don't write that way anymore. *Why* are there so few of you left?

HENRY (hurt but unruffled):
Miss Nash, to tell you the truth, I didn't exactly come here to be admired as a museum piece.

PEGGY:
Now, Jonesy, don't be touchy!

HENRY:
Anyway, Miss Nash—

PEGGY:
"Peggy."

HENRY (a gentleman of the old school):
Anyway, Peggy—I'm sure it's a waste of time to talk about the past when the present can be so lovely that one anticipates a most delightful future.

PEGGY:
Oh, *thank* you, Jonesy. What a difference! You know, the moment you meet somebody of today, he says, "How about it, babe—where do we have supper?" And the next moment he pulls out a diamond bracelet, and before you know it *there* it is on your *wrist.* Oh, how crude—how crude!

HENRY:
Yes, very crude. And let me tell you: a bracelet presented hastily is usually selected hastily. Whereas a bracelet chosen with care—

PEGGY:
Has better stones?

HENRY:
The very best.

PEGGY:
Oh, Jonesy, it all sounds so wonderful. But how could I explain such a gift to . . . (She hesitates prettily.)

HENRY:
To whom? (She goes to a table and stops before a framed photograph. Henry joins her, looking with interest at the picture.) Oh—friend of yours?

PEGGY:
Very much so.

HENRY:
Serious?

PEGGY:
I'm afraid it is.

HENRY:
Is there anything I could do to make you forget this young man?

PEGGY:
Jonesy, you're asking a lot. Just look at him!

HENRY:
He seems very young.

PEGGY:
Not too young.

HENRY:
Would it be indiscreet of me to ask who this young man is?

PEGGY (letting him have it):
Now come on, Mr. Van Cleve—don't you know your own son? (Henry is staggered.) No, I didn't fall into your trap. You know, Mr. Van Cleve, girls are awfully smart these days. It must be rather sad for the great cavalier of the Gay Nineties to find that his technique is getting rusty . . . Yes, I've heard all about the daring Henry. I understand in my mother's day you were—and I'm sure you had—a very dashing figure. And now you're . . . a kind of retired Casanova! (That kills Henry.) It's always the same with men when they retire. Some grow flowers—and some grow a tummy.

HENRY (pulling himself together; getting down to business):
Miss Nash, my son means very much to me.

PEGGY:
He means very much to me, too.

HENRY:
How much?

PEGGY (pretended indignation):
Oh, yes—that's right! Of course! In your day, girls used to wait for the old-fashioned father to come with a big checkbook to pay off.

HENRY:
I'm sure that happened.

PEGGY (smiling):
Well, that's *one* thing that hasn't changed.

HENRY (wasting no more time):
Shall we say five thousand?

PEGGY:
Five thousand! Jonesy, you underestimate me. I'm much worse than that. To get rid of someone as terrible as me is worth . . . Well, I'll give you a bargain—twenty-five thousand.

HENRY (who knows reality when he sees it):
I'll send you the money.

PEGGY:
Before lunch?

HENRY:
Before lunch! . . . Well, goodbye, Miss Nash.

PEGGY (giving him her hand):
You've been charming.

HENRY:
And so have you.

PEGGY:
And you hope never to see me again?

HENRY (laughs):
I wouldn't say that! (A thought comes to him; he is at the door, turns back.) Miss Nash, now that our problem has been solved, I'd like to ask just one slight question—not that it matters, but I'm curious, and I'd appreciate an honest answer.

PEGGY (being honest):
I give you my word.

HENRY:
Suppose you didn't know I was Jack's father, and you happened to see me on the street, or in a restaurant—this is purely an academic question—how old would you say I am?

PEGGY:
Well . . . I'd say . . . about fifty.

HENRY (wounded):
That old?

PEGGY:
> Oh, I'm sorry. I didn't mean to hurt you.

HENRY:
> No, no—that's perfectly all right. Thank you very much.

PEGGY:
> Excuse me, but—how old *are* you?

HENRY (wryly):
> Fifty. (He goes.)

FADE OUT

FADE IN
LIBRARY   VAN CLEVE HOUSE
Same evening. After-dinner atmosphere. The furniture is different in small ways, indicating passage of time. Henry is in a comfortable arm-chair, Martha on the sofa. Both are reading. A domestic idyll.

HENRY (gets up; there is something on his mind):
> Martha—this is going to be a bit unpleasant. I've tried to keep it from you for some time, but now I think I'd better tell you.

MARTHA (used to Henry's big problems):
> You don't love me anymore.

HENRY:
> Don't try to be funny. It's about Jack.

MARTHA (much more a modern parent than Henry):
> Will you please stop worrying about Jack? If he wants to stay out late, what of it? If he's ever going to have some fun, now's the time. Don't spoil it.

HENRY:
> Martha, this is serious—very, very serious. I happened to learn that the boy got into the clutches of a certain girl, and I went to a great deal of trouble—believe me, it wasn't easy—but I managed to find out who the girl was.

MARTHA (casually):
> You mean Peggy Nash?

HENRY (bowled over):
> Where did you—how did you know?

MARTHA:
> Oh, I forget—someone told me—you go to lunch and you hear things.

HENRY:

Why didn't you tell me? How can you be so placid about a thing like that?

MARTHA (motherly):

Darling, why should I excite you? I know you so well. Certain little things get you all worked up. Then you don't sleep. Then you have to take a pill. Then you don't *want* to take a pill . . . Believe me, Henry, the less attention you pay—really these things work themselves out.

HENRY (superior):

Martha, that's one of your greatest charms. After almost twenty-five years in New York, you're still the innocent little girl from Kansas. But fortunately, I've had experience with show girls—and it's the father's function to save his son from the mistakes *he* made. If we ignore matters like this—do you know how our boy will end up?

MARTHA:

Just like you—with a girl like me!

HENRY (embracing her):

I have no illusions about myself. Martha, if I hadn't met you I hate to think where I'd be right now.

MARTHA:

Well—probably outside some stage door—or even inside the dressing room—and having a wonderful time.

HENRY:

Now, Martha!

MARTHA:

Give me a kiss and don't worry about it anymore. (They kiss, then sit and are about to read.)

HENRY (feeling silly about the whole thing):

I just want to get your viewpoint. Do you think it would be a bad idea—just to be safe—if I look up the girl and—

MARTHA:

And what?

HENRY:

Well, maybe—just to avoid complications, ask her to leave the boy alone. And, if necessary, buy her off.

MARTHA:

Henry—don't even *consider* anything as foolish as that.

HENRY:

All right, all right—it was only a thought. If you want me to, I'll drop it.

MARTHA:

Good . . . How much did you pay the girl?

HENRY:

What do you mean?

MARTHA:

Don't I know my Henry and his innocent eyes? (A new butler, James, enters.)

JAMES:

I beg your pardon, sir. You told me to let you know when Mr. Jack arrives.

HENRY:

Thank you. (Butler leaves. Henry looks at his watch. Martha doesn't pay much attention, returns to her book.) See, Martha? He's home early for the first time in weeks. I'll tell you why. He went to the theater as usual, and she gave him his walking papers.

MARTHA:

And the poor boy is probably all upset.

HENRY:

I hope he is. Don't you baby him, Martha—don't you spoil what I did.

Jack enters. He is twenty-two. A good-looking young man. Instead of being depressed, he is in high spirits.

JACK:

Mother!

MARTHA (as he kisses her):

Hello, Jack.

JACK:

And, Father . . .

HENRY (very smooth, playing detective):

How are you, Jack?

JACK (smiling):
Fine.

HENRY:
You look a little depressed.

JACK:
Me? I never felt better in my life.

HENRY:
Good.

JACK:
And besides that, I could use a hundred dollars.

HENRY:
A hundred dollars . . . What for?

JACK:
Well, I just want to throw a little party tonight—take someone out.

HENRY (falsely casual):
I see . . .

MARTHA (trying to help Henry):
Tell me—who do you go around with these days?

HENRY (a super-detective):
Now, Martha—that's Jack's personal life, and we shouldn't pry into it . . . Here's your hundred dollars.

JACK:
Thanks, Father.

HENRY:
And have a good time.

JACK:
Thank you.

HENRY (as Jack starts to go):
And I'm not interested in who you're going to take out. I'm sure she's all right. (Martha chuckles.) Anyway, it's none of our business whether it's Mary Jones, Helen Smith, Mitzi Glutz, or Peggy Nash—

JACK (stopping):
Peggy Nash? Father, what is this? Are you trailing me? Where did you ever hear that name?

HENRY:
I don't know . . . Martha, where *did* we hear that name?

MARTHA (fed up):
I don't know—and don't ask me.

HENRY (lightly):
Well, one has friends—one goes to lunch . . . Isn't she a Follies girl
who is famous for coming down—I think it's a staircase?

JACK (after a slight pause):
Look—we're all grown up, aren't we?

HENRY (expecting a confession):
Why, certainly!

JACK:
Well—I had a crush on her.

HENRY:
And why not? (To Martha.) Why shouldn't he?

MARTHA:
I don't know—and don't ask me.

HENRY:
I understand she's a *very* attractive girl.

JACK:
She *is*—and I took her pretty seriously.

HENRY (looks at Martha triumphantly):
Oh, you did, eh?

JACK:
Yes, very. And then, after a little time—

HENRY (high):
Yes?

JACK:
I got tired of her.

HENRY (low):
Oh—you did?

JACK:
So then I faced the problem of how to get rid of her. You know,
things like that aren't easy, Father.

HENRY (up again; to Martha):
I should say not!

MARTHA:
Don't ask *me!*

HENRY:
I didn't ask you. I merely made a statement. Go on, Jack.

JACK:
Well, anyhow, this afternoon I made up my mind, and I went to her. I said to myself, I must get this over with. I was expecting a big scene—

HENRY (eagerly):
Naturally.

JACK:
But, after all, what could she do—I hadn't promised her anything.

MARTHA (gives Henry a look):
You hadn't?

JACK:
I should say not! I wasn't the first romance in her life. I'm no baby.

HENRY (fighting hard):
But nevertheless you went to her, expecting a lot of trouble?

JACK:
Yes. But, to my surprise, she was so *big* about the whole thing—and let me off so easily . . .

HENRY (up again):
She did, eh? (To Martha.) Isn't that *fortunate?*

JACK:
Yes, she was so wonderful about the whole thing—that I pretty nearly fell in love with her again. (Henry is now completely down. Martha has to hold back her laughter.) But it's all over now, and I'm glad of it.

MARTHA:
And so am I.

HENRY (with relief):
And so am I! As a matter of fact, I never was happier in my life

. . . And since we're on the subject, Jack, I think you're getting to the age where you should start to look around for a really nice girl.

JACK:
I don't have to look around. I've met her.

HENRY:
You *have?*

JACK:
A wonderful girl—the most wonderful I ever met in my life.

HENRY (dubious again):
Really? Well, isn't that nice!

MARTHA:
Tell me, who is the young lady? Is she someone I might know—a New York girl, perhaps?

JACK:
No. She comes from Philadelphia.

MARTHA (impressed):
Oh, from Philadelphia!

HENRY:
Somehow, Philadelphia always sounds right—doesn't it, Martha?

MARTHA:
Yes, it does. Tell us who she is?

HENRY (up again):
Yes, tell us!

JACK (after a pause):
Well—have you been to Earl Carroll's Vanities? (Henry and Martha are dumbfounded.)

HENRY:
You mean this girl comes down a staircase, too!

JACK (proudly):
I should say not! Not this girl! This one slides down the banisters and falls into the orchestra and lands—bang!—right on the big drum. Oh, you'll be crazy about her! . . . Well, see you tomorrow. Have to run along. (He goes.)

CLOSE SHOT   MARTHA AND HENRY

HENRY (completely defeated):
What's the *matter* with that boy?

MARTHA:
He's young, Henry, that's all. Come, dear. It's time to go to bed.
(They walk toward the door.)

MARTHA'S BEDROOM
Henry and Martha enter. Martha starts to get undressed.

HENRY (worried):
Martha, I want to ask you something—and don't spare my feelings. Be absolutely frank.

MARTHA:
I always am.

HENRY:
If you didn't know me, and you saw me for the first time, on the
street, or in a restaurant . . . Martha, do you think I'm getting a
little heavy?

Martha stops her undressing, goes to him, and comforts him with great
sweetness. But, without meaning to, she is giving him the final blow
in a day full of blows.

MARTHA:
Don't let that worry you. As a matter of fact, I like it. Let me tell
you something. Nearly fifteen years ago, when you and Grandfather brought me back from Kansas, I still didn't feel that you
really belonged to me—and only to me. I can't put my finger on
anything definite. But still, whenever I wasn't with you, I was always uncertain and nervous about my little Casanova. And one
day I noticed that you began to have a little—well, just a little
tummy. *Then I knew I was safe.* From that moment on, you were
really mine. You had settled down. (Kissing him.) Now go to bed,
darling. You've had a hard day.

HENRY (crushed):
Yes, Martha, yes . . . Good night, dear.

MARTHA:
Good night, dear. (Henry goes into his bedroom.)

FADE OUT

FADE IN

LIVING ROOM   JUST BEFORE A BIG PARTY

A large array of beautiful presents covers a table. Center is a decoration piece with the number 25.

HENRY'S VOICE:

Yes, we were married twenty-five years. We were celebrating our silver wedding anniversary.

DISSOLVE

LONG SHOT   HALL

It is the night of the twenty-fifth anniversary. Music of a small orchestra. In living room we see guests dancing, all in formal dress. Henry comes out of living room and looks around.

SHOT OF HENRY

as he walks about hall. Butler—still James—comes with a tray, headed for dining room.

HENRY:

Have you seen Mrs. Van Cleve?

BUTLER:

No, sir. (Henry starts toward stairway and sees Jack coming down.)

HENRY:

Jack, is your mother upstairs?

JACK:

I haven't seen her, Dad. (Camera moves with Henry as he goes across the hall toward library.)

LIBRARY

Henry enters, discovers Martha resting in an armchair. Martha doesn't seem to feel well, but pulls herself together the moment she sees Henry.

HENRY (worried):

Darling, what are you doing here all alone?

MARTHA:

Nothing, I just wanted to take a little rest. It's been such an exciting evening.

HENRY:
>Nothing wrong, is there?

MARTHA:
>No, nothing, dear.

HENRY:
>Are you sure?

MARTHA:
>Yes, dear.

HENRY:
>Martha, you're feeling all right, aren't you?

MARTHA:
>Of course, darling. I'm just—

HENRY:
>Just what?

MARTHA:
>To tell you the truth, I'm being a little sentimental. So I came in here for a few minutes.

HENRY (recapturing the mood of twenty-five years ago):
>Yes, this is where it all started.

MARTHA (getting up):
>Twenty-five years ago.

HENRY:
>I was standing here by the desk.

MARTHA (trying to be gay):
>No, you were sitting in the chair.

HENRY:
>That's right. And then you came in. *You* went over to the desk—

MARTHA:
>Then suddenly you started walking toward me—very slowly . . . I could count every step.

HENRY (happy):
>Oh, you were such a frightened little girl. And the closer I came, the more frightened you were.

MARTHA:
   Darling—I want to make a confession.

HENRY (a little worried):
   What is it, Martha?

MARTHA:
   I wasn't frightened at all.

HENRY:
   You weren't?

MARTHA:
   Not at all. And when you were walking toward me so slowly, do you know what was in my mind? I thought: What's the *matter* with him? Can't he walk *faster?* (Henry takes her in his arms and kisses her as he did twenty-five years ago. As they come out of it:) And then I *ran* into the hall—

HENRY:
   But you came back!

MARTHA:
   Only because I had to sneeze. (Door is opened by the butler.)

BUTLER (in discreet tone):
   Madame, you're wanted on the telephone.

MARTHA (trying to hide her nervousness; into phone):
   Hello? . . . Yes, I called you. Well, it's really not important. Yes— everything is all right now. I'll call you soon. Very well, tomorrow. (She hangs up.)

HENRY:
   Who was that?

MARTHA:
   Oh, nothing special. Let's go back to our guests, shall we?

HENRY:
   Darling, who was that on the phone?

MARTHA:
   I'll tell you all about it some other time.

HENRY:
   Why not now?

MARTHA:
Sweetheart, our guests must be wondering where we are.

HENRY:
Now, Martha, *who was that?*

MARTHA (trying to be gay):
All right, I'll tell you. This is another confession . . . My lover.

HENRY:
I don't think that's funny at all.

MARTHA:
Are you jealous?

HENRY (troubled):
Don't be silly. But why can't you tell your husband who you talked to over the telephone? And besides—I wouldn't have brought it up right now, but just the same—for the last several weeks you've been going out in the afternoon, and you always manage to avoid telling me where you were.

MARTHA:
You *are* jealous! Henry! At last! Thank you, darling!

HENRY:
Martha—*who did you talk to?*

MARTHA:
Don't be a baby. What dashing young cavalier would be pursuing me?

HENRY:
Plenty.

MARTHA (puts her arm around him):
Henry, I don't think you realize how sweet you're being at this moment. No husband could have said anything lovelier to his wife on their twenty-fifth anniversary. Imagine—if twenty-five years ago I hadn't sneezed, I wouldn't be the happiest woman in the world right now.

HENRY:
Are you?

MARTHA:
Yes, Henry.

HENRY (takes her in his arms, caresses her; then abruptly):
Now—who was it?

MARTHA:
I'll tell you tomorrow. (She wants to go.)

HENRY (sits down):
I'm not going to leave this room until you tell me.

MARTHA (sitting close to him):
Well, knowing my obstinate little boy—you promise to be sensible and not make a mountain out of a molehill?

HENRY:
I promise. Now—

MARTHA:
Well, you know how women are. We have too much time on our hands, and we begin to imagine things are wrong with us—and I'm no exception. So I've been going to a doctor—that's all.

HENRY (with great relief; laughing; getting up):
Darling, I certainly feel like a fool. Now I must tell you: I really was jealous. (Goes to door; suddenly stops, alarmed.) Martha, what did you see the doctor for? What's wrong?

MARTHA:
Nothing—really.

HENRY:
So that's why you came in here—you weren't feeling well . . . Darling, is it serious?

MARTHA:
I tell you it's nothing at all—just a little dizzy spell. Now, you promised to be sensible. (We hear the orchestra in the living room playing a waltz.) Come—let's dance!

HENRY (holding off):
What did the doctor say?

MARTHA:
Listen, dear—if I take five drops three times a day, and if you don't worry too much about me—we'll both live to celebrate our golden anniversary. Now—let's dance! (Henry takes her in his arms and they dance out into the hall.)

371

HALL   MUSIC FROM LIVING ROOM

They are waltzing alone in the hall. We see the rest of the party waltzing in the living room. Henry draws Martha close. Camera pulls away to a long shot from high above. They become two small dancing figures in the large, festive, empty hall. Against this:

HENRY'S VOICE:

I didn't know it then, but this was our last anniversary. It was the last time we danced together. There were only a few months left for Martha, and she made them the happiest of our lives together.

FADE OUT

FADE IN

THE NUMBER 60 ENGRAVED ON A PARCHMENTLIKE FOLDER

Camera pulls back, disclosing whole folder. At bottom, date of Henry's sixtieth birthday is engraved. Henry's hand opens folder. We see a typical group picture of the guests at the birthday party, almost all elderly relatives.

As Henry's voice narrates, we show close shots of Cousin William, Cousin John, and Aunt Minetta. After these we return to the group picture. Camera now includes part of table as Henry's hand takes folder and locks it in a table drawer.

HENRY'S VOICE:

I was sixty! Jack had insisted on celebrating . . . And here are my relatives, who came to make this birthday an occasion of riotous gaiety . . . Cousin William, seventy-three. Cousin John, seventy-eight. And Aunt Minetta, who admitted to eighty-four . . . The total age of this scintillating assemblage was over fourteen hundred years. I believe Jack gave this party on purpose—to remind me that I was contributing sixty to that fourteen hundred.

DISSOLVE

ENTRANCE HALL   VAN CLEVE HOUSE   VERY EARLY MORNING

The furniture is almost the same as it was ten years ago; perhaps one or two alterations. James, older and still the butler, opens the door to Miss Ralston, the middle-aged secretary.

MISS RALSTON:

Good morning.

BUTLER:

Good morning, Miss Ralston.

MISS RALSTON (crisp and efficient):
Is Mr. Van Cleve down yet?

BUTLER:
Oh, yes—he's at breakfast. (She goes into dining room, where Jack is at the table.)

DINING ROOM

MISS RALSTON:
Good morning, Mr. Van Cleve.

JACK (a crisp, mature businessman):
Good morning, Miss Ralston. Sorry I got you up so early, but I want these two letters on the nine thirty plane.

MISS RALSTON:
Yes, Mr. Van Cleve.

JACK (as he signs the letters):
And when you're at the office, will you please see that I get a complete domestic report from every department before noon. I may have to go to Chicago.

MISS RALSTON:
Very well. (Tactfully.) Now, there's one little thing—it's—well, a letter came from your father addressed to the board of directors . . .

JACK (annoyed):
Is he trying to go over my head again?

MISS RALSTON:
Oh, I'm sure he didn't mean it that way.

JACK:
What does he want? We live together in the same house, and he writes letters to the board of directors! . . . What's the old gentleman trying to put over this time?

MISS RALSTON (a wee bit on Henry's side):
He wants the board of directors to vote him a bonus.

JACK:
A bonus!

373

MISS RALSTON:

He talked to me yesterday confidentially. In case that bonus doesn't go through, he wanted me to persuade you to give him at least an advance on his monthly check.

JACK:

He shouldn't go to you.

MISS RALSTON:

But—

JACK:

Well . . . I'm going to give him a lesson.

HALLWAY AT FRONT DOOR

Henry, in evening clothes, comes sneaking in, guilty and scared. He is sixty and looks sixty. However, he has lost his bulge and is rather haggard.

MISS RALSTON'S VOICE (nearing the hall):

Yes, Mr. Van Cleve. (Miss Ralston comes out of dining room. She sees Henry, who can't find a place to hide.)

MISS RALSTON:

Why, Mr.—!

HENRY:

Shh! (Whispering.) Is he in a bad mood?

MISS RALSTON (friendly whisper):

Terrible!

HENRY:

Now look, Miss Ralston—will you do me a very great favor?

JACK'S VOICE:

Father!

Henry turns, sees Jack in dining room doorway. Miss Ralston leaves as Jack enters hall.

HENRY (a sad effort at a smile):

Good morning, Jack!

JACK (brusquely):

I'd like to talk to you, Father. (With hardly a glance at Henry, he strides into the library, assuming that Henry will follow. But Henry hesitates.)

JACK'S VOICE (from library):
Father! (Henry hastens after Jack.)

LIBRARY
Henry enters, trying to behave like a social equal.

HENRY:
Jack, I heard a very funny joke—you'll love it. It'll start your day off with a laugh.

JACK (severely; father to son):
You should be ashamed—coming home at all hours—making a wreck of yourself. How long do you think you can keep this up?

HENRY (like a little boy):
Please, Jack—don't scold me.

JACK (with conviction):
Any day now you're going to collapse.

HENRY (caught):
Do I look that bad?

JACK:
You look like a ghost.

HENRY (another shift):
I know you're right, Jack. I shouldn't be living this kind of life. But, my boy, put yourself in my place. I'm lonesome . . . You're always away somewhere on business . . . And being alone in this big house, night after night—you don't know what it's like.

JACK:
Neither do you—because you're never at home.

HENRY:
But I can *imagine* what it's like—and Jack, it's horrible! (With an air of out-and-out common sense.) I *must* have a talk with you. I'm not fooling myself—I'm not getting any younger. And I think the time has come to change *my whole way of living*.

JACK:
That makes sense, Father . . . Now what are you driving at, you old fox?

HENRY:

Jack, don't be harsh. (Dolorously.) I've been a lonely widower for almost ten years.

JACK (tough):

Who is she?

HENRY (innocent):

Who?

JACK:

The girl you want to marry.

HENRY:

Who said anything about getting married? That's the last thing I was thinking of. And listen, Jack—I know how you feel. (Shrewdly.) If I came in with a pretty young blonde the way so many men of my age do—and they *do* it, Jack—anyway, you'd be outraged, wouldn't you?

JACK:

I certainly would.

HENRY:

And you're *right*, my boy! No, no—what I had in mind was something entirely different. You know, Jack, when a man gets to be sixty, the blood doesn't flow so fast anymore. Instead of a wild mountain stream, it becomes a quiet little brook. The other day when I was all alone in the house, you know what I felt like doing?

JACK (not trusting Henry for a second):

What?

HENRY:

Jack, I wanted to sit down in a comfortable chair—and read, and read, and read.

JACK:

Well, why didn't you? The library is full of books, and you haven't read a single one of them.

HENRY:

Jack, the eyes can't take it anymore.

JACK:

Why don't you go to an oculist?

HENRY (cornered):

I suppose I should—yes, yes . . . (Twisting again.) On the other hand, what do you think of the idea of . . . Well—of some kind of *reader?* You know, someone with a pleasant voice . . . and good diction . . .

JACK (mercilessly amenable):
I know *just* what you want! You mean, one of those nice, quiet fellows from Yale or Harvard. They're easy to get . . . Now—*who is she?*

HENRY (righteously):
You have the most suspicious mind!

JACK:
Come on—*how old is she?*

HENRY (coming out into the open; with dignity):
Well, she's an unusually adult young woman. I met her at old Wilson Weatherby's house. She was *his* reader.

JACK:
Just exactly what did she do?

HENRY:
What *does* a reader do?

JACK:
I don't know.

HENRY:
She *reads.*

JACK:
Hmmm . . . Sounds a little fishy . . .

HENRY (getting stronger):
Jack, why do you want to deprive your old father of a little cultural pleasure? (Takes book at random from shelf and gestures with it.) I can think of nothing more dignified and homelike than sitting in front of the fireplace and having someone read a fine book to me . . . (He glances at title of book, but has to focus his aging eyes.) Something worthwhile—something which— (He stops suddenly.)

CLOSE SHOT
on book, then back to Henry. The book is *How to Make Your Husband Happy.* The lettering has faded. Henry starts to lay book aside and go out. Jack stops him.

CLOSE SHOT   HENRY AND JACK

Henry's mood has changed. Martha has spoken to him. Jack looks at
the book as Henry puts it quietly back on the shelf. He sits quietly
down. Jack, touched, sits by his father.

JACK:

Father, her last thought was that you should be happy. I promised
her that I'd see to it. So if you want this young lady to read to
you—go ahead, with my blessing. (Henry smiles sadly, pats his
son's hand gratefully.)

HENRY:

I couldn't do it. When a man gets to be sixty, his life—

JACK:

Is not over, Father. It doesn't have to be over. If a man is lonely
and he feels he needs—well—

HENRY (an infinitesimal gleam in his eye):
The feminine touch?

JACK:

That's natural. . . . (Gently.) But I think he should find someone
closer to his own age.

HENRY (agreeing):
Maybe . . .

JACK:

Not a girl of—

HENRY (confessing):
Twenty-four.

JACK (delicately):
That would be a little out of proportion.

HENRY (convinced and sad):
I'm afraid so.

JACK:

But if, for instance, he should meet a cultured woman—

HENRY:

Right! With dignity—

378

JACK:
A woman, say, of about fifty, or fifty-one—

HENRY:
Or fifty-*three*—or fifty-*five*—or even fifty-*seven*.

JACK:
That's more like it!

HENRY (after a moment):
Jack, my future looks pretty depressing. (He leans back in his chair and closes his eyes. James, the butler, comes in.)

BUTLER:
Mr. Van Cleve, you're wanted on the telephone. (Henry, eyes still closed, hardly hears the butler.)

JACK (goes to the nearby telephone):
Hello . . . (Puzzled.) What? . . . Just a moment. (To his father.) It's for you, poochie! (Henry sits up, embarrassed, rises, and goes very nervously toward the telephone.)

HENRY (into phone; in a very meek voice):
Hello.

DISSOLVE

CLOSE SHOT   NEW YORK NEWSPAPER INSERT
Girl lying on couch in very smart negligee, legs displayed, book in hand. Camera pulls back for headline:
READER'S CONTRACT SETTLED
FOR HUNDRED THOUSAND DOLLARS

FADE OUT

FADE IN
HENRY'S BATHROOM
Camera moves to medicine cabinet.

HENRY'S VOICE:
As a man grows older, his medicine cabinet grows, too. (Henry's hand opens cabinet. It is filled to overflowing.) That's me at seventy.

DISSOLVE

UPPER LANDING IN FRONT OF HENRY'S BEDROOM   EVENING
Doctor, Jack, and Jane come out, close door. Jack is forty-five. Jane, his

379

wife, a handsome woman, is forty. They are in evening clothes. As they walk toward the staircase—

DOCTOR:
Now, really, there's nothing to worry about. But Mrs. Van Cleve, *please*—

JANE (contritely):
I know! But it was his seventieth birthday, and I didn't have the heart to keep him from celebrating a little.

JACK:
I hate to go out and leave the old man alone.

JANE:
I'd just as soon stay home.

DOCTOR:
No, no—it's perfectly all right for you to go. The fewer people around him, the better off he'll be.

DISSOLVE

HENRY'S BEDROOM
Henry is asleep. Nurse sits close to bed, back to camera. She takes a thermometer, taps Henry's hand gently. Apparently in a dream, he smiles brightly and pats her hand.

NURSE:
Now, Mr. Van Cleve—I'm sorry to wake you up, but it has to be done.

CLOSE-UP   HENRY
He comes out of dream still smiling. His eyes begin to open.

CLOSE-UP   NURSE
We see her for the first time. She is unattractive; also she wears glasses.

CLOSE SHOT   NURSE AND HENRY
Sight of nurse has jarred Henry awake.

HENRY (grouchily):
Huh?

NURSE:
Now, open your mouth, please.

She tries to put thermometer in his mouth. (During following, nurse tries several times to insert thermometer, but Henry always fends her off.)

HENRY:

Go away! Leave me alone! What was that dream about? Oh, I was having such a good time!

NURSE:

Just open your mouth.

HENRY (to himself):

What was it about? Oh, yes—the door opened and a man stepped out of a rowboat. He said, "Henry, I'm going to take you on a trip from which you'll never come back."

NURSE:

Now, please don't get excited.

HENRY:

I said, "My good fellow, if I ever take a trip like that, it'll be in a deluxe cabin and not in a dinky little rowboat that doesn't even have a bar." So I threw him out, rowboat and all.

NURSE (trying to put thermometer in his mouth):

Good, good.

HENRY:

So what do you think he did? He came back with a big luxury liner, floating on an ocean of whiskey and soda, and instead of funnels there were big black cigars. And on top, in a lifeboat, sat the most beautiful blonde, in a Merry Widow costume. She dived into the whiskey and swam right over to my bedside. "Henry," she said, "how about a little dance?" And suddenly the man from the boat took an accordion and played the "Merry Widow Waltz"—and the girl held her arms out to me and started to dance. Well, with him playing, and her dancing, and me up to my neck in whiskey any-how . . . I put my arms around the beautiful girl and was just about to dance away with her when, of all people, you cut in— *you, yes, you!*

NURSE (very patiently):

Just open your mouth . . .

HENRY:

> Oh, go away—and take that thermometer with you! (Knock at bedroom door. As nurse goes toward door—)

CLOSE SHOT AT DOOR
Nurse opens door softly to James, the butler.

BUTLER:

> The night nurse is here. (Butler goes. Nurse picks up handbag and leaves.)

UPPER HALL   HENRY'S DOOR
Nurse comes out, closes door gently. Camera pans with her as she goes toward staircase. As she reaches staircase night nurse comes up. She is a beautiful blonde. As they pass each other

DAY NURSE:

> Good evening.

NIGHT NURSE:

> Hello. (Day nurse indicates door of Henry's bedroom.) Thank you.

Camera pans with night nurse. She pauses at mirror, fixes her hair and face, then goes into bedroom, closes door behind her. Camera stays outside. In a little while we hear the "Merry Widow Waltz" played on an accordion. Camera pulls back from door, tilts down to lower hall, and sinks slowly down and apparently through the floor.

DISSOLVE

HIS EXCELLENCY'S OFFICE   HENRY AND HIS EXCELLENCY AT DESK

HENRY:

> I had fallen asleep again, and I was awakened by a caressing touch on my forehead. I opened my eyes—and there she was, sitting on the edge of my bed . . . Nellie Brown, registered nurse . . . Your Excellency, one look at her and it didn't matter whether she was registered or not! And then Nellie took out a thermometer, and she said, "Open your mouth." Who wouldn't for Nellie? Then she put the thermometer in, and my temperature went up to a hundred and ten. Who could ask for a more beautiful death? (Pause.) Well, Your Excellency, that's the story of my life . . . (He gets up.) And now I'd be grateful if you'd push that button and have it over with.

EXCELLENCY (gets up; with mock severity):

No—definitely no. I hope you will not consider me inhospitable if I say: Sorry, Mr. Van Cleve, but we don't cater to your class of people. Please make your reservations somewhere else.

HENRY:

Somewhere *else?* But, Your Excellency, if I even walk into the lobby of the other place—

EXCELLENCY:

You mean above?

HENRY:

I know what will happen. The man behind the desk will say, "Can't you read the sign?" and there it'll be right up on the wall: Clientele Restricted. They might not even let me register. The doorman might not even let me in.

EXCELLENCY (he seems to like Henry):

Well, you never can tell—it's worth trying. Sometimes they have a small room vacant in the annex—not exactly on the sunny side, not so very comfortable. The bed may be hard, and you might have to await a few hundred years until they move you into the main building. It all depends on how your story appeals to the Man Behind the Desk. (As he escorts Henry toward a little hall with a private elevator.) After all, they may inquire about you among the residents in the main building, and I think a lot of people may give you a good reference—and that always helps. (They have reached the elevator.) For instance, there were several young ladies—

HENRY (not sure):

Yes? What about them?

EXCELLENCY:

Well, some of them *might* be up there. And, from what you have told me beyond words, I wouldn't be surprised if you made them all pretty happy. I'm sure they'd like to see you happy, too . . . And your grandfather—

HENRY (with feeling):

Ah, yes—grandfather!

EXCELLENCY:

Don't you think *he'll* be waiting for you?

HENRY:
He might.

EXCELLENCY:
He *will*—and not with a baseball bat. (Gently.) And then there is someone else . . .

HENRY (with deep feeling):
Yes, she's there . . .

EXCELLENCY (quietly):
She will plead for you.

HENRY (fighting back the tears):
Do you think so?

EXCELLENCY (even more quietly):
You know she will . . . (Reassuringly.) Mr. Van Cleve, I'd say you have a chance. (Presses elevator button.) Anyway, it's worth trying. (Elevator door is opened by uniformed boy.) Goodbye!

HENRY:
Goodbye, Your Excellency—and thank you!

EXCELLENCY (as Henry steps into the elevator):
Good luck!

HENRY:
I'll need it.

ELEVATOR BOY:
Down?

EXCELLENCY:
No—up.

As door closes camera rests on Excellency, who looks pleased.

FADE OUT

THE END

Production Credits

Produced and directed by	Ernst Lubitsch
Screenplay by	Samson Raphaelson
Based on the play	
Szuletesnap, by	Laszlo Bus-Feketè
Photography by	Edward Cronjager
Set Designers	James Basevi and
	Leland Fuller
Set Decorators	Thomas Little
	Walter M. Scott
Music by	Alfred Newman
Technicolor Color Director	Natalie Kalmus
Edited by	Dorothy Spencer
Costumes by	René Hubert
Makeup by	Guy Pearce
Special Photographic Effects	Fred Sersen
Sound by	Eugene Grossman and
	Roger Heman
Assistant Director	Henry Weinberger

Studio: 20th Century-Fox
Shooting: February 1 to April 10, 1943
Running Time: 112 minutes
New York Premiere: August 11, 1943

Cast

Martha	Gene Tierney
Henry Van Cleve	Don Ameche
Hugo Van Cleve	Charles Coburn
Mrs. Strabel	Marjorie Main
His Excellency	Laird Cregar
Bertha Van Cleve	Spring Byington
Albert Van Cleve	Allyn Joslyn
E. F. Strabel	Eugene Pallette
Mademoiselle	Signe Hasso
Randolph Van Cleve	Louis Calhern
Peggy Nash	Helene Reynolds
James	Aubrey Mather
Jack Van Cleve	Michael Ames
Flogdell	Leonard Carey
Jasper	Clarence Muse
Henry Van Cleve, age 15	Dickie Moore
Albert Van Cleve, age 15	Dickie Jones
Jane	Trudy Marshall
Mrs. Craig	Florence Bates
Grandmother	Clara Blandick
Mrs. Cooper-Cooper	Anita Bolster
Jack as a boy	Nino Pepitone
Miss Ralston	Claire Du Brey
Nurse	Maureen Rodin-Ryan
Coachman	Frank Orth
Albert's father	Alfred Haller
Albert's mother	Grace Hampton
Smith	Gerald Oliver Smith
Clerk in Brentano's	Charles Halton
Policemen	James Flavin, Arthur Foster
Maids	Libby Taylor, Bernice Pilot
Henry, age 15 months	Michael McLean

Cast

Doctor	Edwin Maxwell
Henry, age 9	Scotty Beckett
Mary	Marlene Mains
Elevator boy	Gerald Pierce
Nurse	Doris Merrick

Several filmographies also list:

Ziegfeld Girls	Claire James, Rose-Anne Murray, Marian Rosamond, Adele Jurgens, Ruth Brady

Author's Notes

The title "Heaven Can Wait" has been used recently on a movie that in no way resembles our original film. I don't know why this was done.

Heaven Can Wait, written in the spring of 1942, was Lubitsch's first color picture. His use of color was deliberately unobtrusive, and even today stands as an example of lucidity against the savage blurrings and blazings with which many directors attempt to achieve distinction.

I have spoken elsewhere in this volume of the time when *Heaven Can Wait* was written, calling it a blithe experience. That is how I felt about it then, in the early 1940s. But I saw it again years later, on television, and in 1977, as a guest of the New York Museum of Modern Art—one of a series shown before audiences with the critic Richard Corliss as host. I found myself still enamored with the first three-quarters of the story but not so hot about where it all went. Interviewed by Mr. Corliss, I told him and the audience how the picture affected (and still affects) me. The interview was taped and transcribed, and published in *The Writer's Guild Monthly*; I feel that part of it should stand here so that, for readers of today, my today's attitude will be on record. Here it is:

RICHARD CORLISS: What do you think of this movie we just saw . . . ?

SAMSON RAPHAELSON: Well, my wife liked it very much. I saw it on TV and before that I hadn't seen it for about thirty years. I liked it last time up to a certain point. Tonight I liked it about seven or eight minutes past that point. But I got a little tired of the variations on lechery . . . My wife, who is, I'd say offhand, less lecherous than I am, seemed to like it all the way. There was an occasional difference between Lubitsch and me in our outlook on human behavior. I wasn't going to do this picture at first. He gave me a notion of what he expected. He was looking forward with great glee to this 13-year-old American boy being seduced by a voluptuous 18-year-old double-buttocked kitchen wench—Fifth Avenue mansion, 1889. No French maid was then in either of our minds. I didn't care for the 13-year-old brat or how he felt about the wench or how she felt about him. I *could* see it, of course, *ala* Wedekind, in terms of a poetic and tragic sex awakening. Anyway, while Lubitsch and I were hollering away, I think it was I who started horsing around and got the idea of the French girl. I like to believe it was I, anyway. I really can't remember. Besides, when two men are working together, the look in one man's eye might inspire the spoken words of the other. Maybe I contributed the kindling look. But once the concept—French maid; this is 1889, not 1888, and you don't *have* to marry the girl you kiss—once that came in, the whole seduction took on style.

Although there were often differences of opinion between him and me, as we worked together we had more and more respect for each other. There was never a falling out. He was only about four or five years older than I. We had a tacit understanding that when one of us objected to something, we would work on it until we both liked it. So I must have liked the last part of *Heaven Can Wait*. Still, when Ameche goes to that blonde, and we reveal with a bit of theatrical ingenuity that he isn't out to seduce her but to salvage his son . . . I don't remember, but I hope I said, "Oh, God, haven't we had enough of this . . . these variations on oo-la-la? Let's open it up. Either make him a real horny old bastard, or let's introduce another facet of character. He's a pretty monotonous old Casanova by now."

Now I don't know if I said or even felt that at the time. I know I wasn't just following along against my convictions. It was never like that between Lubitsch and me (except in the first picture we worked on and the last; that's irrelevant here). I must have agreed then. But I'm not agreeing now.

RC: Aren't you taking a moral stance here? Isn't this a story that's having fun with the stuffiness of Victorian New York: Isn't it your cheerful "message" that Heaven rewards Ameche for having been a gallant lover of the ladies rather than a run-of-the-mill unromantic young man of virtue?

SR: Oh, sure. But about three-fourths of the way through, I feel, "Come on, Henry. Skip the next chick of your dreams. Let's not donate all the charm to grandpa. What does grandpa like about *you*, anyway, beyond your bungling infidelity?"

RC: You want to see him in Wall Street dominating men? Or crusading for woman suffrage?

SR: Maybe . . . I'd like an edge to him, personality, flavor. I wouldn't mind his being a talented playboy who fulfilled the early promise of the kid who got cockeyed with the French maid and dropped nickels down Mrs. Astorbilt's decolletage. I'd call it a success story if that boy grew up into a hilarious champagne-guzzler who beats up the husky driver of a sanitation truck, takes charge of the truck, piles a bevy of chorus girls on top, including a five-piece band with a piano, and drives the whole shebang up Fifth Avenue at dawn, sprinkling sidewalks right and left, to the tune of "Wait Till the Sun Shines, Nellie." And, when the cops get him, he announces that he is running for mayor, that his platform is, "Sanitation and Syncopation,"—or "Water, Woman and Song." Something like that, or—

RC: Needs a little work.

SR: —or he might win a sexual intercourse tournament—

RC: That would need a little work, too.

SR: But let him be a champ at *something* . . . and I wish there were more bells ringing about his wife at the end. Hearing it tonight, when Ameche is talking to the Devil, I said, "Huh? Don't tell me he's going to meet some cuties up *there*, too—who remember him piously for his bedroom benevolences!" And finally the Devil—an *afterthought*—remarks that *grandpa* is up there. As for the lovely wife, the Devil (and Lubitsch and I) damn near forgot her. She is barely mentioned. I don't know what was the matter with me or with the great Lubitsch, to be so lacking in grace in the moment when a man is dead and should have a little dignity . . . Maybe my present advanced age has changed my view . . . Still, I wouldn't mind having a little fun at my *own* funeral. And I'm sure my first stop too would be more down- stairs than up. But to be received by Laird Cregar!

RC: How would *you* cast your Other-World receptionist?

SR: Well . . . not in that *maître d'hôtel* cutaway, or with that toothpaste-commercial smile. I'd feel obligated to slip him a $50 tip—which is more punishment than I honestly think I'd de- serve.

RC: Did you have a ration of door scenes—scenes involving doors—doors slightly open, doors closed, people walking into doors. . . .

SR: No . . . no . . . Lubitsch never sat down and said we will do variation Number 68 on my door trick. If you write at all for actors—and I have written a good deal and directed some of my plays—there's always a point where the actor has to go out; and if he goes out, 900 times out of 901 he goes through a door. That moment, going out—that moment has punctuation power. That moment, if you are an experienced craftsman—I'm talking the- ater now—if you have the cunning of an artist, then you know he doesn't just go out and shut the door . . . That is a moment when something can be said. And what is said is going to be heard; it's your chance to score. (There are times in a play when things are spoken but not remembered—as if they hadn't been written at all.) So usually, if you're any good, you'll study each doorway as you come to it. Now, of course, in a movie, there are greater possibilities.

RC: Those were the days of the Hays censorship, I believe.

SR: I think so.

RC: Yet in this picture—and even more so in several others you did with Lubitsch—there are wicked sexual . . . implica- tions. Did Hays object? Or make you tone down your original scripts?

SR: I don't recall making changes. We instinctively reached for the naughtiest way, the most oblique way—and it always came without the glimpse of a single pubic hair.

RC: If you had it to do over again, knowing what you know now—what would you have done?

SR: I would have rewritten the last 15 minutes of *Heaven Can*

Wait marvelously, and Lubitsch would have been so happy about it that he would never have had those heart attacks and would be here tonight having a very good time.

TEXT DESIGNED BY GARY GORE
COMPOSED BY GRAPHIC COMPOSITION, INC., ATHENS, GEORGIA
MANUFACTURED BY FAIRFIELD GRAPHICS, FAIRFIELD, PENNSYLVANIA
TEXT AND DISPLAY LINES ARE SET IN PALATINO

Library of Congress Cataloging in Publication Data
Raphaelson, Samson, 1896–
Three screen comedies.
Contents: Freundschaft : how it was with Lubitsch
and me—Author's notes—Trouble
in paradise—The shop around the corner—[etc.]
I. Title.
PS3535.A66A6   1983   812'.52   81–50948
ISBN 0–299–08780–8

PROPERTY OF
GLENBROOK SOUTH SPEECH TEAM
4000 WEST LAKE AVE.
GLENVIEW, ILL. 60025
(312) 729-2000